MW00851194

AIR WARRIORS
WORLD WAR ONE
VOLUME 1

CALIBER
COMICS

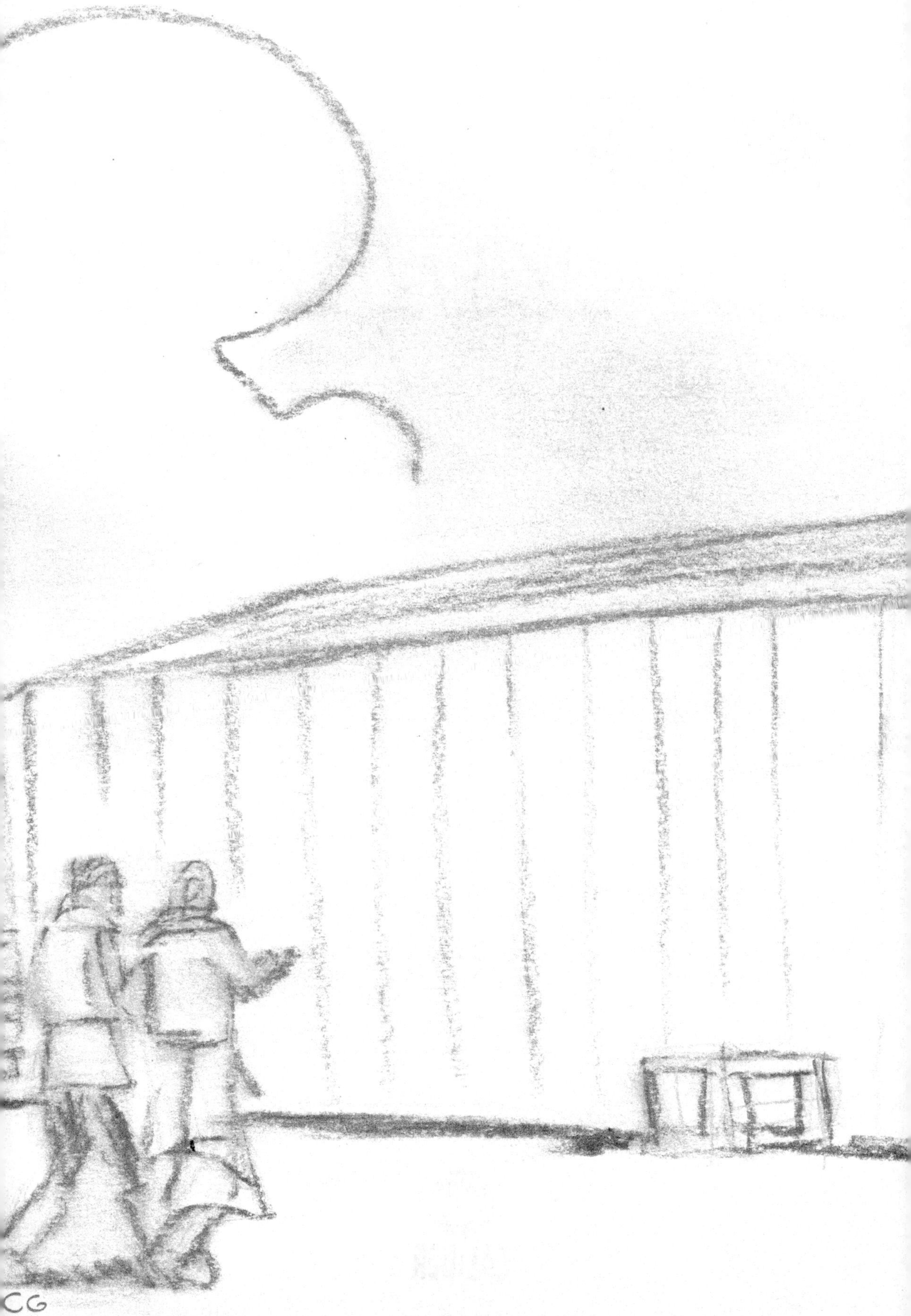
CG

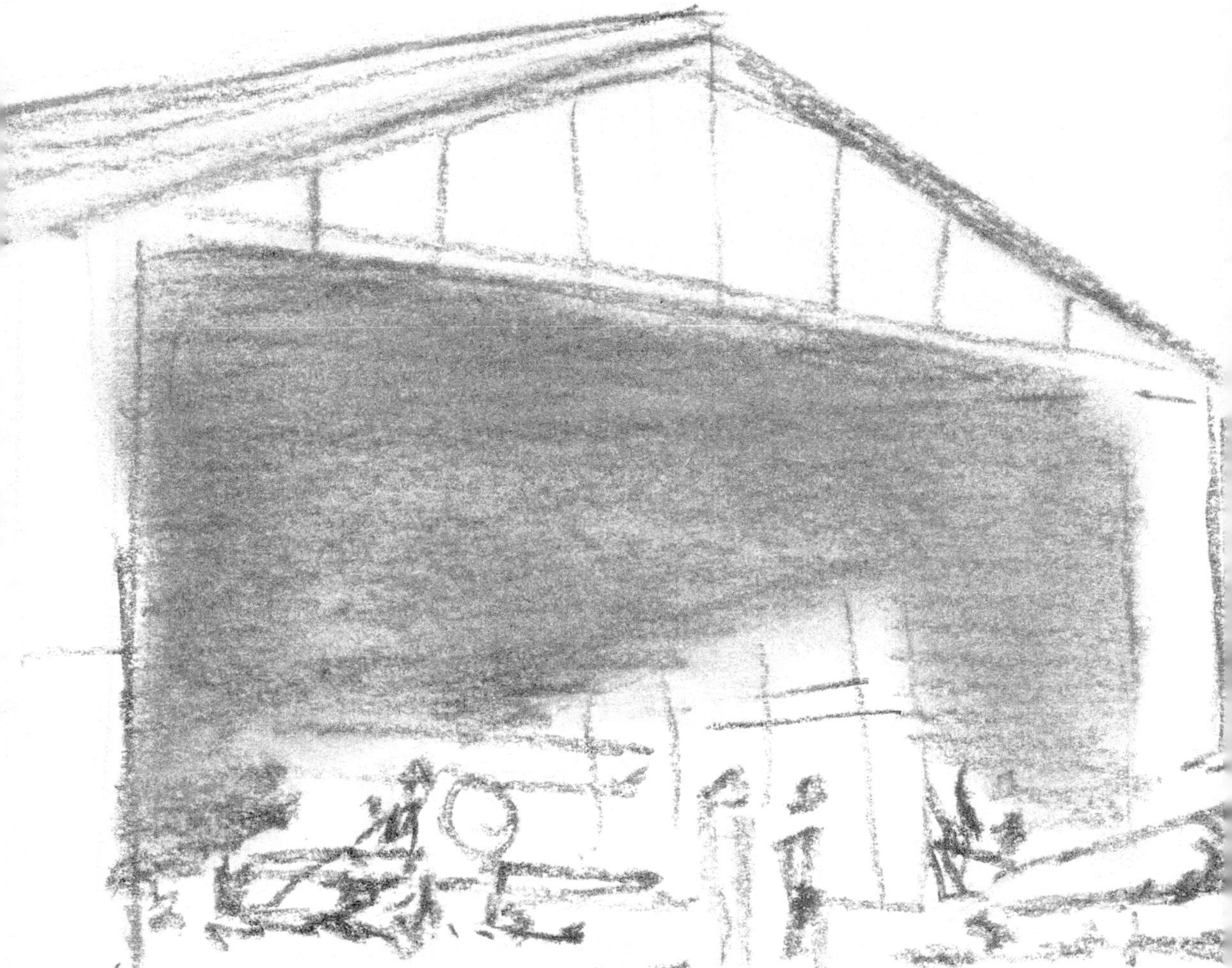

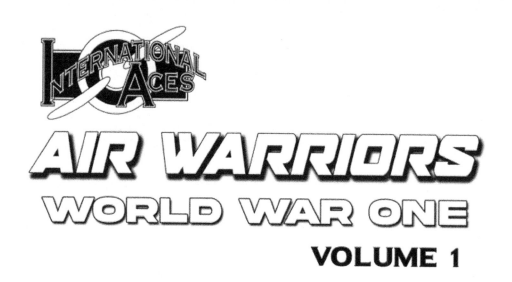

AIR WARRIORS
WORLD WAR ONE
VOLUME 1

INTERNATIONAL ACES CAPTURES THE TRUE STORIES OF THE WORLD'S FIRST GREAT FIGHTER PILOTS.

EACH STORY IS BASED ON CAREFULLY RESEARCHED HISTORICAL EVENTS. OF COURSE, ALL STORY-TELLING IS SUBJECTIVE AND REFLECTS A PARTIAL VIEW OF WHAT REALLY HAPPENED.

THIS SERIES HAS TAKEN NEARLY FOUR YEARS TO COMPLETE. INDEPENDENTLY CREATED TO COMMEMORATE 100 YEARS SINCE THE FIRST WORLD WAR, WE HOPE YOU FIND THESE TRUE STORIES INFORMATIVE AND INSPIRING.

SINCERELY,

CHRIS GEARY

WRITTEN AND ILLUSTRATED BY

CHRIS GEARY

COVER ART BY JAY HOWSE

BACK COVER ART BY ANTONIS KARIDIS COURTESY OF 777 STUDIOS

AIR WARRIORS - WORLD WAR ONE: INTERNATIONAL ACES VOLUME 1. Published by Caliber Comics, a division of Caliber Entertainment LLC.

AIR WARRIORS
WORLD WAR ONE
VOLUME 1

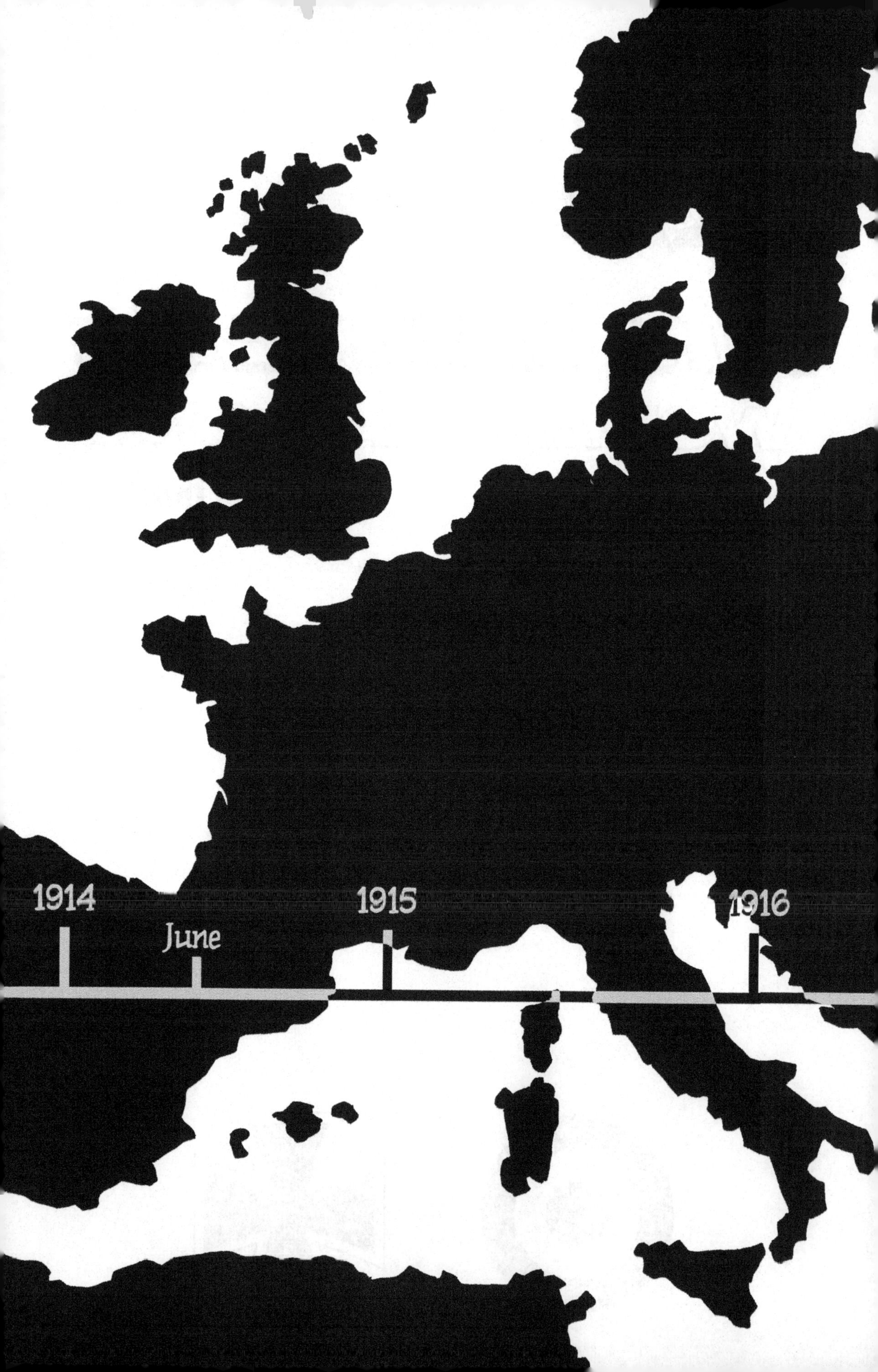

1914
June
1915
1916

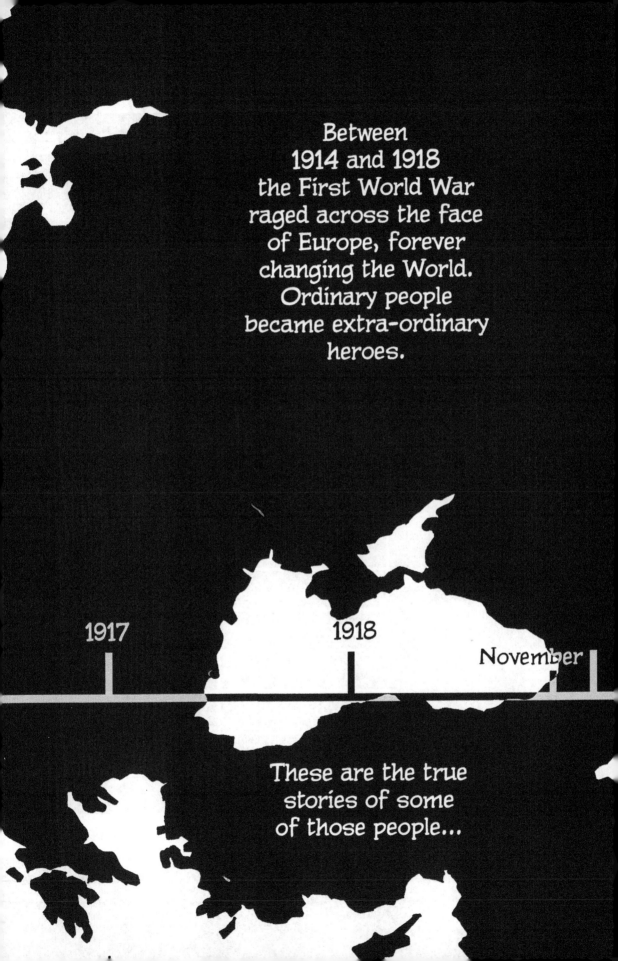

Between
1914 and 1918
the First World War
raged across the face
of Europe, forever
changing the World.
Ordinary people
became extra-ordinary
heroes.

1917

1918

November

These are the true
stories of some
of those people...

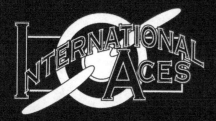

AIR WARRIORS
WORLD WAR ONE

Germany
Von Richthofen
Canada
Bishop
South Africa
Beauchamp-Proctor
Australia
Little
Austro-Hungary
Brumowski
USA
Rickenbacker
Russia
Kozakov

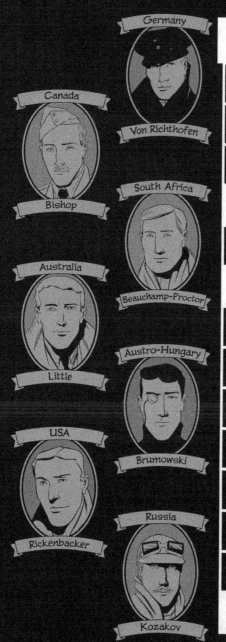

NATION :	ACES :
GERMANY	VON RICHTHOFEN
FRANCE	FONCK
CANADA	BISHOP
ENGLAND	MANNOCK
SOUTH AFRICA	BEAUCHAMP-PROCTOR
IRELAND	McELROY
AUSTRALIA	LITTLE
BELGIUM	COPPENS
AUSTRO-HUNGARY	BRUMOWSKI
ITALY	BARACCA
U.S.A.	RICKENBACKER
NEW ZEALAND	CALDWELL
RUSSIA	KOZAKOV
INDIA	LADDIE

YOUNG PILOTS FROM ACROSS THE WORLD TOOK TO THE SKIES IN NEWLY INVENTED FLYING MACHINES. LOCKED IN FEARFUL COMBAT, THEY EARNED 'VICTORIES' WITH EVERY ENEMY AIRCRAFT THEY SHOT DOWN.

VOLUME 1: INDIA - IRELAND - ENGLAND

:	RANK	: VICTORIES
	RITTMEISTER	80
	CAPITAINE	75
	LIEUTENANT COLONEL	72
	MAJOR	61
	CAPTAIN	54
	CAPTAIN	47
	CAPTAIN	47
	MAJOR	37
	HAUPTMANN	35
	MAGGIORE	34
	CAPTAIN	26
	MAJOR	25
	POLKOVNIK	20
	2ND LIEUTENANT	10

France
Fonck

Ireland
McElroy

Italy
Baracca

India
Laddie

England
Mannock

Belgium
Coppens

New Zealand
Caldwell

Indra Lal 'Laddie' Roy
Born in India
Royal Flying Corps/Royal Air Force
10 victories

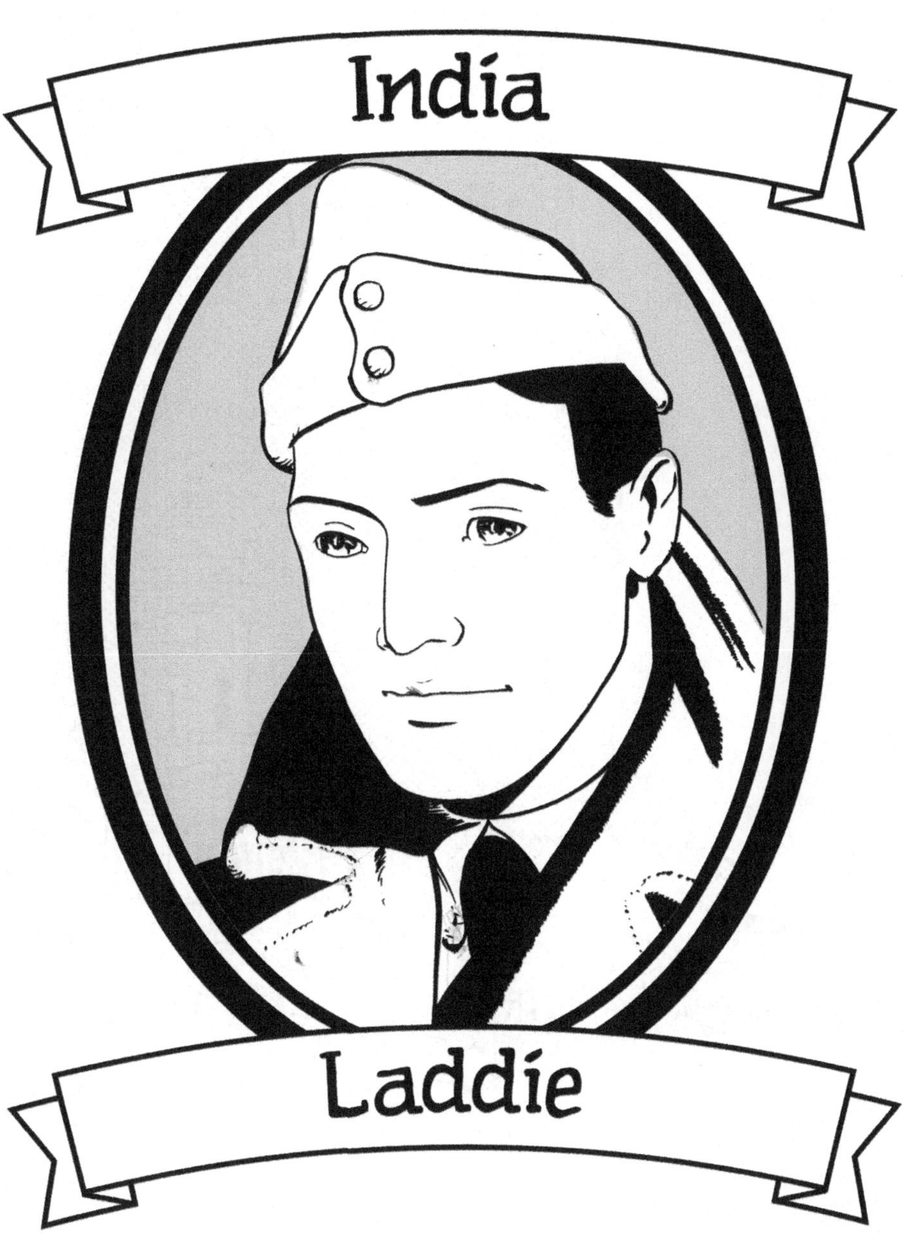
India
Laddie

Laddie

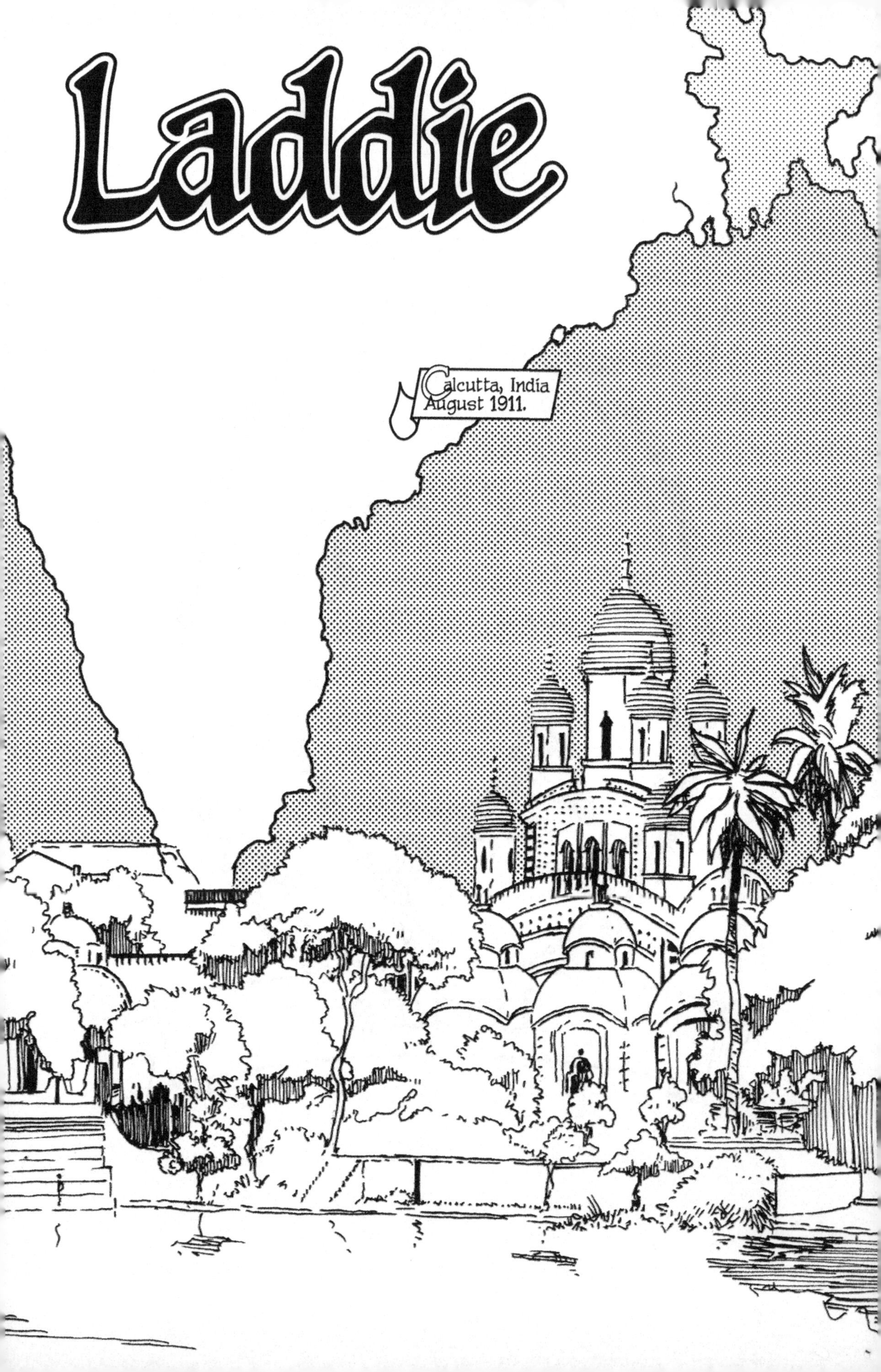
Calcutta, India
August 1911.

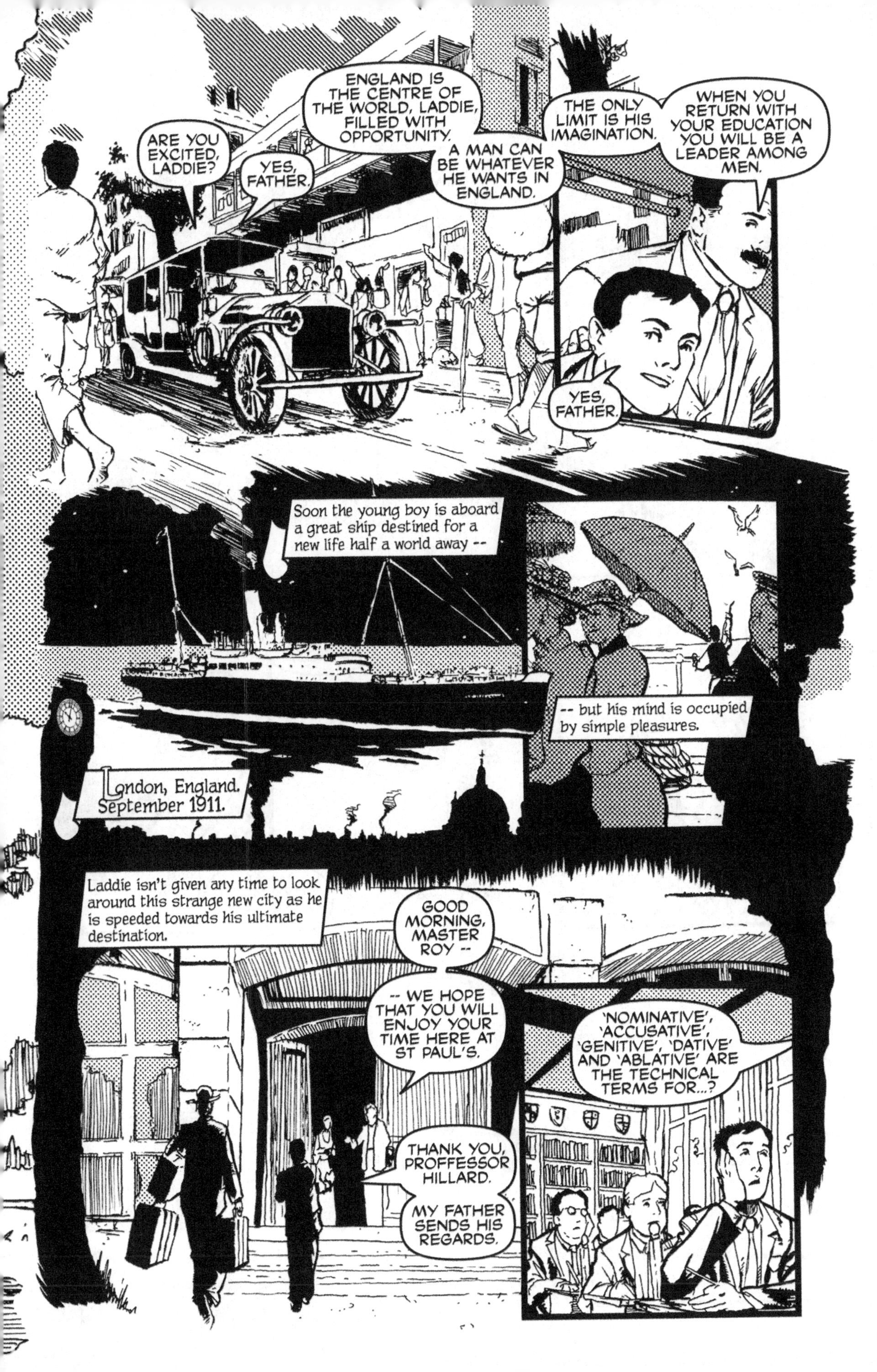
ARE YOU EXCITED, LADDIE?
YES, FATHER.
ENGLAND IS THE CENTRE OF THE WORLD, LADDIE, FILLED WITH OPPORTUNITY.
A MAN CAN BE WHATEVER HE WANTS IN ENGLAND.
THE ONLY LIMIT IS HIS IMAGINATION.
WHEN YOU RETURN WITH YOUR EDUCATION YOU WILL BE A LEADER AMONG MEN.
YES, FATHER.
Soon the young boy is aboard a great ship destined for a new life half a world away --
-- but his mind is occupied by simple pleasures.
London, England. September 1911.
Laddie isn't given any time to look around this strange new city as he is speeded towards his ultimate destination.
GOOD MORNING, MASTER ROY --
-- WE HOPE THAT YOU WILL ENJOY YOUR TIME HERE AT ST PAUL'S.
THANK YOU, PROFFESSOR HILLARD.
MY FATHER SENDS HIS REGARDS.
'NOMINATIVE', 'ACCUSATIVE', 'GENITIVE', 'DATIVE' AND 'ABLATIVE' ARE THE TECHNICAL TERMS FOR...?

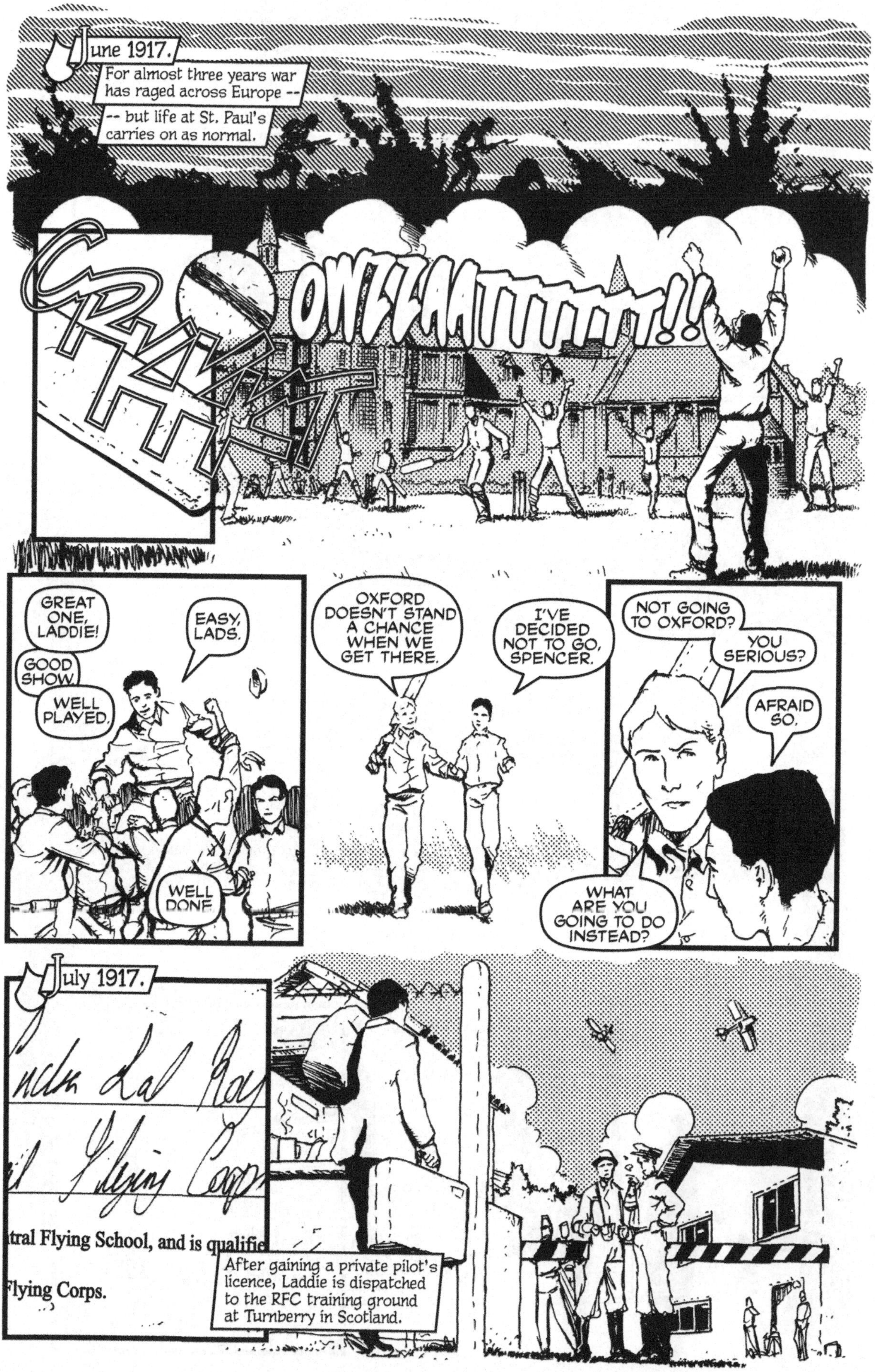
June 1917.
For almost three years war has raged across Europe --
-- but life at St. Paul's carries on as normal.
CRAAAACK!
OWZZAATTTTTT!!
GREAT ONE, LADDIE!
EASY, LADS.
GOOD SHOW.
WELL PLAYED.
WELL DONE.
OXFORD DOESN'T STAND A CHANCE WHEN WE GET THERE.
I'VE DECIDED NOT TO GO, SPENCER.
NOT GOING TO OXFORD?
YOU SERIOUS?
AFRAID SO.
WHAT ARE YOU GOING TO DO INSTEAD?
July 1917.
tral Flying School, and is qualifie
Flying Corps.
After gaining a private pilot's licence, Laddie is dispatched to the RFC training ground at Turnberry in Scotland.

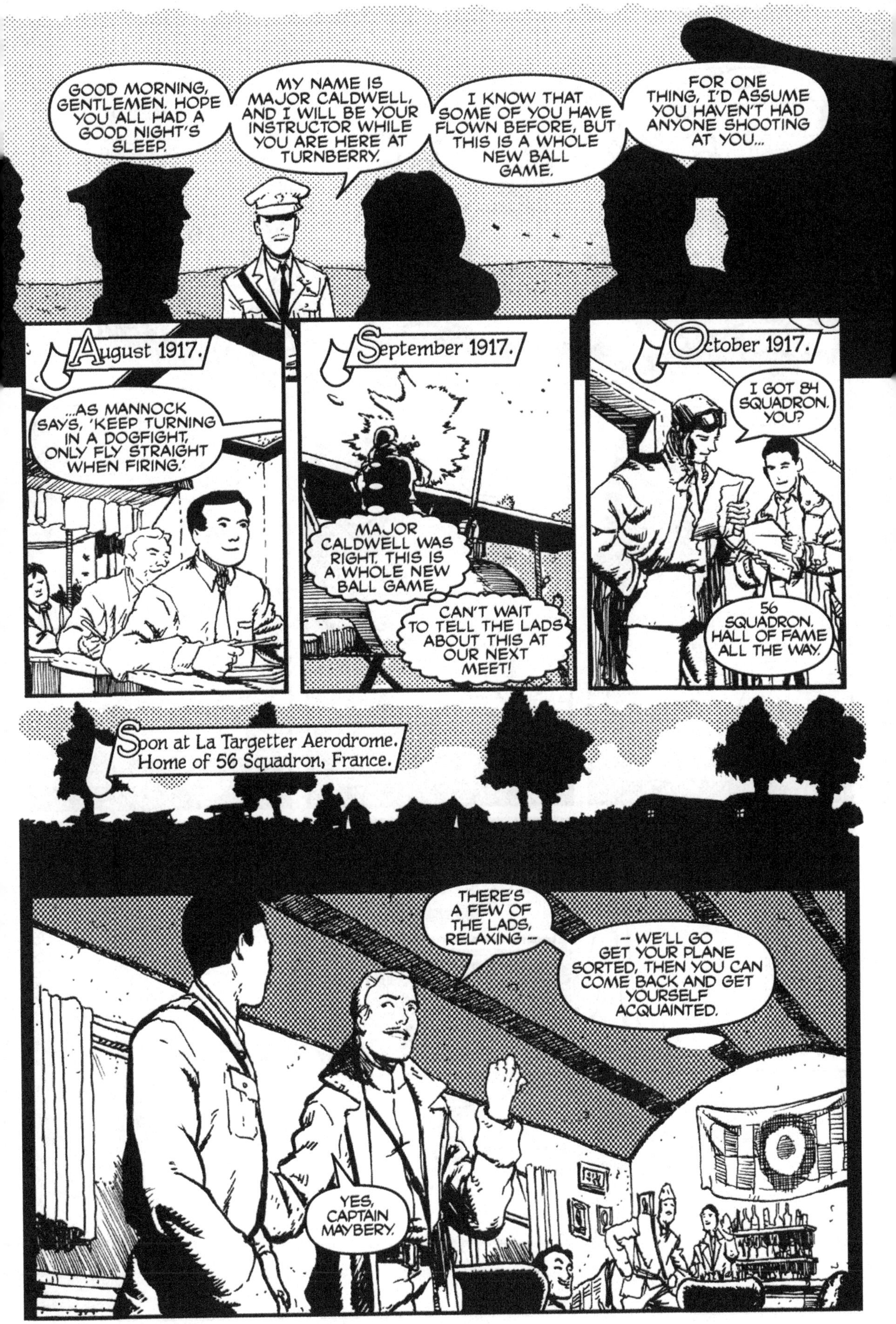
GOOD MORNING, GENTLEMEN. HOPE YOU ALL HAD A GOOD NIGHT'S SLEEP.
MY NAME IS MAJOR CALDWELL, AND I WILL BE YOUR INSTRUCTOR WHILE YOU ARE HERE AT TURNBERRY.
I KNOW THAT SOME OF YOU HAVE FLOWN BEFORE, BUT THIS IS A WHOLE NEW BALL GAME.
FOR ONE THING, I'D ASSUME YOU HAVEN'T HAD ANYONE SHOOTING AT YOU...
August 1917.
...AS MANNOCK SAYS, 'KEEP TURNING IN A DOGFIGHT, ONLY FLY STRAIGHT WHEN FIRING.'
September 1917.
MAJOR CALDWELL WAS RIGHT. THIS IS A WHOLE NEW BALL GAME.
CAN'T WAIT TO TELL THE LADS ABOUT THIS AT OUR NEXT MEET!
October 1917.
I GOT 84 SQUADRON. YOU?
56 SQUADRON. HALL OF FAME ALL THE WAY.
Soon at La Targetter Aerodrome. Home of 56 Squadron, France.
THERE'S A FEW OF THE LADS, RELAXING --
-- WE'LL GO GET YOUR PLANE SORTED, THEN YOU CAN COME BACK AND GET YOURSELF ACQUAINTED.
YES, CAPTAIN MAYBERY.

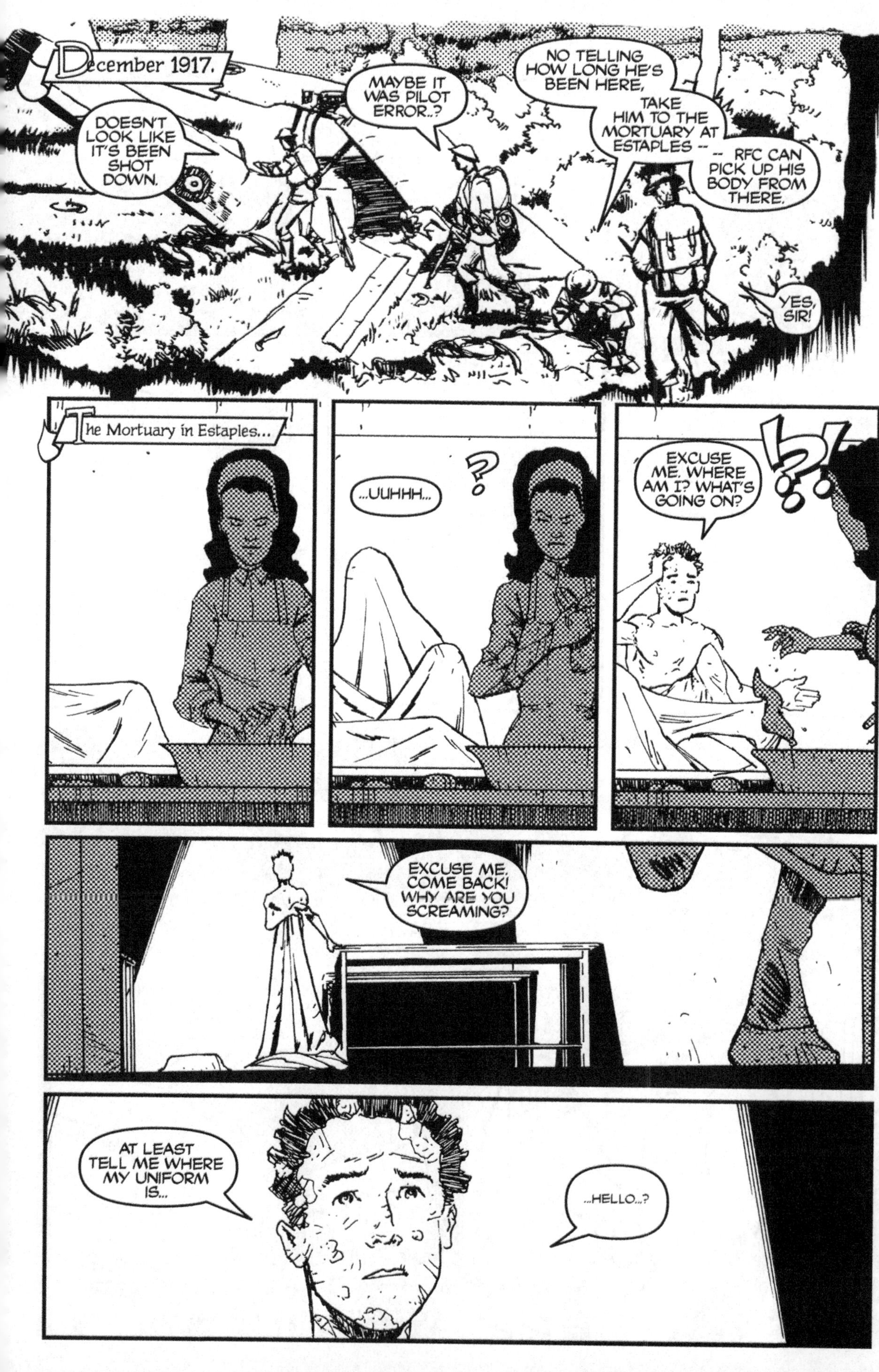
December 1917.
DOESN'T LOOK LIKE IT'S BEEN SHOT DOWN.
MAYBE IT WAS PILOT ERROR..?
NO TELLING HOW LONG HE'S BEEN HERE,
TAKE HIM TO THE MORTUARY AT ESTAPLES --
-- RFC CAN PICK UP HIS BODY FROM THERE.
YES, SIR!
The Mortuary in Estaples...
...UUHHH...
?
EXCUSE ME. WHERE AM I? WHAT'S GOING ON?
!?!
EXCUSE ME. COME BACK! WHY ARE YOU SCREAMING?
AT LEAST TELL ME WHERE MY UNIFORM IS...
...HELLO...?

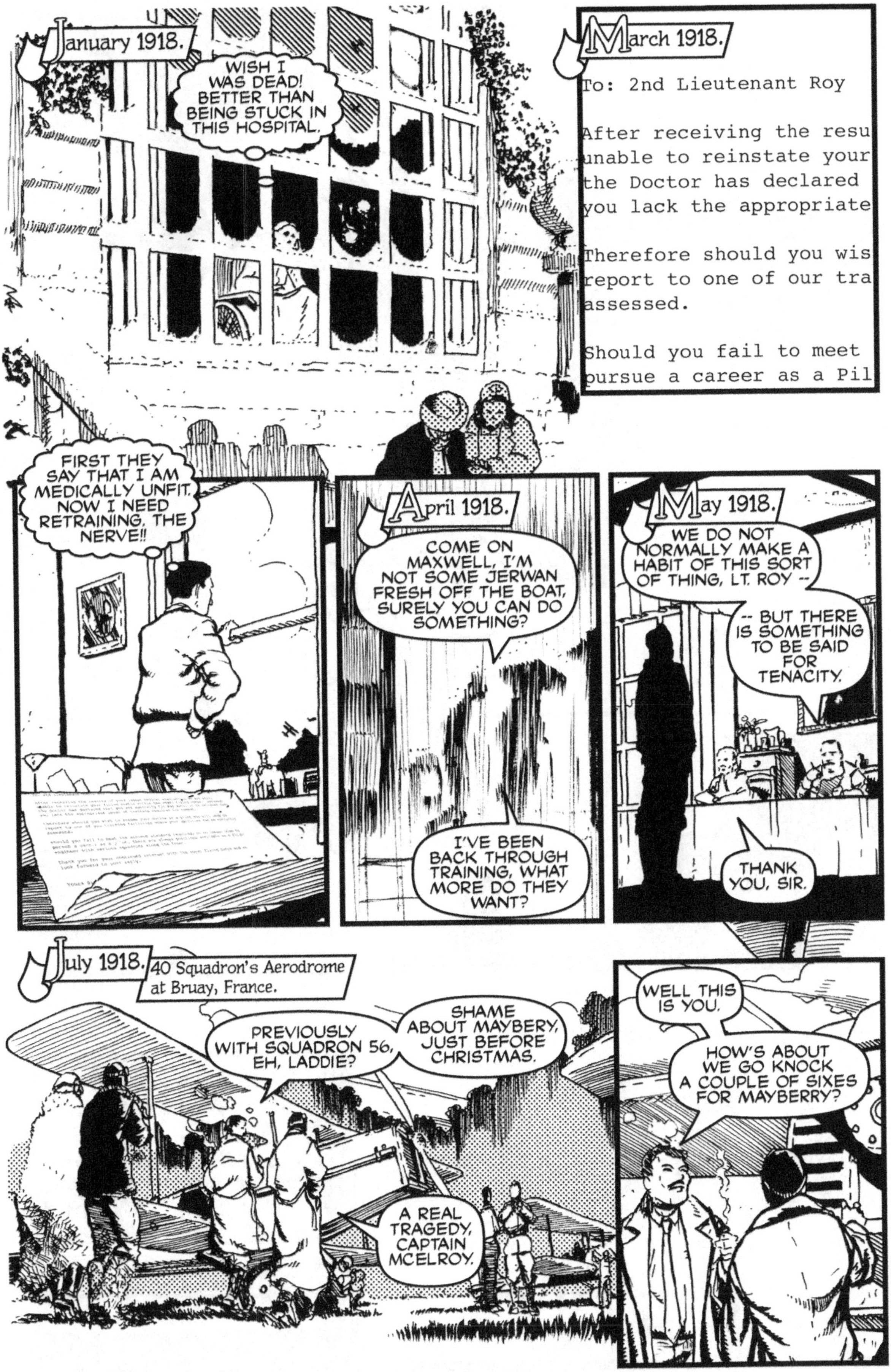
January 1918.
WISH I WAS DEAD! BETTER THAN BEING STUCK IN THIS HOSPITAL.
March 1918.
To: 2nd Lieutenant Roy
After receiving the resu
unable to reinstate your
the Doctor has declared
you lack the appropriate
Therefore should you wis
report to one of our tra
assessed.
Should you fail to meet
pursue a career as a Pil
FIRST THEY SAY THAT I AM MEDICALLY UNFIT. NOW I NEED RETRAINING. THE NERVE!!
April 1918.
COME ON MAXWELL, I'M NOT SOME JERWAN FRESH OFF THE BOAT, SURELY YOU CAN DO SOMETHING?
I'VE BEEN BACK THROUGH TRAINING, WHAT MORE DO THEY WANT?
May 1918.
WE DO NOT NORMALLY MAKE A HABIT OF THIS SORT OF THING, LT. ROY --
-- BUT THERE IS SOMETHING TO BE SAID FOR TENACITY.
THANK YOU, SIR.
July 1918.
40 Squadron's Aerodrome at Bruay, France.
PREVIOUSLY WITH SQUADRON 56, EH, LADDIE?
SHAME ABOUT MAYBERY, JUST BEFORE CHRISTMAS.
A REAL TRAGEDY, CAPTAIN MCELROY.
WELL THIS IS YOU.
HOW'S ABOUT WE GO KNOCK A COUPLE OF SIXES FOR MAYBERRY?

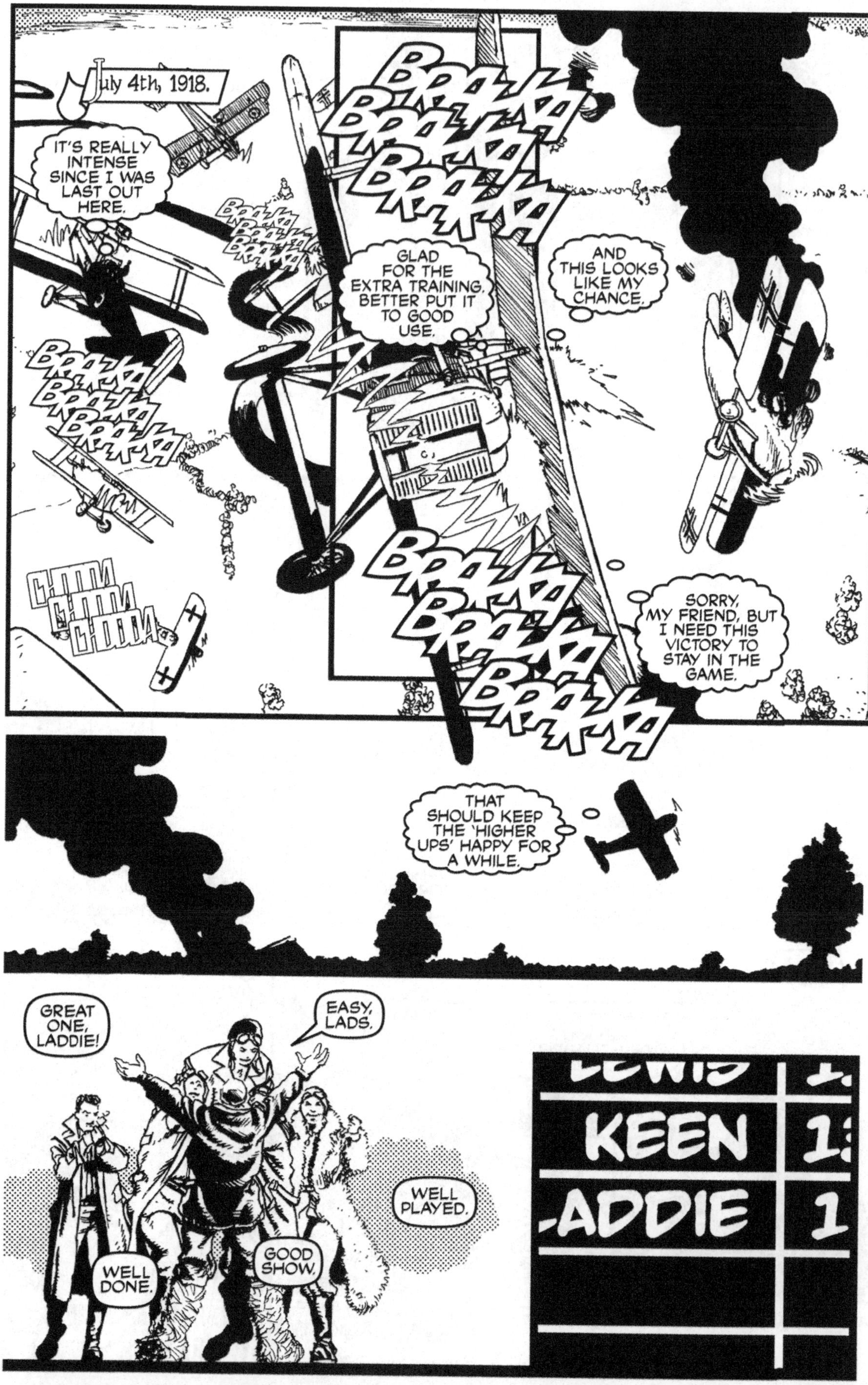
July 4th, 1918.
IT'S REALLY INTENSE SINCE I WAS LAST OUT HERE.
BRAKKA BRAKKA BRAKKA
GLAD FOR THE EXTRA TRAINING. BETTER PUT IT TO GOOD USE.
AND THIS LOOKS LIKE MY CHANCE.
CHODDA CHODDA CHODDA
SORRY, MY FRIEND, BUT I NEED THIS VICTORY TO STAY IN THE GAME.
BRAKKA BRAKKA BRAKKA
THAT SHOULD KEEP THE 'HIGHER UPS' HAPPY FOR A WHILE.
GREAT ONE, LADDIE!
EASY, LADS.
WELL PLAYED.
GOOD SHOW.
WELL DONE.
KEEN
-ADDIE

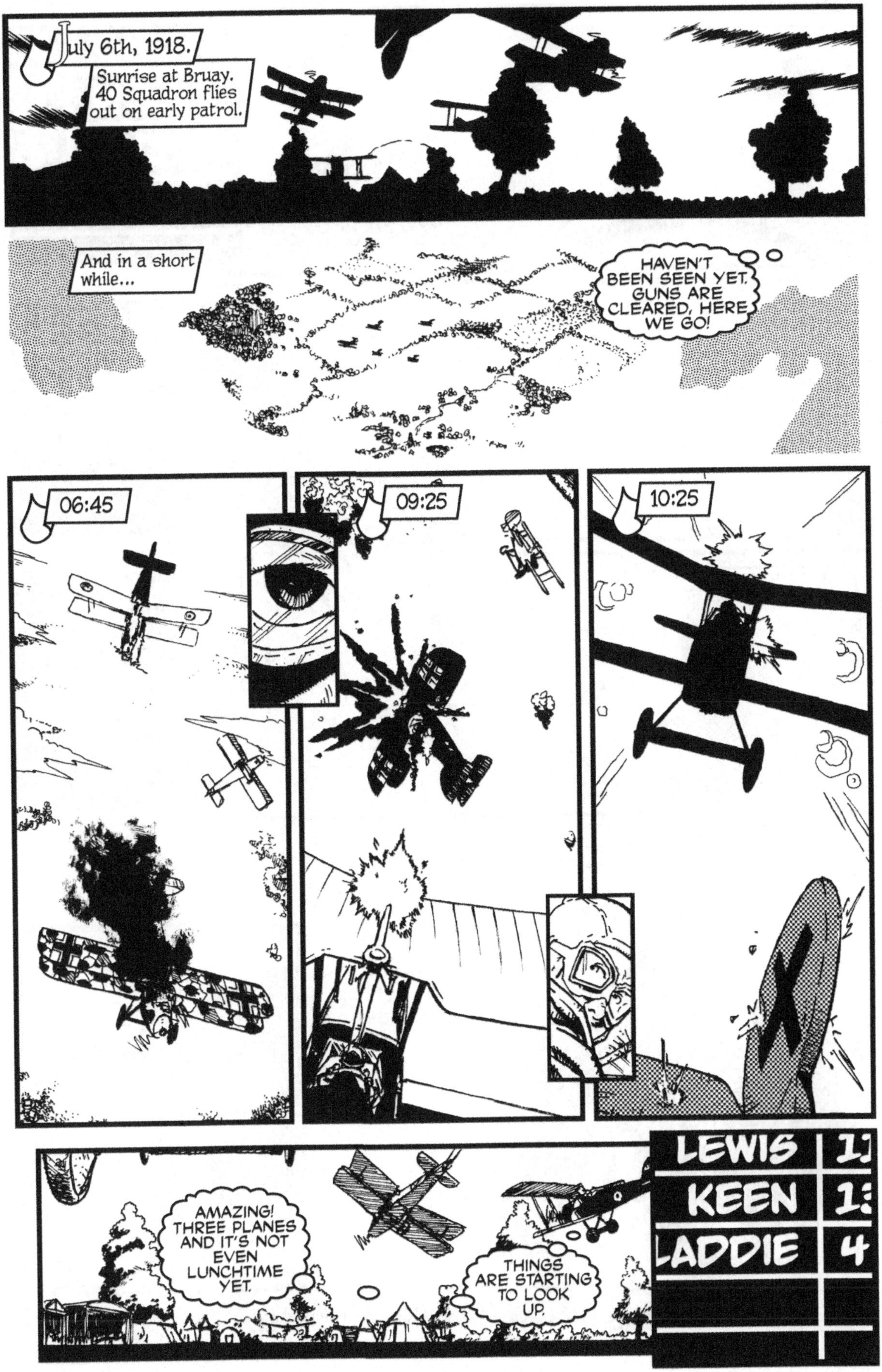
July 6th, 1918.
Sunrise at Bruay. 40 Squadron flies out on early patrol.
And in a short while...
HAVEN'T BEEN SEEN YET. GUNS ARE CLEARED, HERE WE GO!
06:45
09:25
10:25
AMAZING! THREE PLANES AND IT'S NOT EVEN LUNCHTIME YET.
THINGS ARE STARTING TO LOOK UP.
LEWIS
KEEN
LADDIE 4

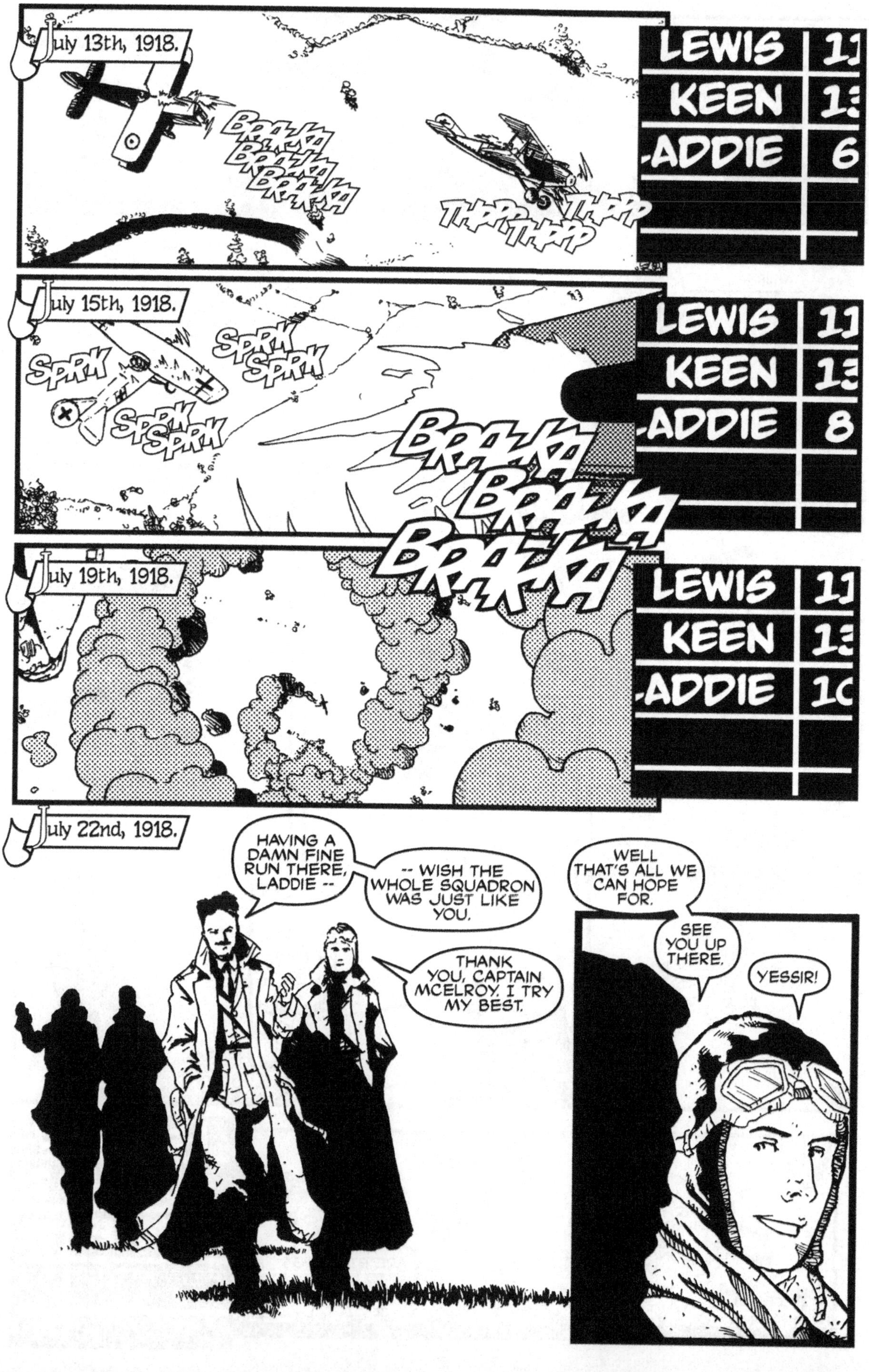
July 13th, 1918.
BRAKKA BRAKKA BRAKKA
THPP THPP THPP THPP
LEWIS 11
KEEN 13
LADDIE 6
July 15th, 1918.
SPRK
SPRK SPRK
SPRK SPRK
BRAKKA BRAKKA BRAKKA
LEWIS 11
KEEN 13
LADDIE 8
July 19th, 1918.
LEWIS 11
KEEN 13
LADDIE 10
July 22nd, 1918.
HAVING A DAMN FINE RUN THERE, LADDIE --
-- WISH THE WHOLE SQUADRON WAS JUST LIKE YOU.
THANK YOU, CAPTAIN MCELROY. I TRY MY BEST.
WELL THAT'S ALL WE CAN HOPE FOR.
SEE YOU UP THERE.
YESSIR!

Soon, over Carvin...

THPPP THPPP

THPPP

GIDDA GIDDA GIDDA GIDDA

CAN'T GET CLEAR OF THIS PILOT --

-- GOING TO NEED SOME HELP ON THIS ONE.

GIDDA GIDDA GIDDA GIDDA

GIDDA GIDDA GIDDA GIDDA

TRY AND LURE HIM TOWARDS THE REST OF THE SQUADRON...

LADDIE!!

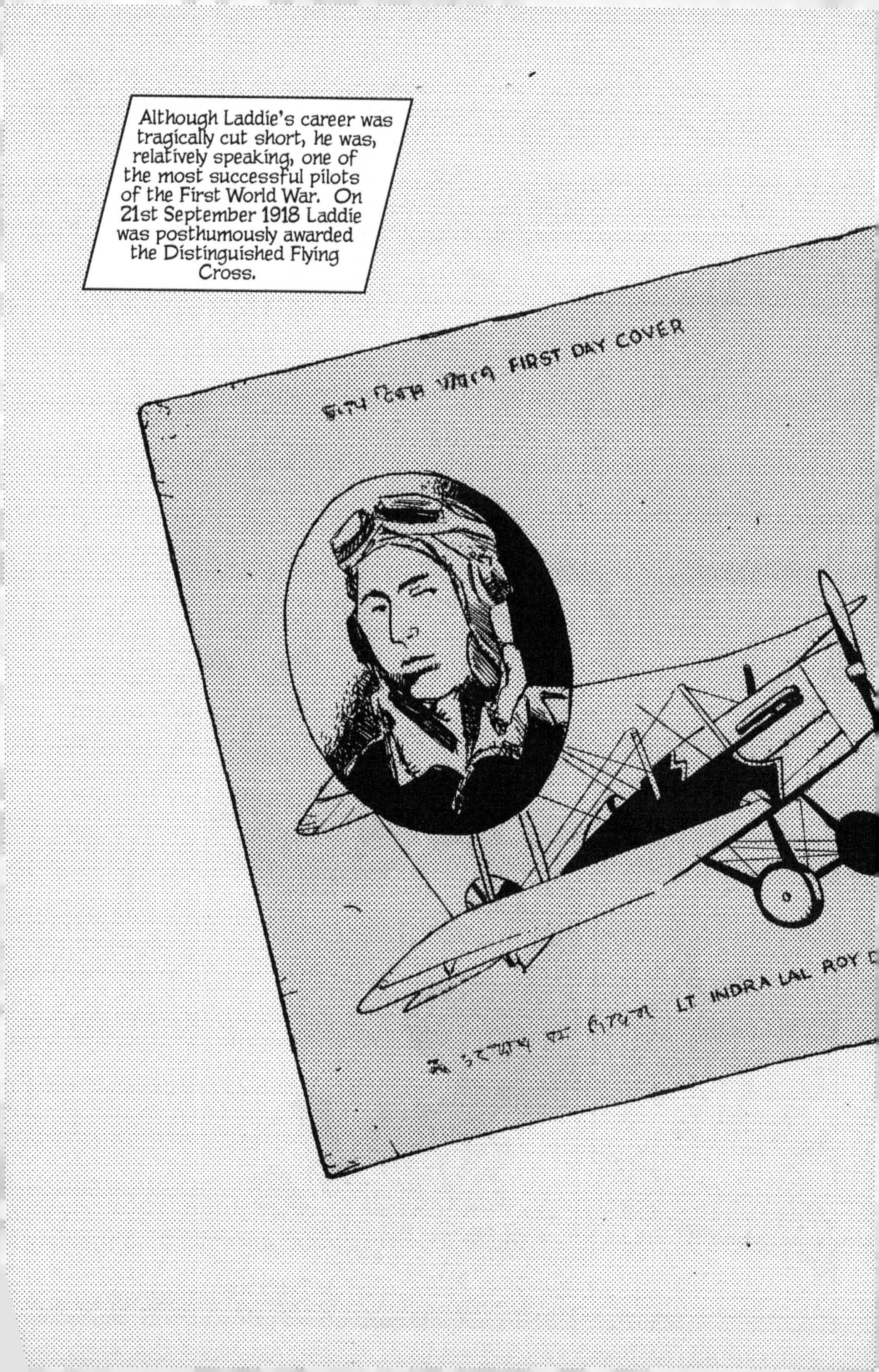
Although Laddie's career was tragically cut short, he was, relatively speaking, one of the most successful pilots of the First World War. On 21st September 1918 Laddie was posthumously awarded the Distinguished Flying Cross.
FIRST DAY COVER
LT INDRA LAL ROY

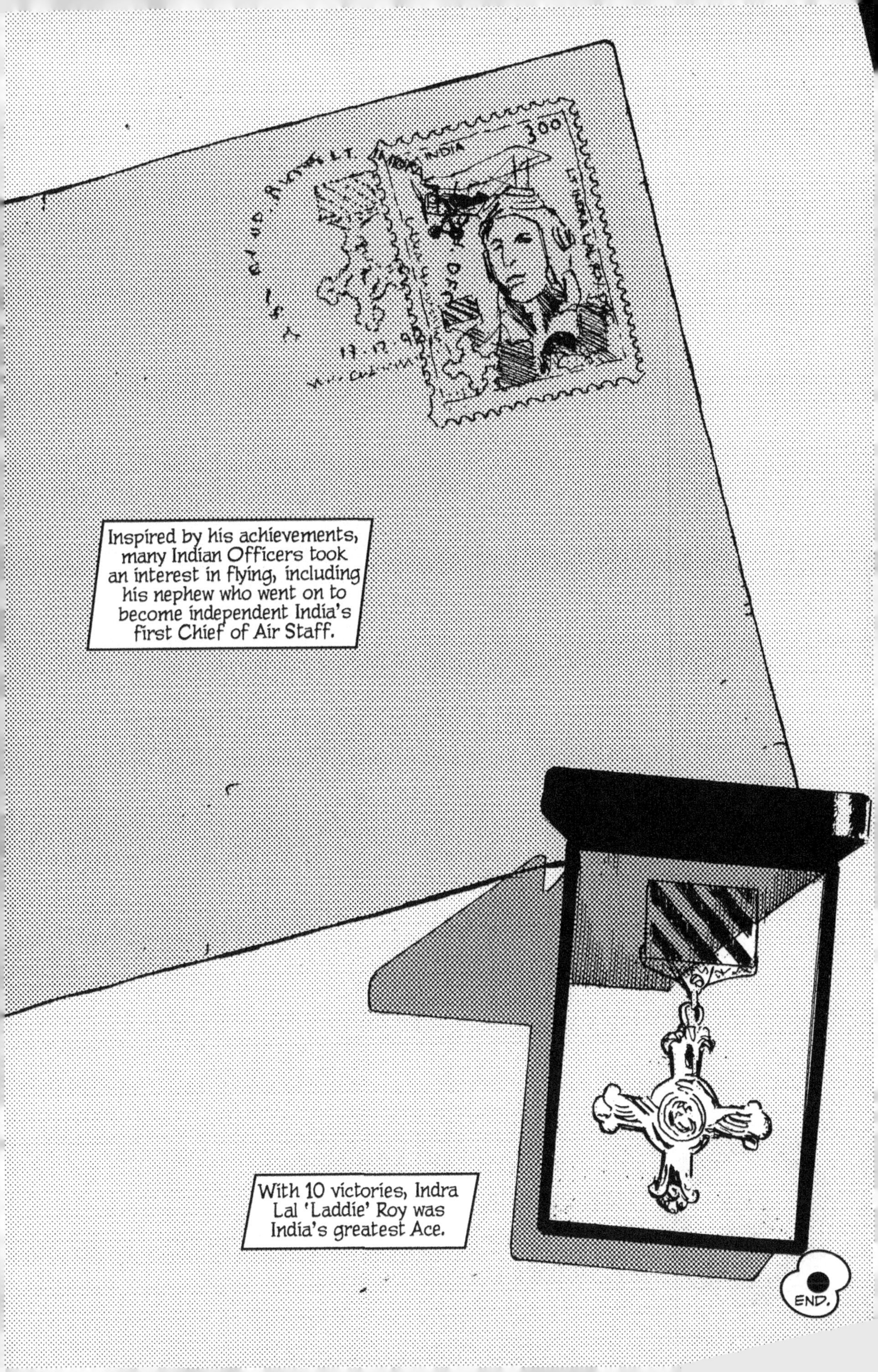
Inspired by his achievements, many Indian Officers took an interest in flying, including his nephew who went on to become independent India's first Chief of Air Staff.
With 10 victories, Indra Lal 'Laddie' Roy was India's greatest Ace.
END.

 George 'McIrish' McElroy
Born in Ireland
Royal Flying Corps/Royal Air Force
47 victories

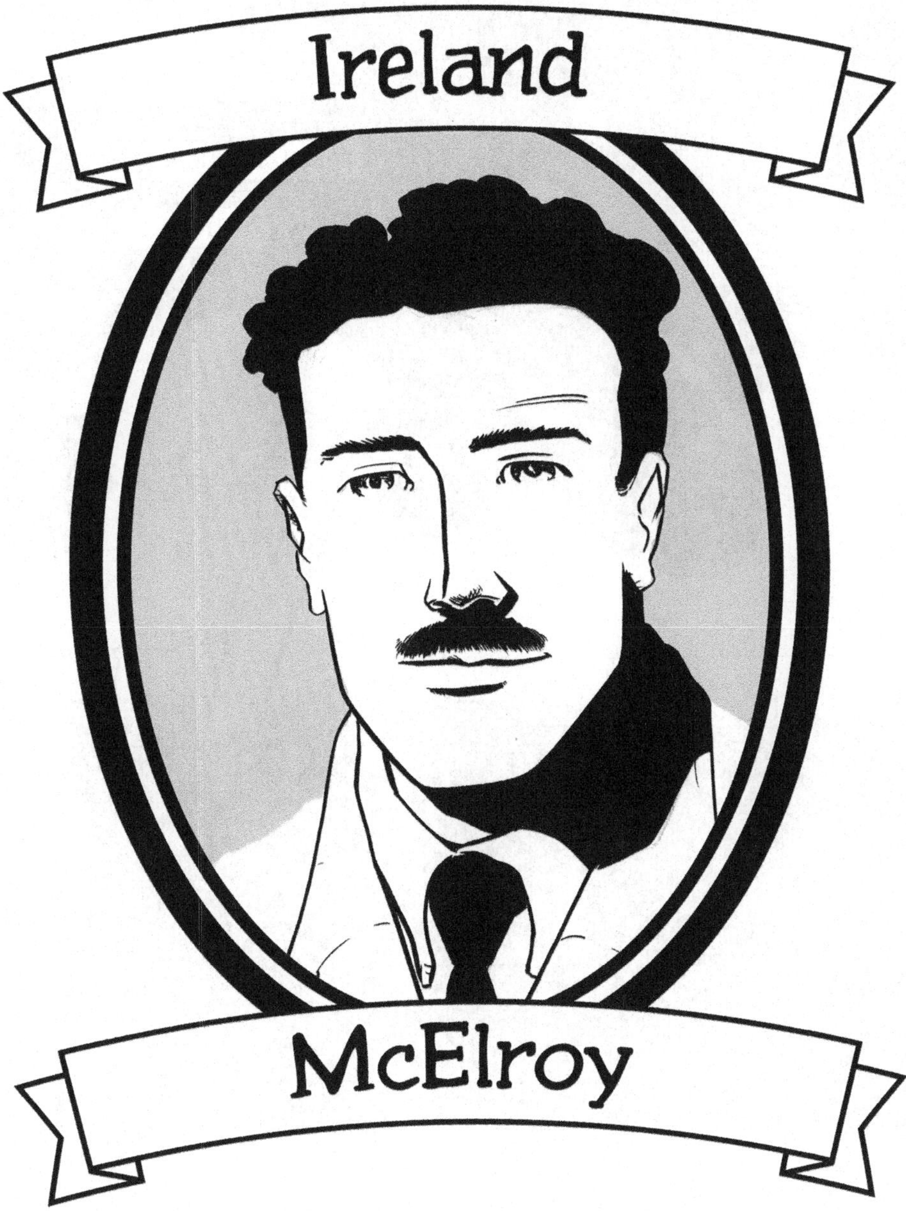
Ireland
McElroy

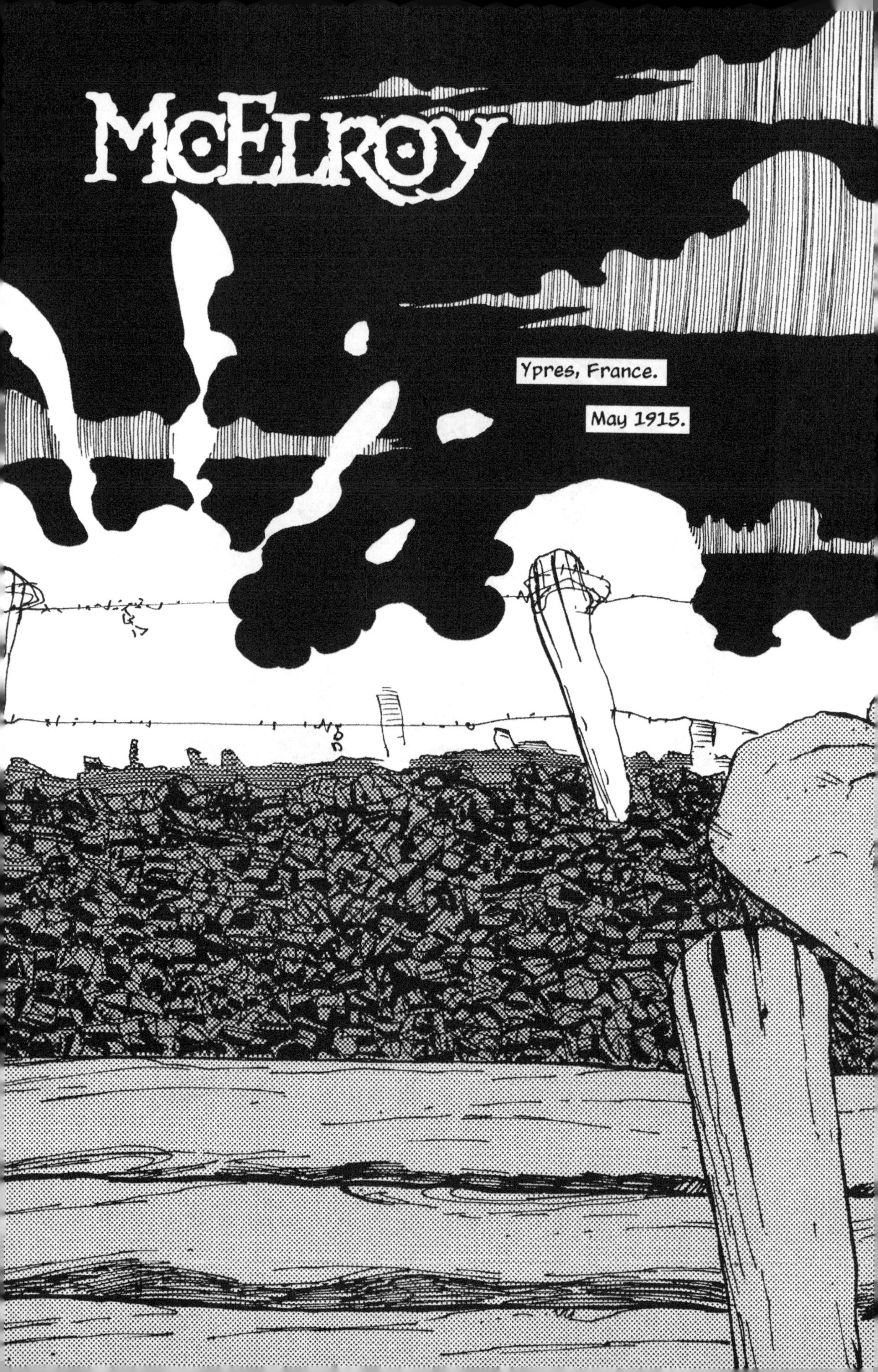
McELROY
Ypres, France.
May 1915.

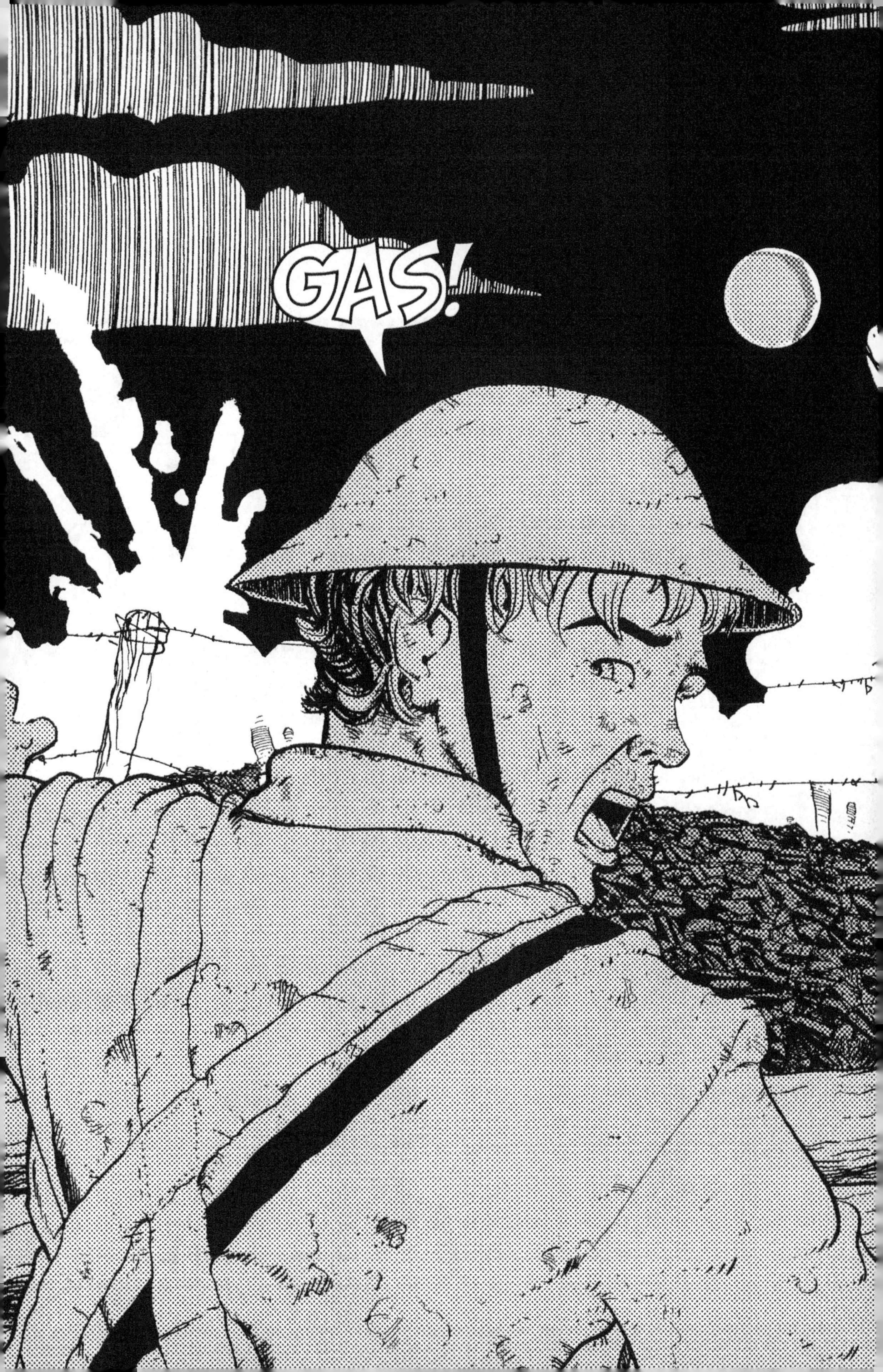
GAS!

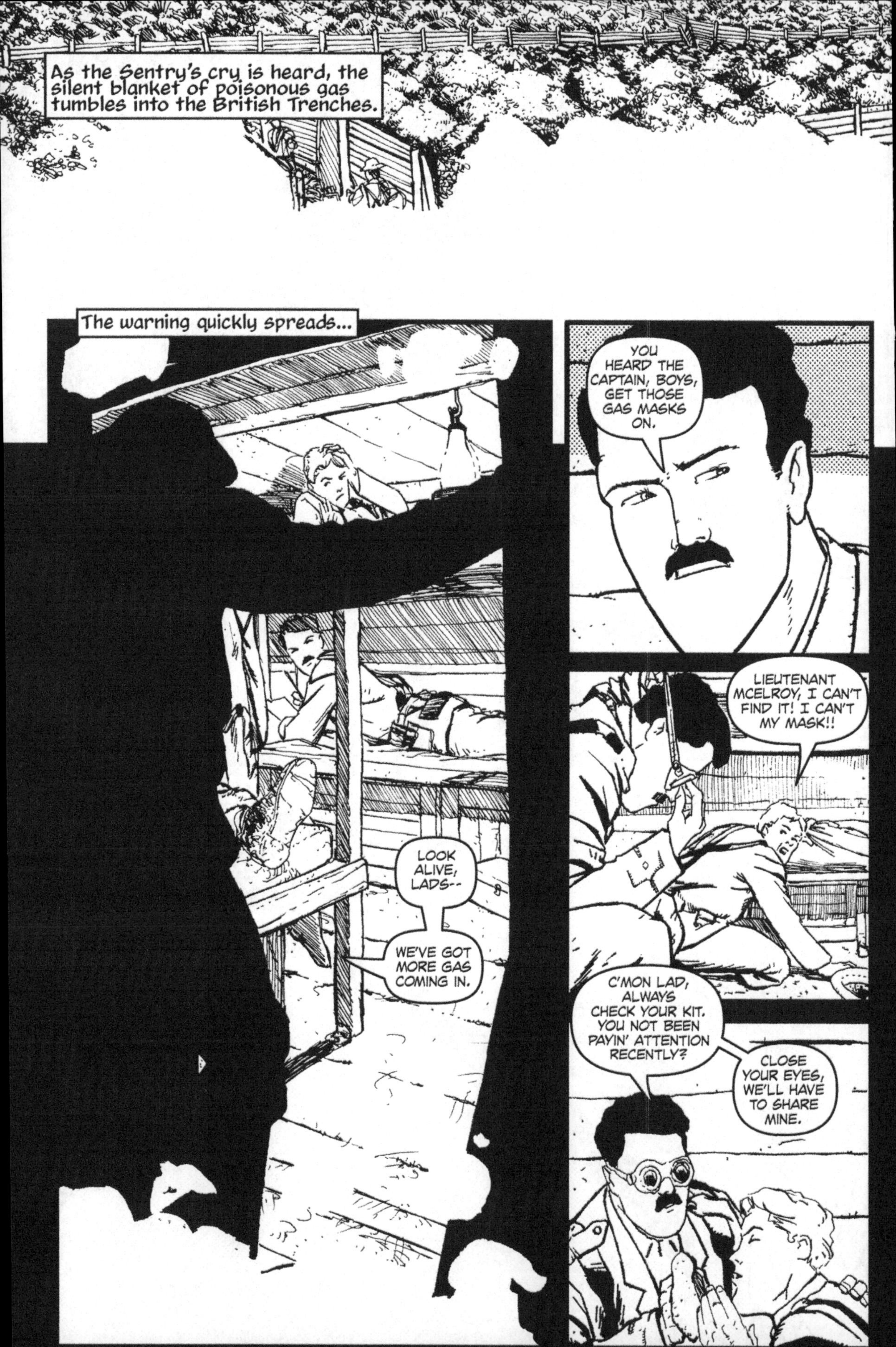
As the Sentry's cry is heard, the silent blanket of poisonous gas tumbles into the British Trenches.
The warning quickly spreads...
LOOK ALIVE, LADS--
WE'VE GOT MORE GAS COMING IN.
YOU HEARD THE CAPTAIN, BOYS, GET THOSE GAS MASKS ON.
LIEUTENANT MCELROY, I CAN'T FIND IT! I CAN'T MY MASK!!
C'MON LAD, ALWAYS CHECK YOUR KIT. YOU NOT BEEN PAYIN' ATTENTION RECENTLY?
CLOSE YOUR EYES, WE'LL HAVE TO SHARE MINE.

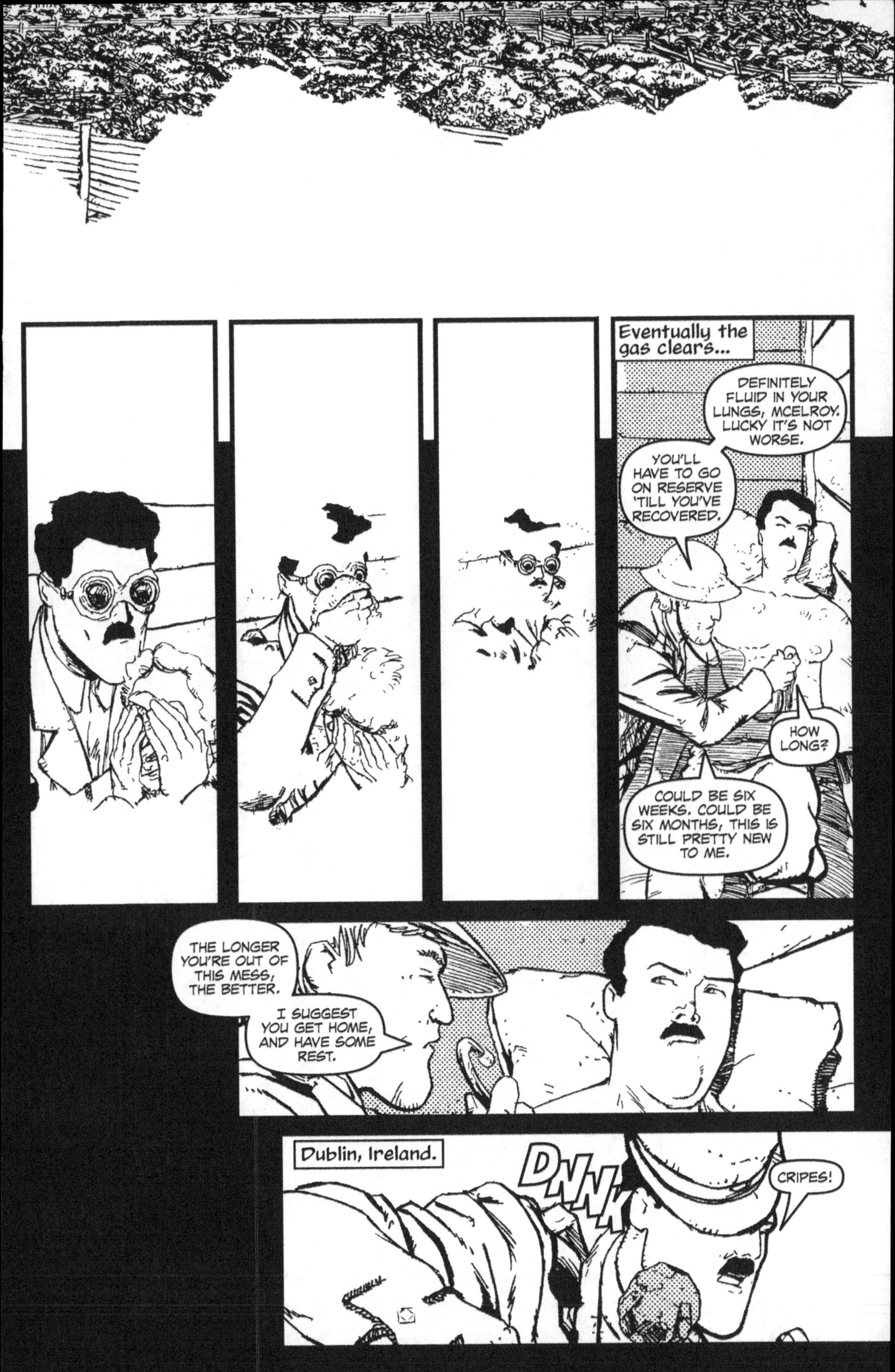
Eventually the gas clears...
DEFINITELY FLUID IN YOUR LUNGS, MCELROY. LUCKY IT'S NOT WORSE.
YOU'LL HAVE TO GO ON RESERVE 'TILL YOU'VE RECOVERED.
HOW LONG?
COULD BE SIX WEEKS. COULD BE SIX MONTHS, THIS IS STILL PRETTY NEW TO ME.
THE LONGER YOU'RE OUT OF THIS MESS, THE BETTER.
I SUGGEST YOU GET HOME, AND HAVE SOME REST.
Dublin, Ireland.
DNNK
CRIPES!

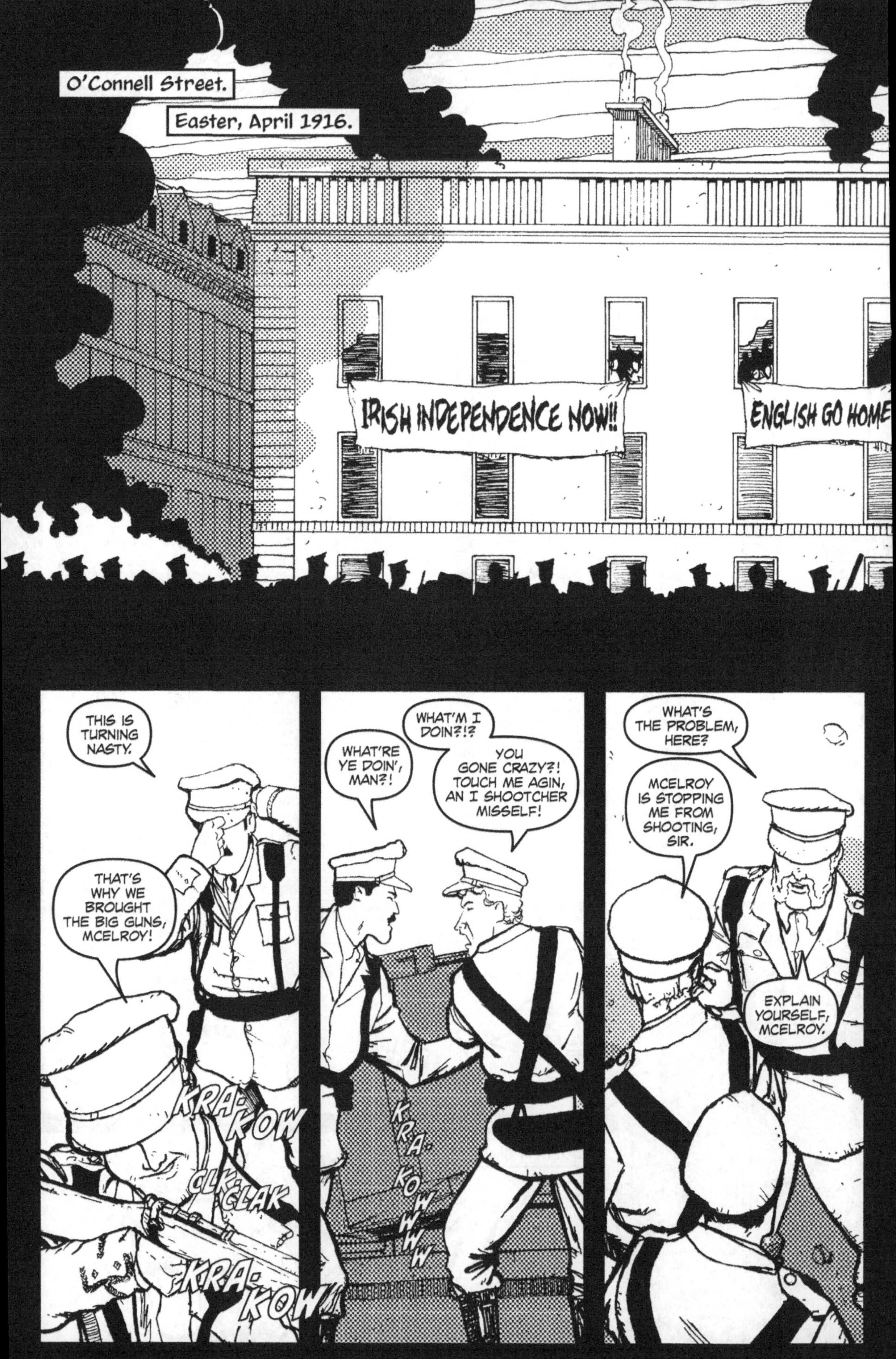
O'Connell Street.
Easter, April 1916.
IRISH INDEPENDENCE NOW!!
ENGLISH GO HOME
THIS IS TURNING NASTY.
THAT'S WHY WE BROUGHT THE BIG GUNS, MCELROY!
KRA-KOW
CLK-CLAK
KRA-KOW
WHAT'RE YE DOIN', MAN?!
WHAT'M I DOIN?!?
YOU GONE CRAZY?! TOUCH ME AGIN, AN I SHOOTCHER MISSELF!
KRA-KOWWWW
WHAT'S THE PROBLEM, HERE?
MCELROY IS STOPPING ME FROM SHOOTING, SIR.
EXPLAIN YOURSELF, MCELROY.

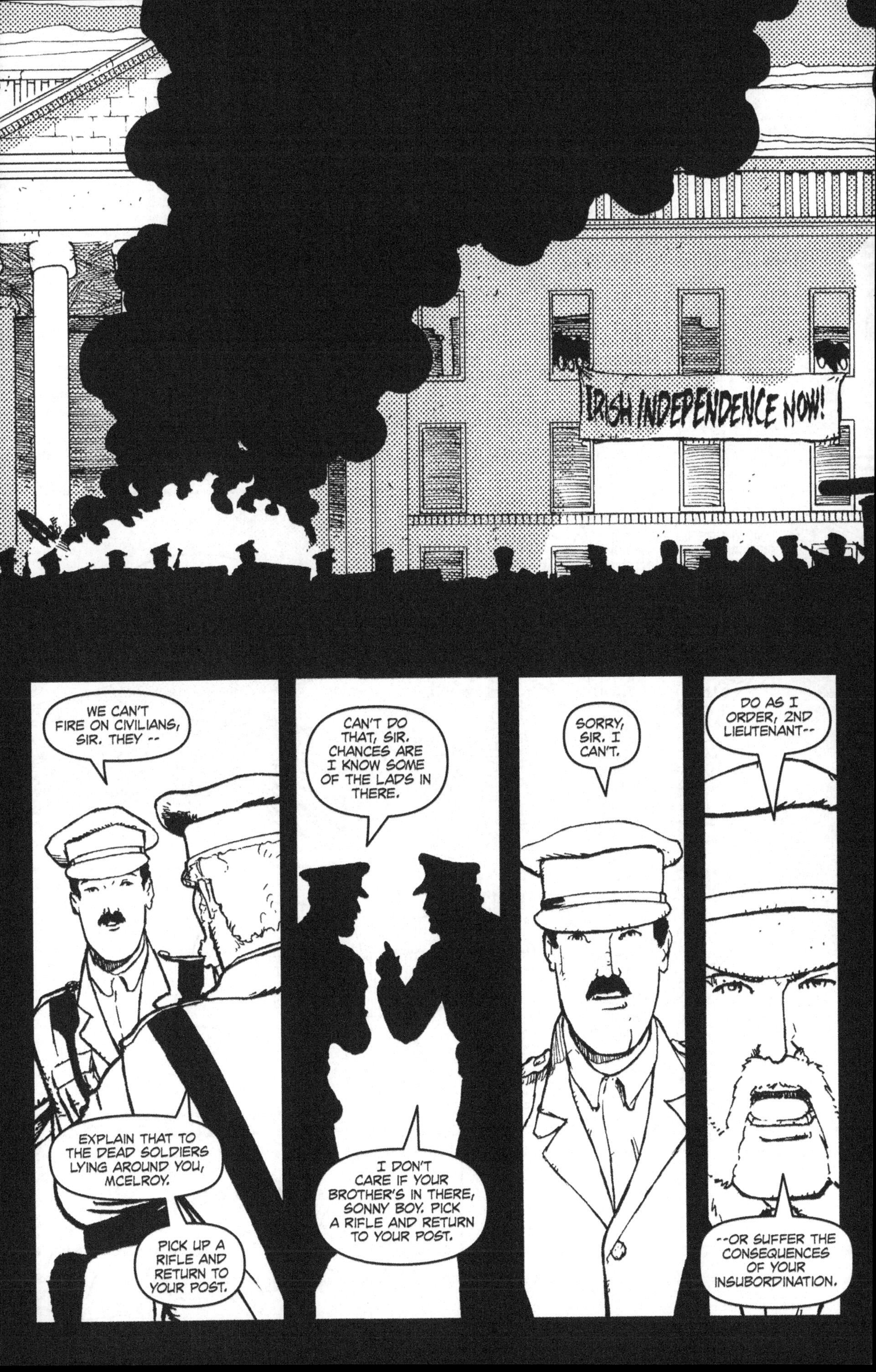
IRISH INDEPENDENCE NOW!
WE CAN'T FIRE ON CIVILIANS, SIR. THEY --
EXPLAIN THAT TO THE DEAD SOLDIERS LYING AROUND YOU, MCELROY.
PICK UP A RIFLE AND RETURN TO YOUR POST.
CAN'T DO THAT, SIR. CHANCES ARE I KNOW SOME OF THE LADS IN THERE.
I DON'T CARE IF YOUR BROTHER'S IN THERE, SONNY BOY. PICK A RIFLE AND RETURN TO YOUR POST.
SORRY, SIR. I CAN'T.
DO AS I ORDER, 2ND LIEUTENANT--
--OR SUFFER THE CONSEQUENCES OF YOUR INSUBORDINATION.

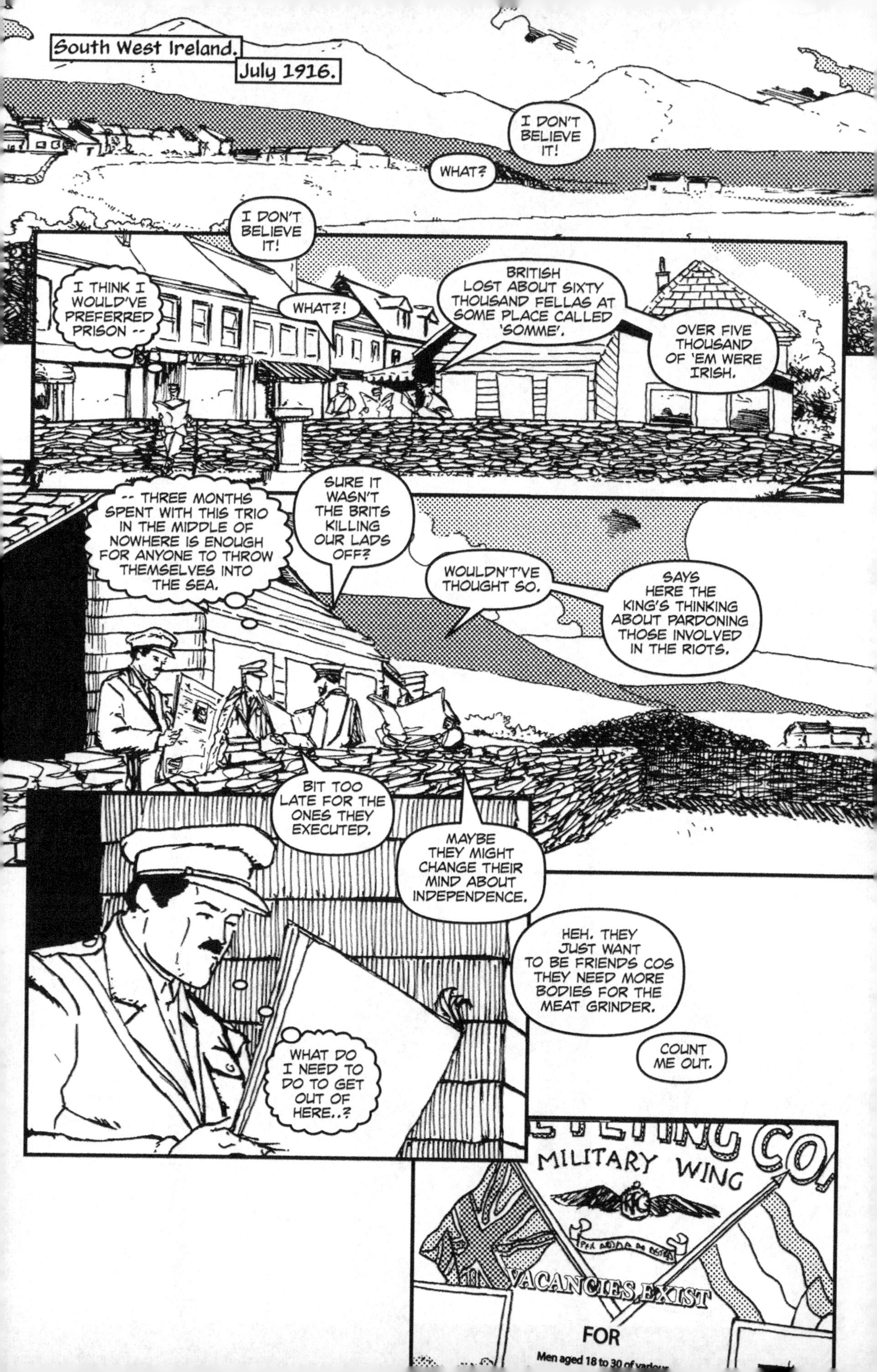
South West Ireland.
July 1916.
I DON'T BELIEVE IT!
WHAT?
I DON'T BELIEVE IT!
I THINK I WOULD'VE PREFERRED PRISON --
WHAT?!
BRITISH LOST ABOUT SIXTY THOUSAND FELLAS AT SOME PLACE CALLED 'SOMME'.
OVER FIVE THOUSAND OF 'EM WERE IRISH.
-- THREE MONTHS SPENT WITH THIS TRIO IN THE MIDDLE OF NOWHERE IS ENOUGH FOR ANYONE TO THROW THEMSELVES INTO THE SEA.
SURE IT WASN'T THE BRITS KILLING OUR LADS OFF?
WOULDN'T'VE THOUGHT SO.
SAYS HERE THE KING'S THINKING ABOUT PARDONING THOSE INVOLVED IN THE RIOTS.
BIT TOO LATE FOR THE ONES THEY EXECUTED.
MAYBE THEY MIGHT CHANGE THEIR MIND ABOUT INDEPENDENCE.
WHAT DO I NEED TO DO TO GET OUT OF HERE..?
HEH. THEY JUST WANT TO BE FRIENDS COS THEY NEED MORE BODIES FOR THE MEAT GRINDER.
COUNT ME OUT.
MILITARY WING
VACANCIES EXIST
FOR
Men aged 18 to 30 of vadour

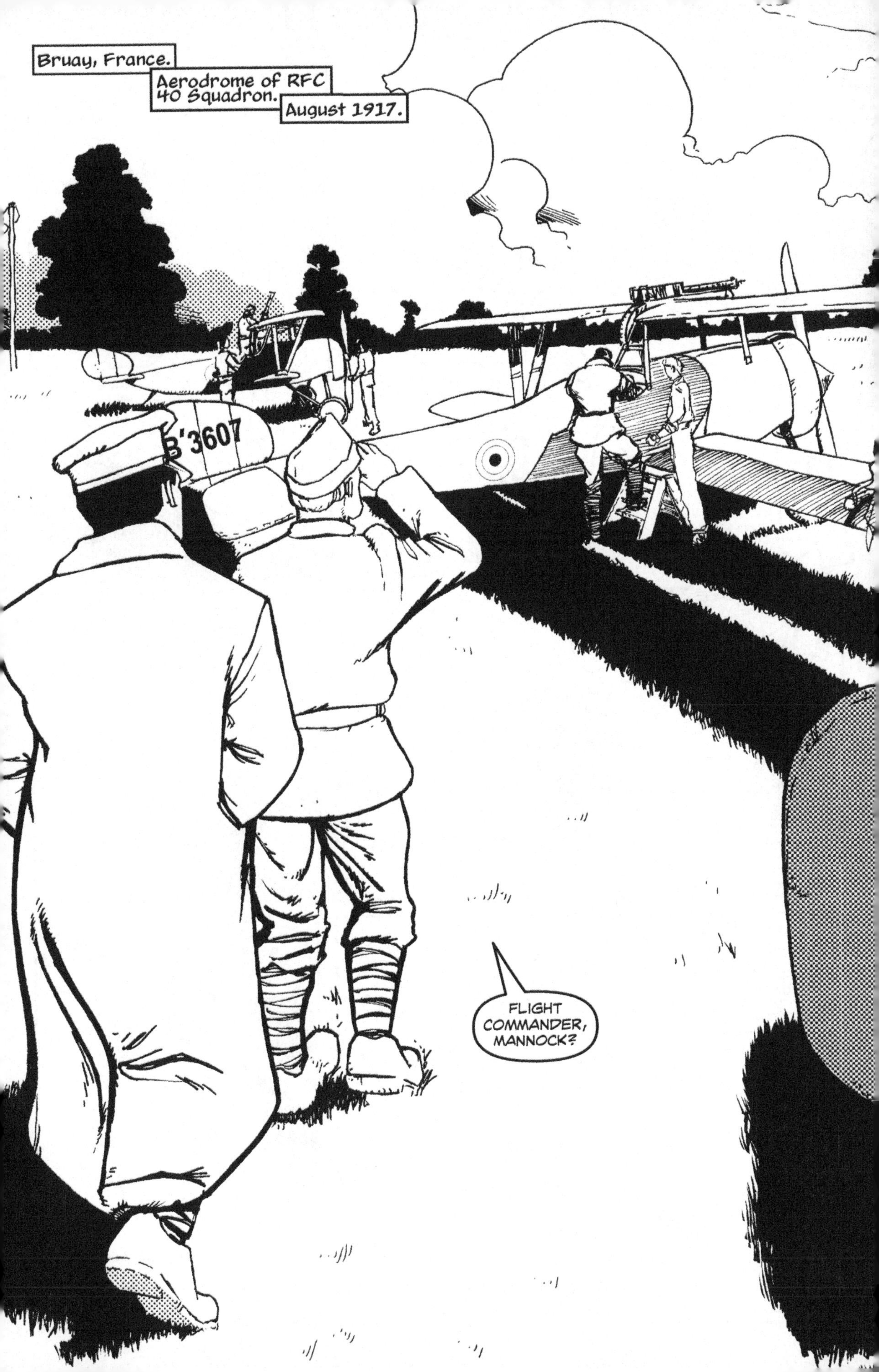

Bruay, France.
Aerodrome of RFC 40 Squadron.
August 1917.
B'3607
FLIGHT COMMANDER, MANNOCK?

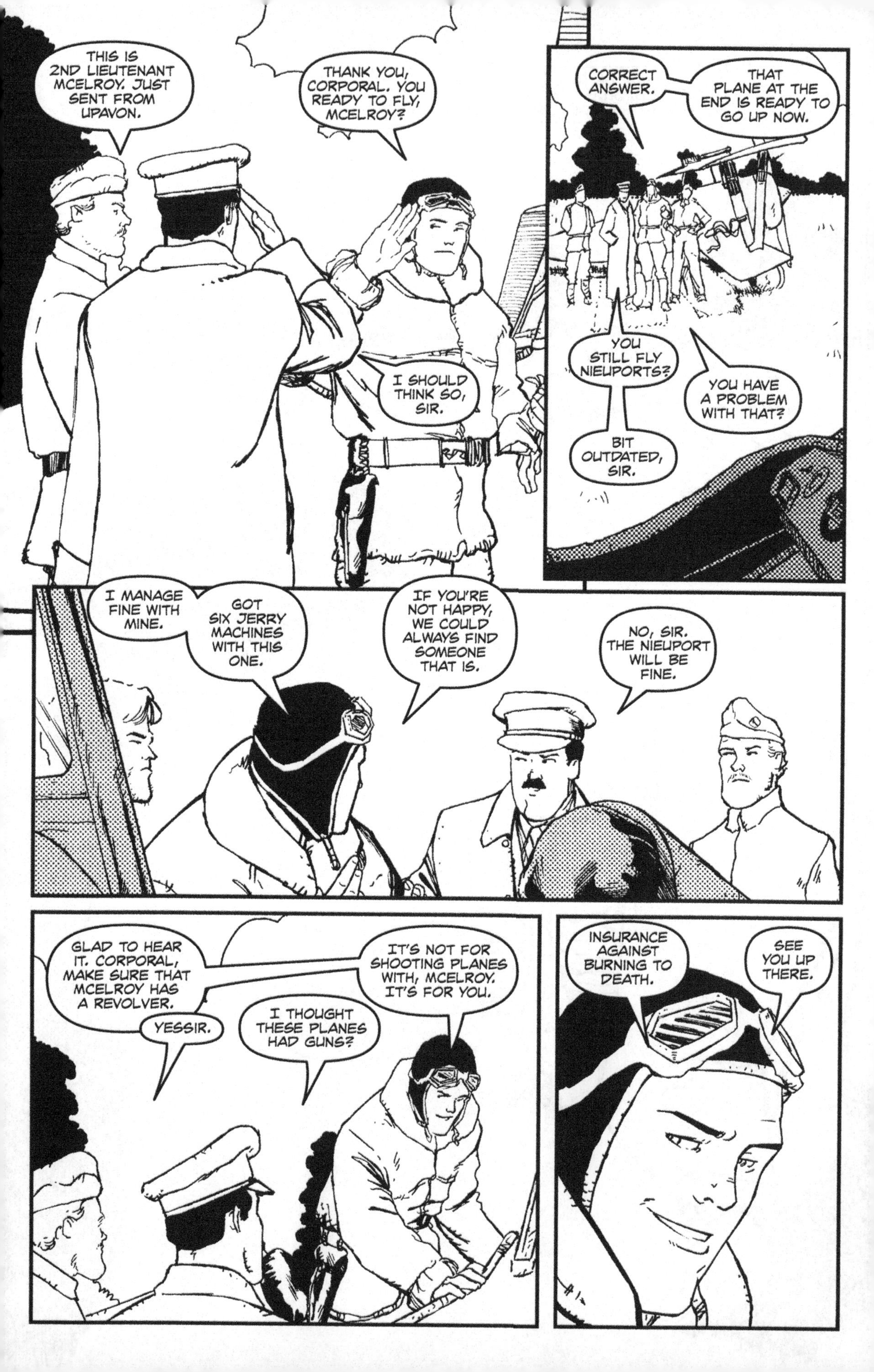

THIS IS 2ND LIEUTENANT MCELROY. JUST SENT FROM UPAVON.
THANK YOU, CORPORAL. YOU READY TO FLY, MCELROY?
I SHOULD THINK SO, SIR.
CORRECT ANSWER.
THAT PLANE AT THE END IS READY TO GO UP NOW.
YOU STILL FLY NIEUPORTS?
BIT OUTDATED, SIR.
YOU HAVE A PROBLEM WITH THAT?
I MANAGE FINE WITH MINE.
GOT SIX JERRY MACHINES WITH THIS ONE.
IF YOU'RE NOT HAPPY, WE COULD ALWAYS FIND SOMEONE THAT IS.
NO, SIR. THE NIEUPORT WILL BE FINE.
GLAD TO HEAR IT. CORPORAL, MAKE SURE THAT MCELROY HAS A REVOLVER.
YESSIR.
I THOUGHT THESE PLANES HAD GUNS?
IT'S NOT FOR SHOOTING PLANES WITH, MCELROY. IT'S FOR YOU.
INSURANCE AGAINST BURNING TO DEATH.
SEE YOU UP THERE.

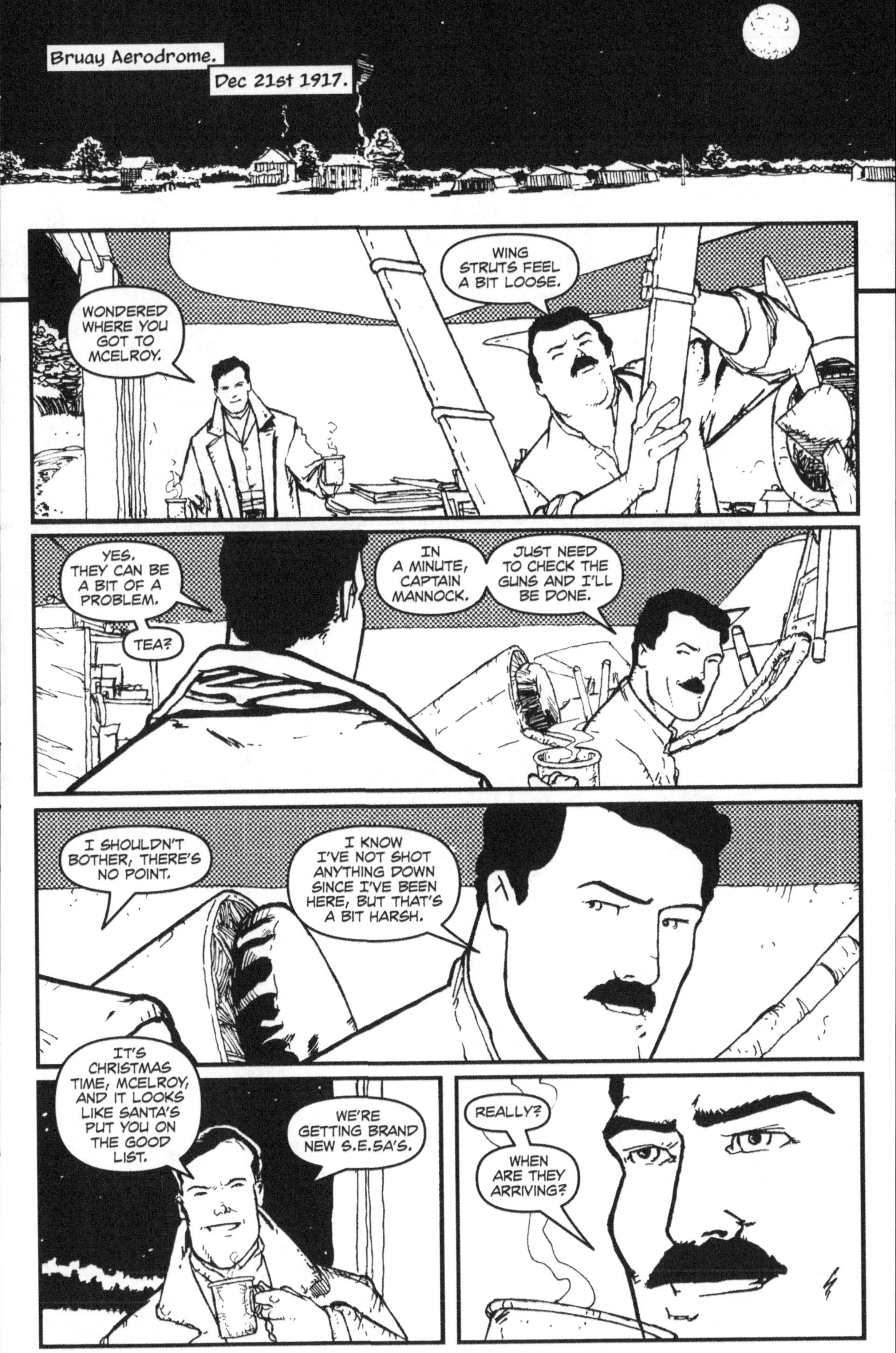
Bruay Aerodrome.
Dec 21st 1917.
WING STRUTS FEEL A BIT LOOSE.
WONDERED WHERE YOU GOT TO MCELROY.
YES. THEY CAN BE A BIT OF A PROBLEM.
TEA?
IN A MINUTE, CAPTAIN MANNOCK.
JUST NEED TO CHECK THE GUNS AND I'LL BE DONE.
I SHOULDN'T BOTHER, THERE'S NO POINT.
I KNOW I'VE NOT SHOT ANYTHING DOWN SINCE I'VE BEEN HERE, BUT THAT'S A BIT HARSH.
IT'S CHRISTMAS TIME, MCELROY, AND IT LOOKS LIKE SANTA'S PUT YOU ON THE GOOD LIST.
WE'RE GETTING BRAND NEW S.E.5A'S.
REALLY?
WHEN ARE THEY ARRIVING?

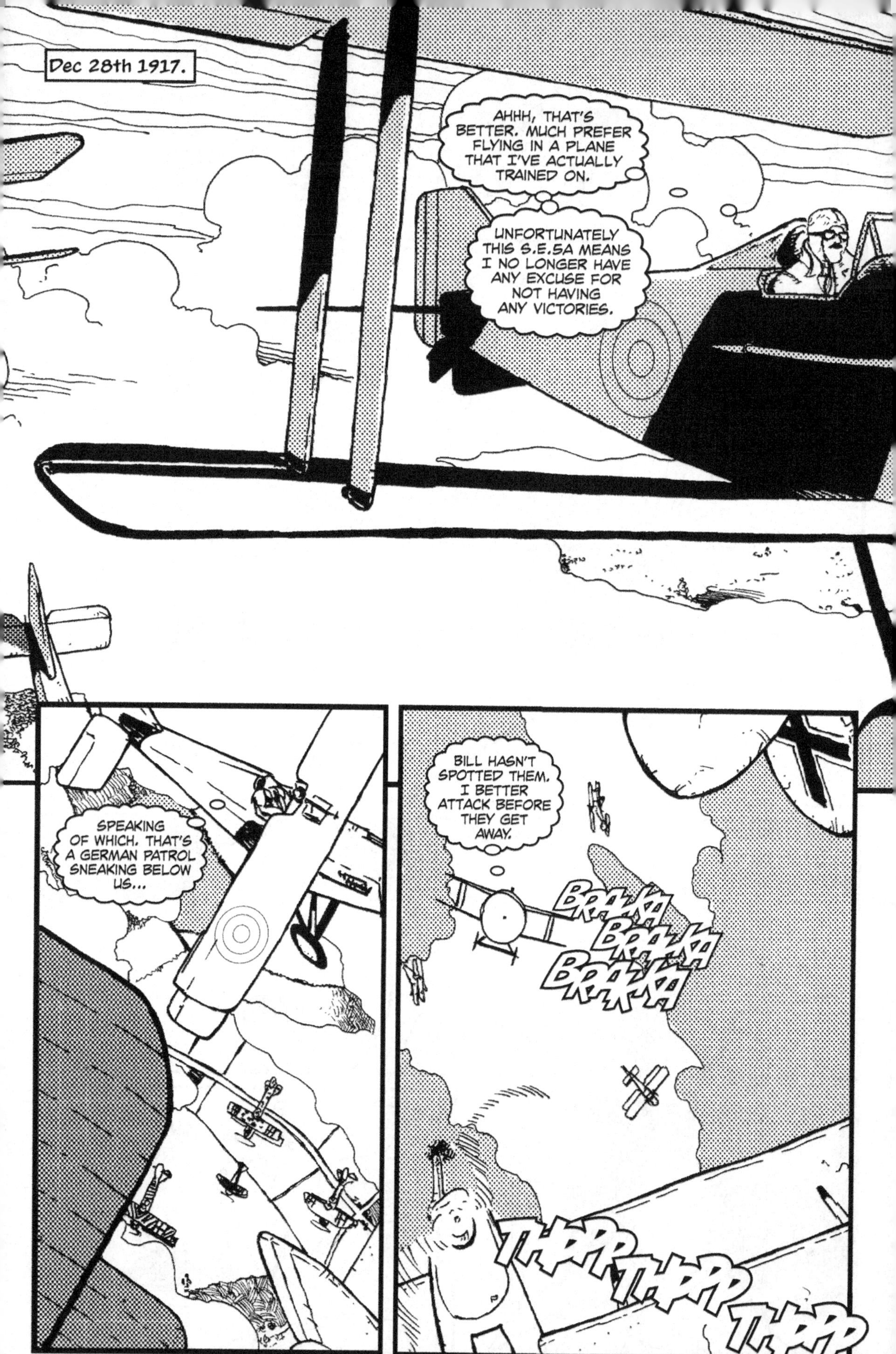
Dec 28th 1917.
AHHH, THAT'S BETTER. MUCH PREFER FLYING IN A PLANE THAT I'VE ACTUALLY TRAINED ON.
UNFORTUNATELY THIS S.E.5A MEANS I NO LONGER HAVE ANY EXCUSE FOR NOT HAVING ANY VICTORIES.
SPEAKING OF WHICH. THAT'S A GERMAN PATROL SNEAKING BELOW US...
BILL HASN'T SPOTTED THEM. I BETTER ATTACK BEFORE THEY GET AWAY.
BRAKA
BRAKA
BRAKA
THPPP
THPPP
THPPP

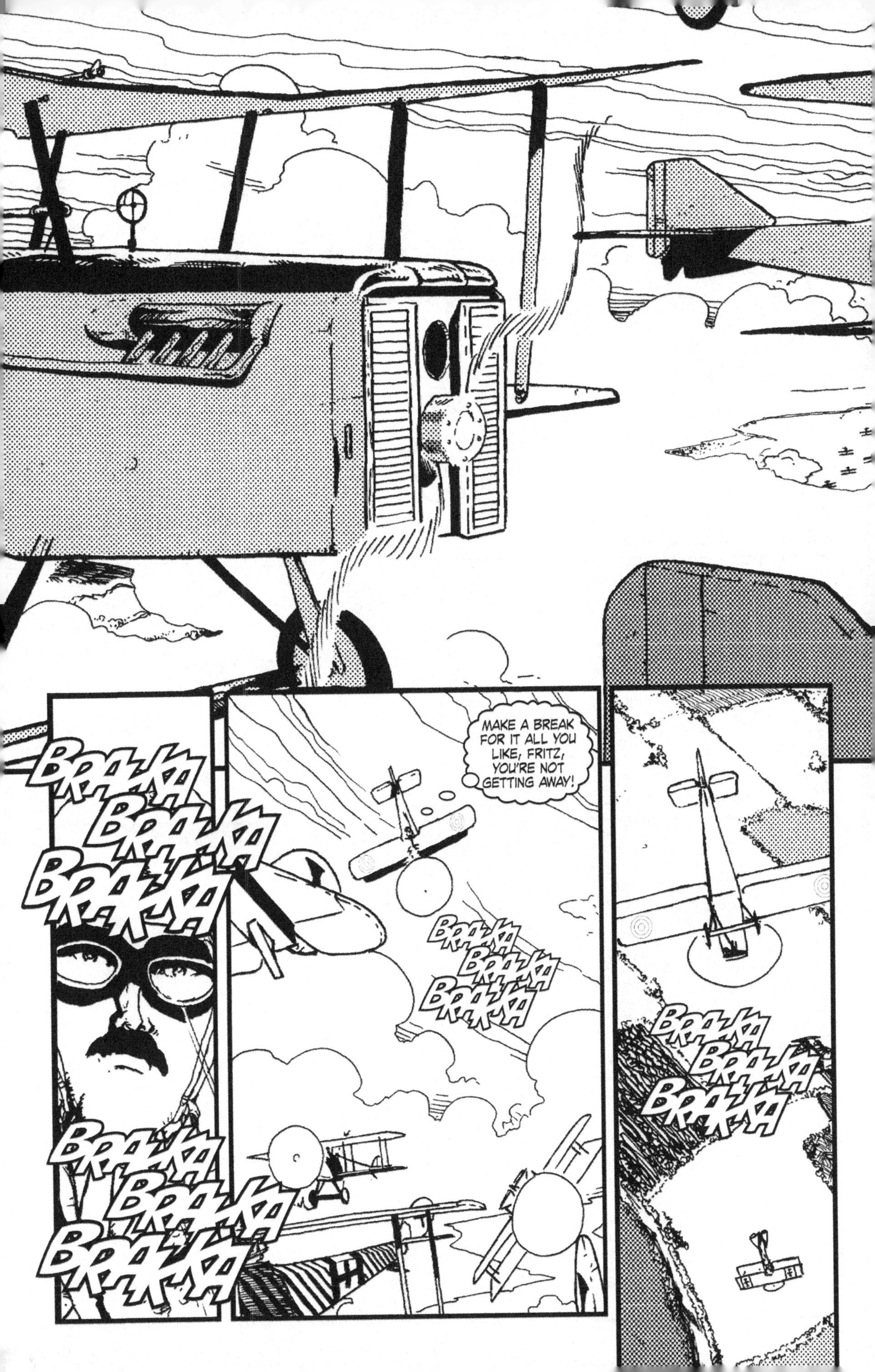
BRAKKA
BRAKKA
BRAKKA
BRAKKA
BRAKKA
BRAKKA
MAKE A BREAK FOR IT ALL YOU LIKE, FRITZ, YOU'RE NOT GETTING AWAY!
BRAKKA
BRAKKA
BRAKKA
BRAKKA
BRAKKA
BRAKKA

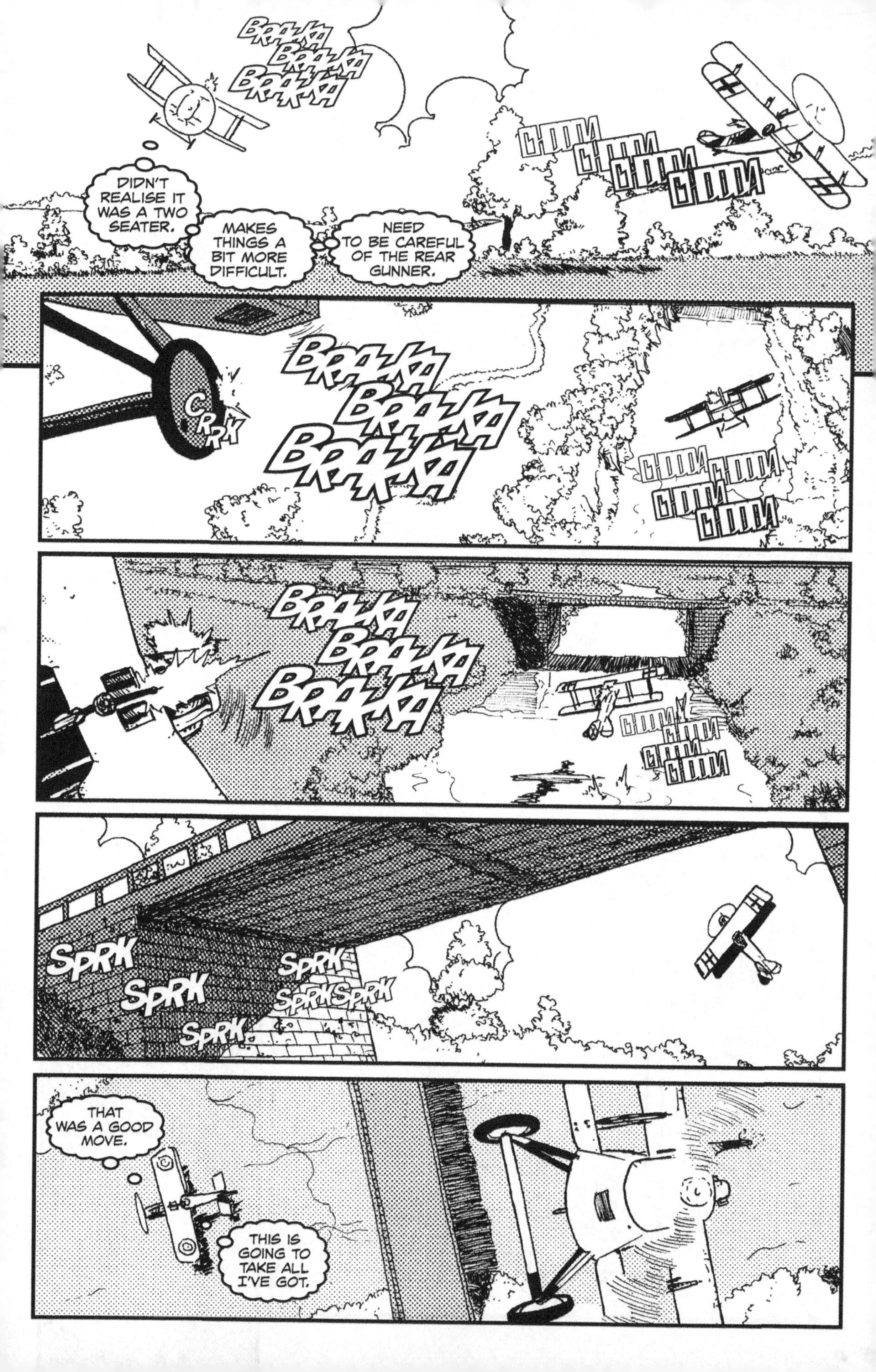
BRAKKA BRAKKA BRAKKA
GIDDDA GIDDDA GIDDDA GIDDDA
DIDN'T REALISE IT WAS A TWO SEATER.
MAKES THINGS A BIT MORE DIFFICULT.
NEED TO BE CAREFUL OF THE REAR GUNNER.
CRRK
BRAKKA BRAKKA BRAKKA
BRAKKA BRAKKA BRAKKA
SPRK SPRK SPRK SPRK SPRK SPRK
THAT WAS A GOOD MOVE.
THIS IS GOING TO TAKE ALL I'VE GOT.

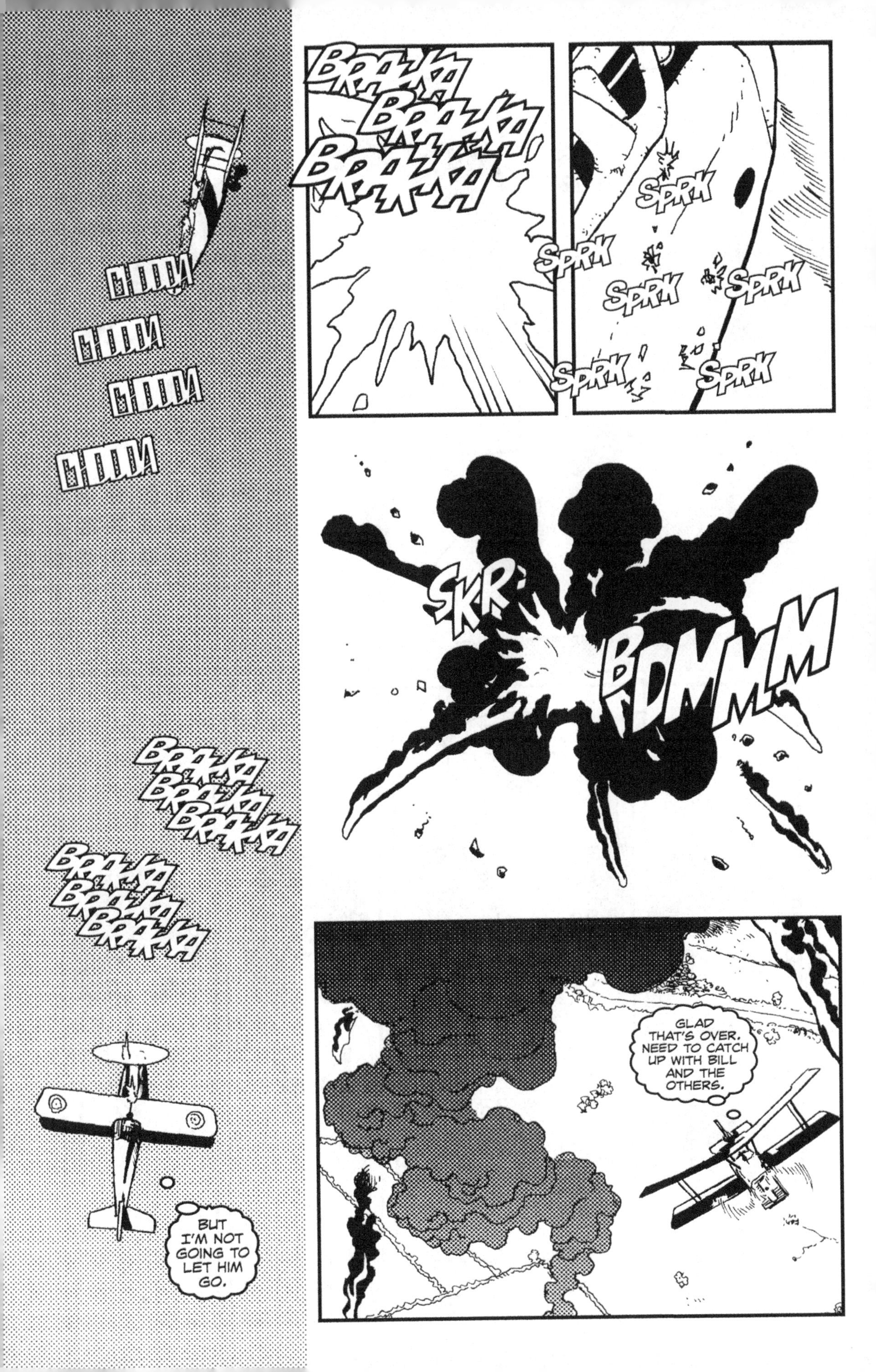
CHOODA
CHOODA
CHOODA
CHOODA
BRAKKA
BRAKKA
BRAKKA
SPRK
SPRK
SPRK
SPRK
SPRK
SPRK
SKR-
BDMMMM
GLAD THAT'S OVER. NEED TO CATCH UP WITH BILL AND THE OTHERS.
BRAKKA
BRAKKA
BRAKKA
BRAKKA
BRAKKA
BRAKKA
BUT I'M NOT GOING TO LET HIM GO.

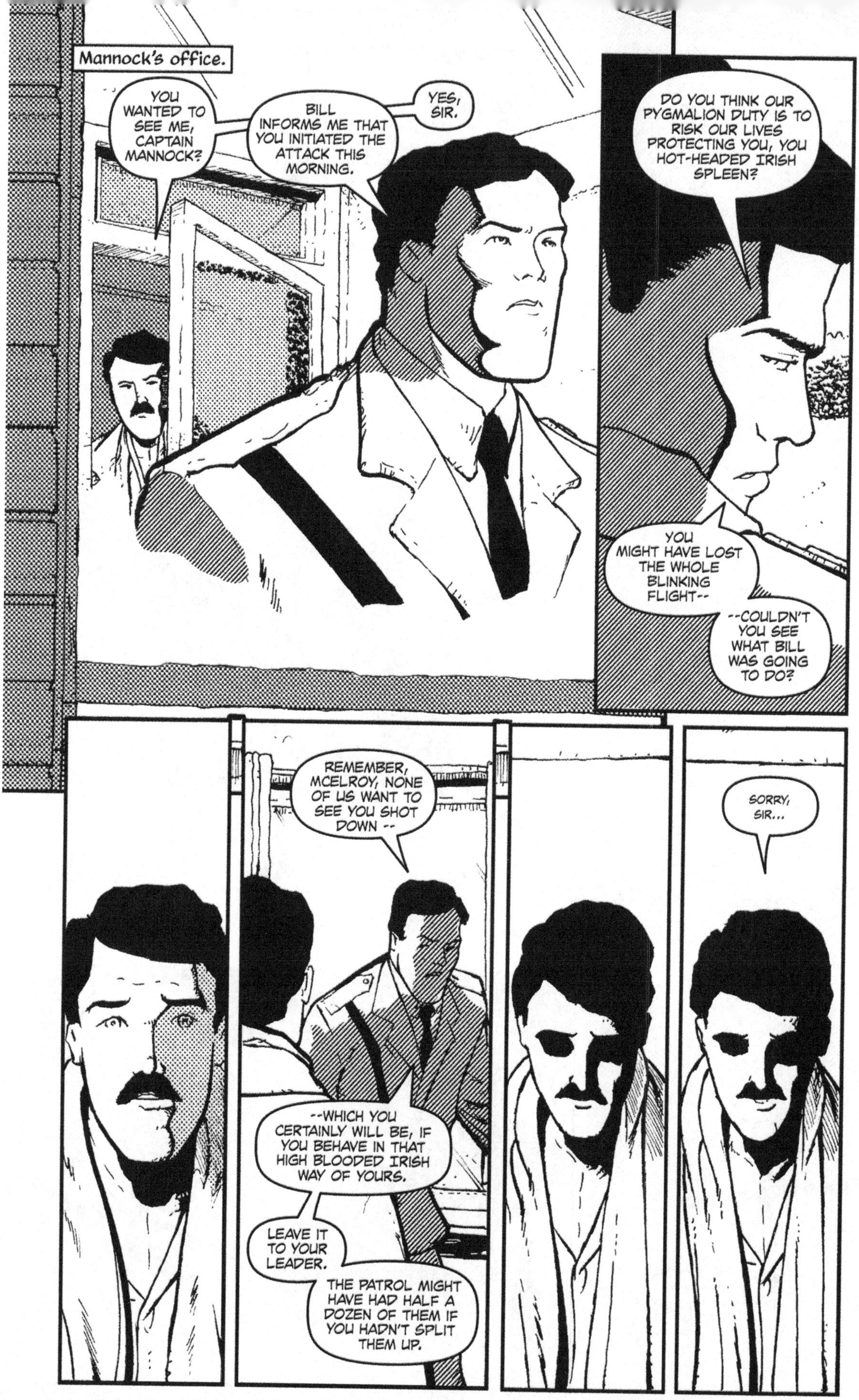
Mannock's office.
YOU WANTED TO SEE ME, CAPTAIN MANNOCK?
BILL INFORMS ME THAT YOU INITIATED THE ATTACK THIS MORNING.
YES, SIR.
DO YOU THINK OUR PYGMALION DUTY IS TO RISK OUR LIVES PROTECTING YOU, YOU HOT-HEADED IRISH SPLEEN?
YOU MIGHT HAVE LOST THE WHOLE BLINKING FLIGHT--
--COULDN'T YOU SEE WHAT BILL WAS GOING TO DO?
REMEMBER, MCELROY, NONE OF US WANT TO SEE YOU SHOT DOWN --
--WHICH YOU CERTAINLY WILL BE, IF YOU BEHAVE IN THAT HIGH BLOODED IRISH WAY OF YOURS.
LEAVE IT TO YOUR LEADER.
THE PATROL MIGHT HAVE HAD HALF A DOZEN OF THEM IF YOU HADN'T SPLIT THEM UP.
SORRY, SIR...

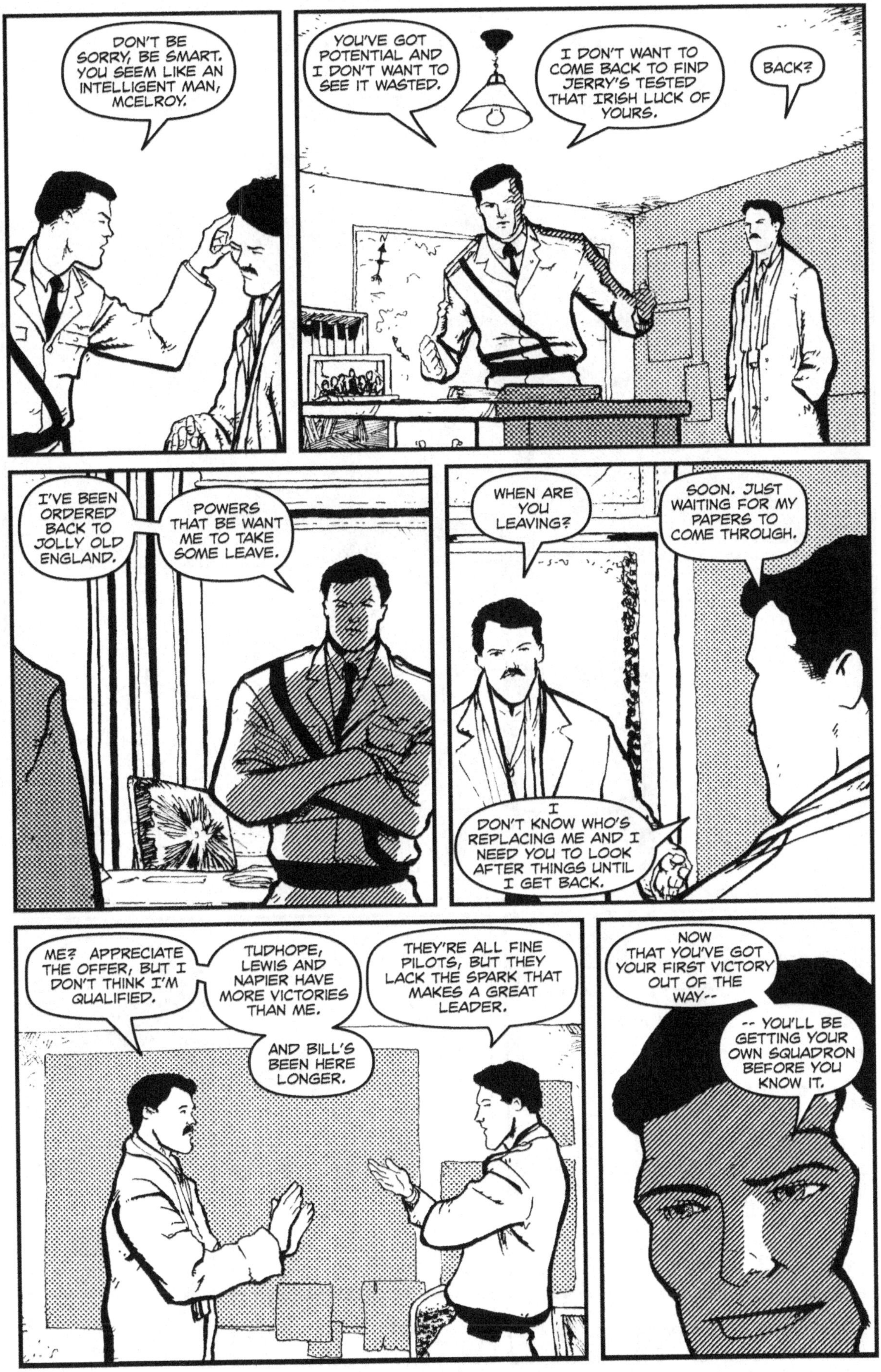
DON'T BE SORRY, BE SMART. YOU SEEM LIKE AN INTELLIGENT MAN, MCELROY.
YOU'VE GOT POTENTIAL AND I DON'T WANT TO SEE IT WASTED.
I DON'T WANT TO COME BACK TO FIND JERRY'S TESTED THAT IRISH LUCK OF YOURS.
BACK?
I'VE BEEN ORDERED BACK TO JOLLY OLD ENGLAND.
POWERS THAT BE WANT ME TO TAKE SOME LEAVE.
WHEN ARE YOU LEAVING?
SOON. JUST WAITING FOR MY PAPERS TO COME THROUGH.
I DON'T KNOW WHO'S REPLACING ME AND I NEED YOU TO LOOK AFTER THINGS UNTIL I GET BACK.
ME? APPRECIATE THE OFFER, BUT I DON'T THINK I'M QUALIFIED.
TUDHOPE, LEWIS AND NAPIER HAVE MORE VICTORIES THAN ME.
AND BILL'S BEEN HERE LONGER.
THEY'RE ALL FINE PILOTS, BUT THEY LACK THE SPARK THAT MAKES A GREAT LEADER.
NOW THAT YOU'VE GOT YOUR FIRST VICTORY OUT OF THE WAY--
-- YOU'LL BE GETTING YOUR OWN SQUADRON BEFORE YOU KNOW IT.

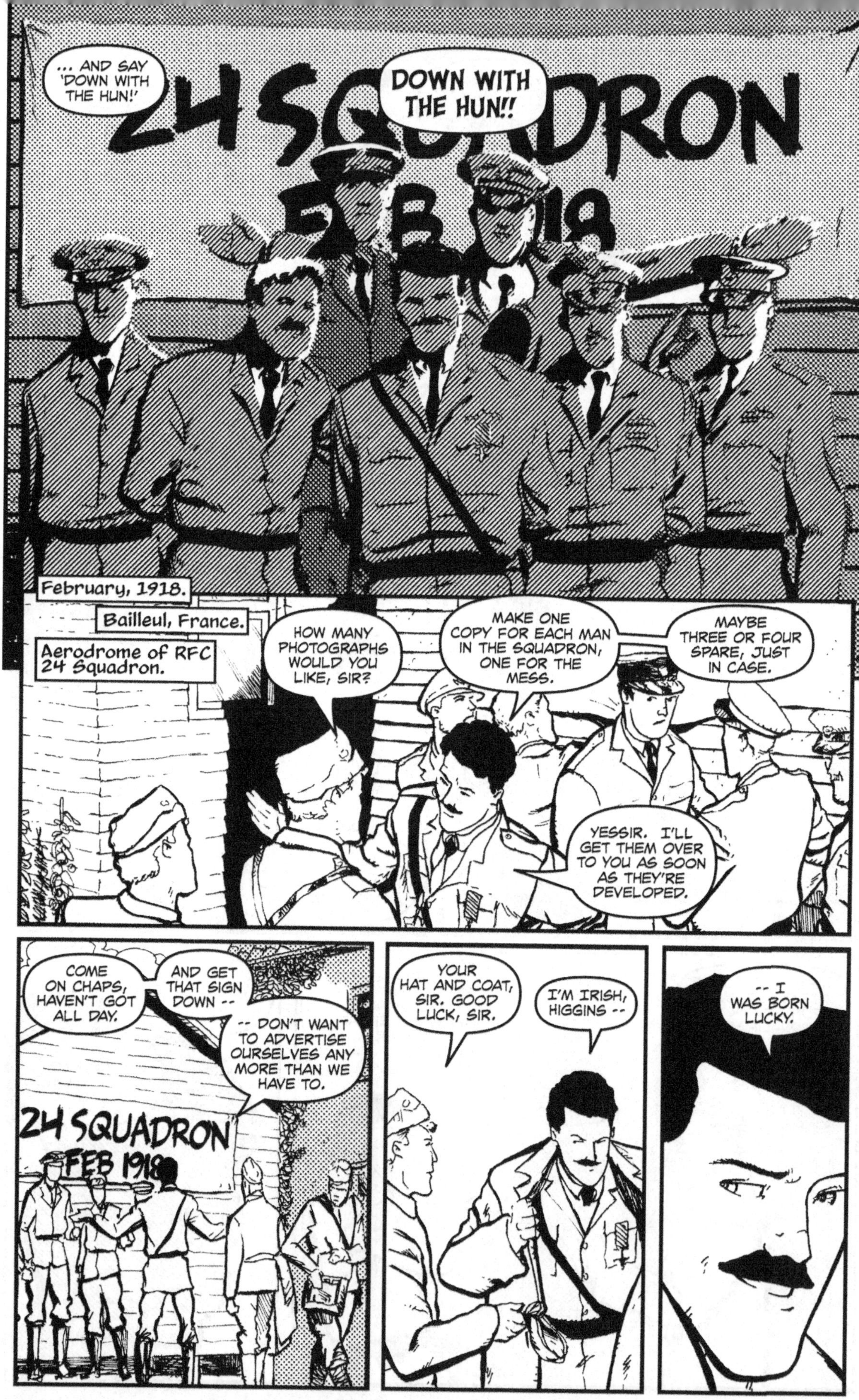
... AND SAY 'DOWN WITH THE HUN!'
DOWN WITH THE HUN!!
24 SQUADRON FEB 1918
February, 1918.
Bailleul, France.
Aerodrome of RFC 24 Squadron.
HOW MANY PHOTOGRAPHS WOULD YOU LIKE, SIR?
MAKE ONE COPY FOR EACH MAN IN THE SQUADRON, ONE FOR THE MESS.
MAYBE THREE OR FOUR SPARE, JUST IN CASE.
YESSIR. I'LL GET THEM OVER TO YOU AS SOON AS THEY'RE DEVELOPED.
COME ON CHAPS, HAVEN'T GOT ALL DAY.
AND GET THAT SIGN DOWN --
-- DON'T WANT TO ADVERTISE OURSELVES ANY MORE THAN WE HAVE TO.
24 SQUADRON FEB 1918
YOUR HAT AND COAT, SIR. GOOD LUCK, SIR.
I'M IRISH, HIGGINS --
-- I WAS BORN LUCKY.

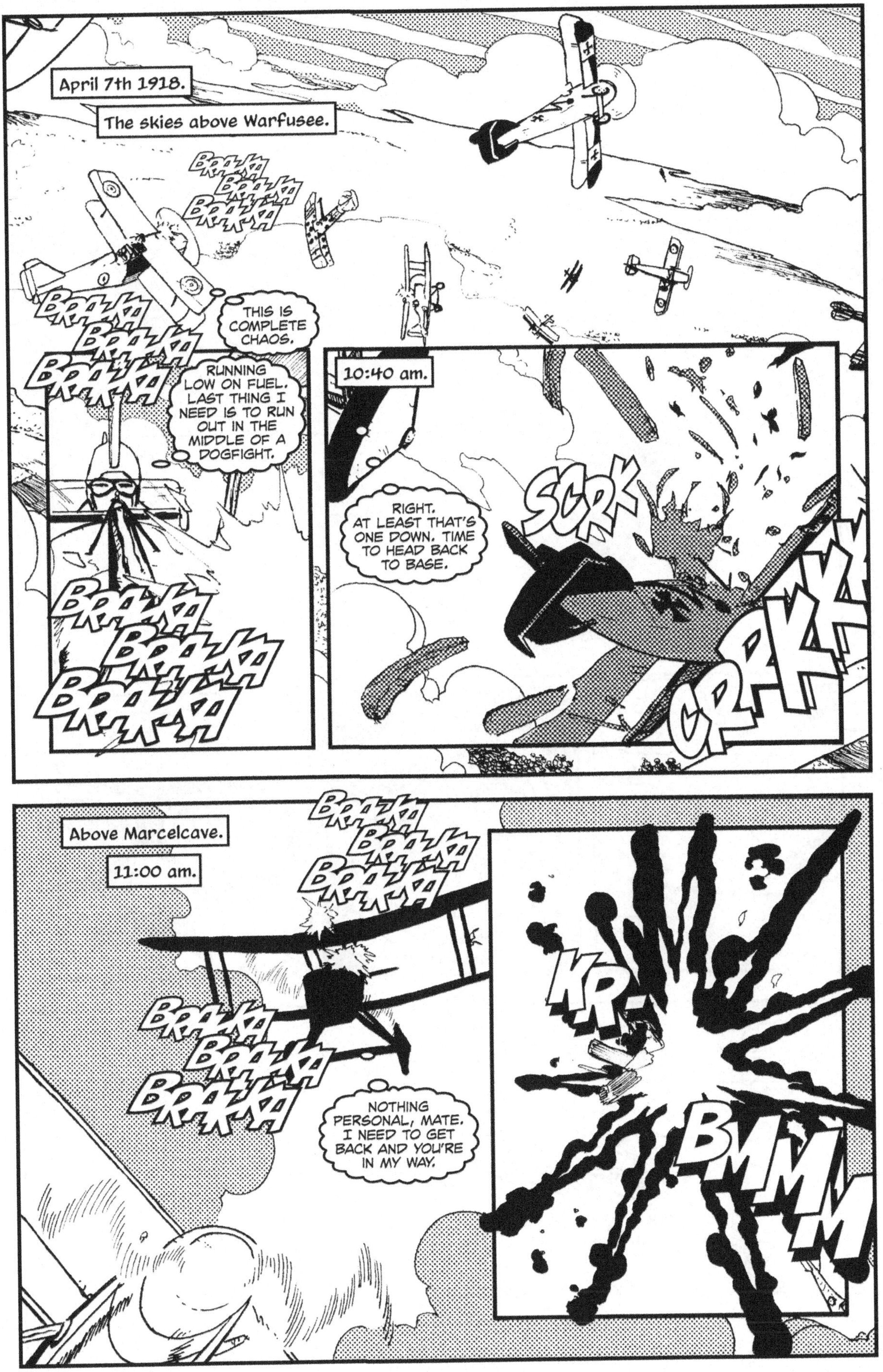
April 7th 1918.
The skies above Warfusee.
BRAKKA BRAKKA BRAKKA
BRAKKA BRAKKA BRAKKA
THIS IS COMPLETE CHAOS.
RUNNING LOW ON FUEL. LAST THING I NEED IS TO RUN OUT IN THE MIDDLE OF A DOGFIGHT.
BRAKKA BRAKKA BRAKKA
10:40 am.
RIGHT. AT LEAST THAT'S ONE DOWN. TIME TO HEAD BACK TO BASE.
SCRK
CRRKK
Above Marcelcave.
11:00 am.
BRAKKA BRAKKA BRAKKA
BRAKKA BRAKKA BRAKKA
NOTHING PERSONAL, MATE. I NEED TO GET BACK AND YOU'RE IN MY WAY.
KR-
BMMM

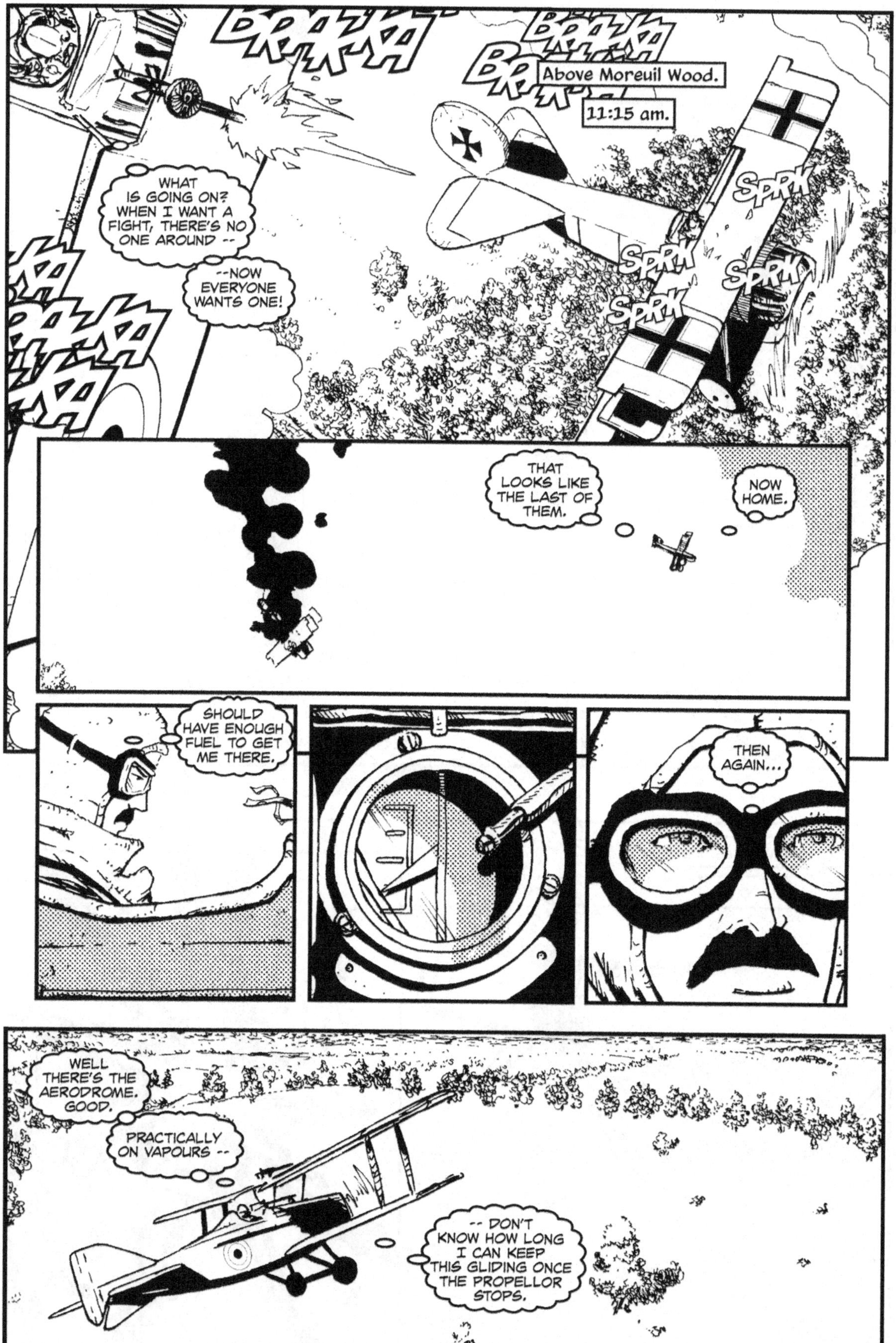
BRRAKKA
BRRAKKA
BRRAKKA
Above Moreuil Wood.
11:15 am.
WHAT IS GOING ON? WHEN I WANT A FIGHT, THERE'S NO ONE AROUND --
--NOW EVERYONE WANTS ONE!
SPRK
SPRK
SPRK
SPRK
THAT LOOKS LIKE THE LAST OF THEM.
NOW HOME.
SHOULD HAVE ENOUGH FUEL TO GET ME THERE.
THEN AGAIN...
WELL THERE'S THE AERODROME. GOOD.
PRACTICALLY ON VAPOURS --
-- DON'T KNOW HOW LONG I CAN KEEP THIS GLIDING ONCE THE PROPELLOR STOPS.

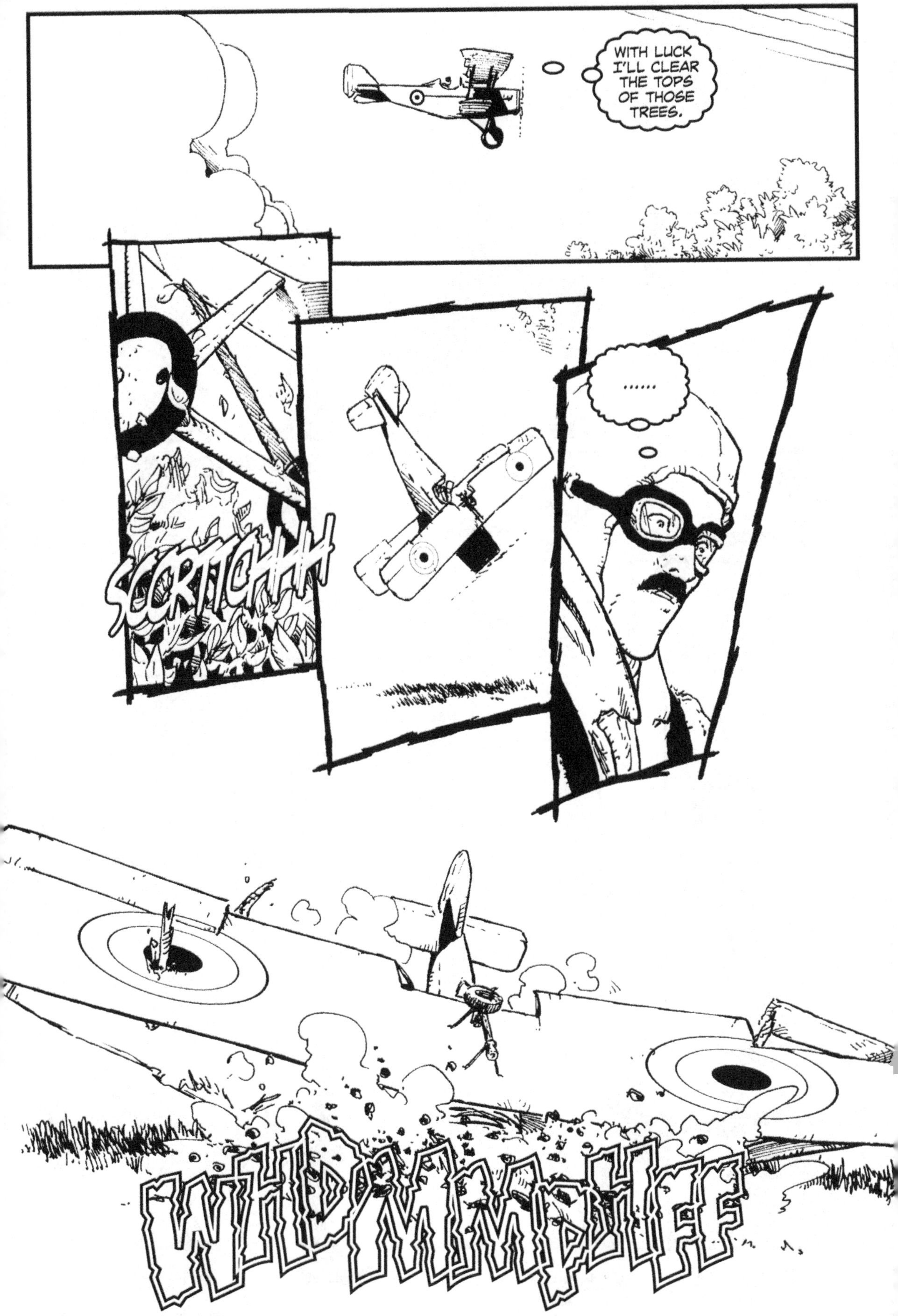
WITH LUCK I'LL CLEAR THE TOPS OF THOSE TREES.
SCRITCHHH
......
WHDRMMPHFF

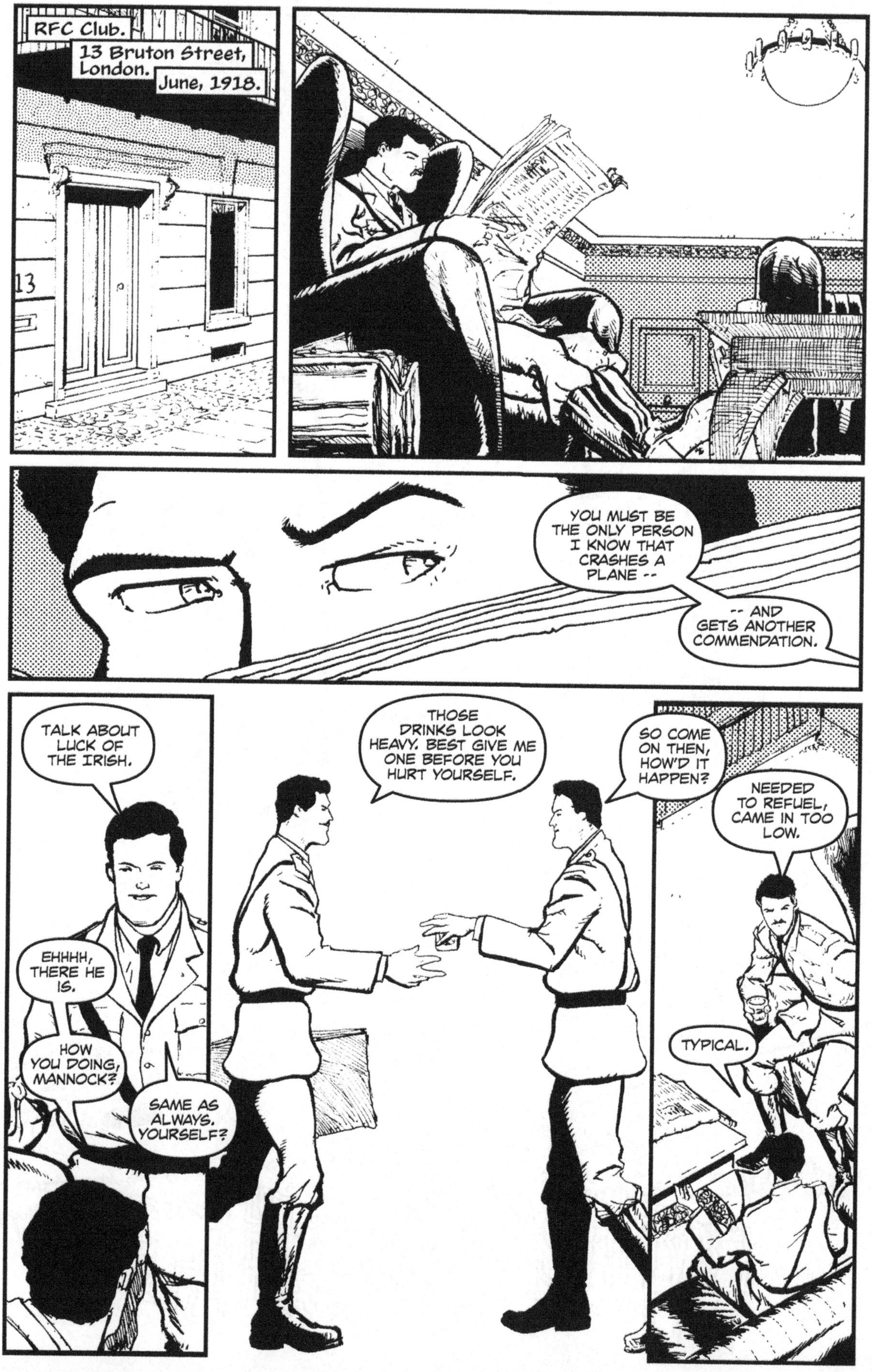
RFC Club.
13 Bruton Street, London.
June, 1918.
YOU MUST BE THE ONLY PERSON I KNOW THAT CRASHES A PLANE --
-- AND GETS ANOTHER COMMENDATION.
TALK ABOUT LUCK OF THE IRISH.
EHHHH, THERE HE IS.
HOW YOU DOING, MANNOCK?
SAME AS ALWAYS. YOURSELF?
THOSE DRINKS LOOK HEAVY. BEST GIVE ME ONE BEFORE YOU HURT YOURSELF.
SO COME ON THEN, HOW'D IT HAPPEN?
NEEDED TO REFUEL, CAME IN TOO LOW.
TYPICAL.

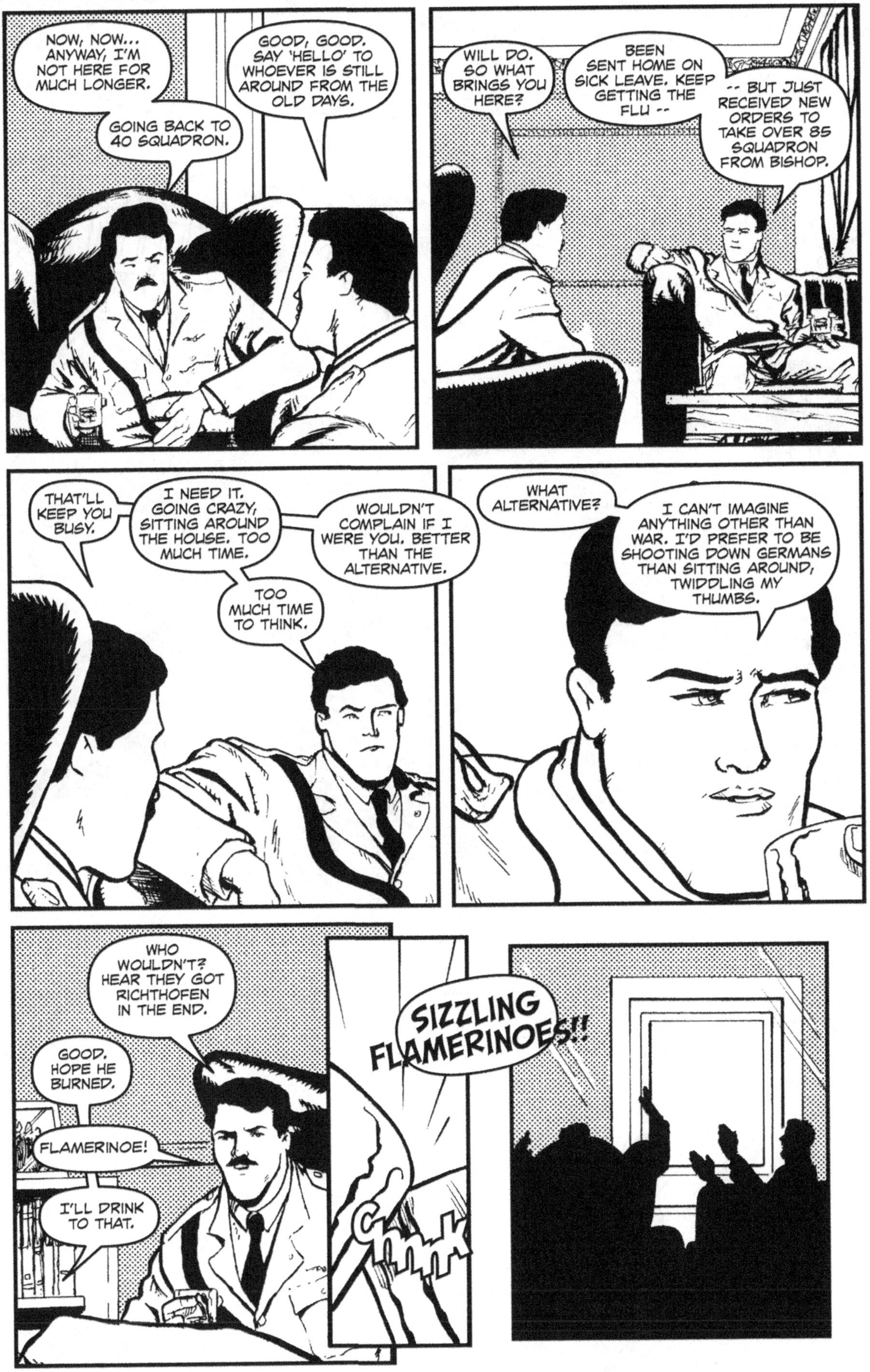
NOW, NOW... ANYWAY, I'M NOT HERE FOR MUCH LONGER.
GOING BACK TO 40 SQUADRON.
GOOD, GOOD. SAY 'HELLO' TO WHOEVER IS STILL AROUND FROM THE OLD DAYS.
WILL DO. SO WHAT BRINGS YOU HERE?
BEEN SENT HOME ON SICK LEAVE. KEEP GETTING THE FLU --
-- BUT JUST RECEIVED NEW ORDERS TO TAKE OVER 85 SQUADRON FROM BISHOP.
THAT'LL KEEP YOU BUSY.
I NEED IT. GOING CRAZY, SITTING AROUND THE HOUSE. TOO MUCH TIME.
TOO MUCH TIME TO THINK.
WOULDN'T COMPLAIN IF I WERE YOU. BETTER THAN THE ALTERNATIVE.
WHAT ALTERNATIVE?
I CAN'T IMAGINE ANYTHING OTHER THAN WAR. I'D PREFER TO BE SHOOTING DOWN GERMANS THAN SITTING AROUND, TWIDDLING MY THUMBS.
WHO WOULDN'T? HEAR THEY GOT RICHTHOFEN IN THE END.
GOOD. HOPE HE BURNED.
FLAMERINOE!
I'LL DRINK TO THAT.
SIZZLING FLAMERINOES!!
Chnnk

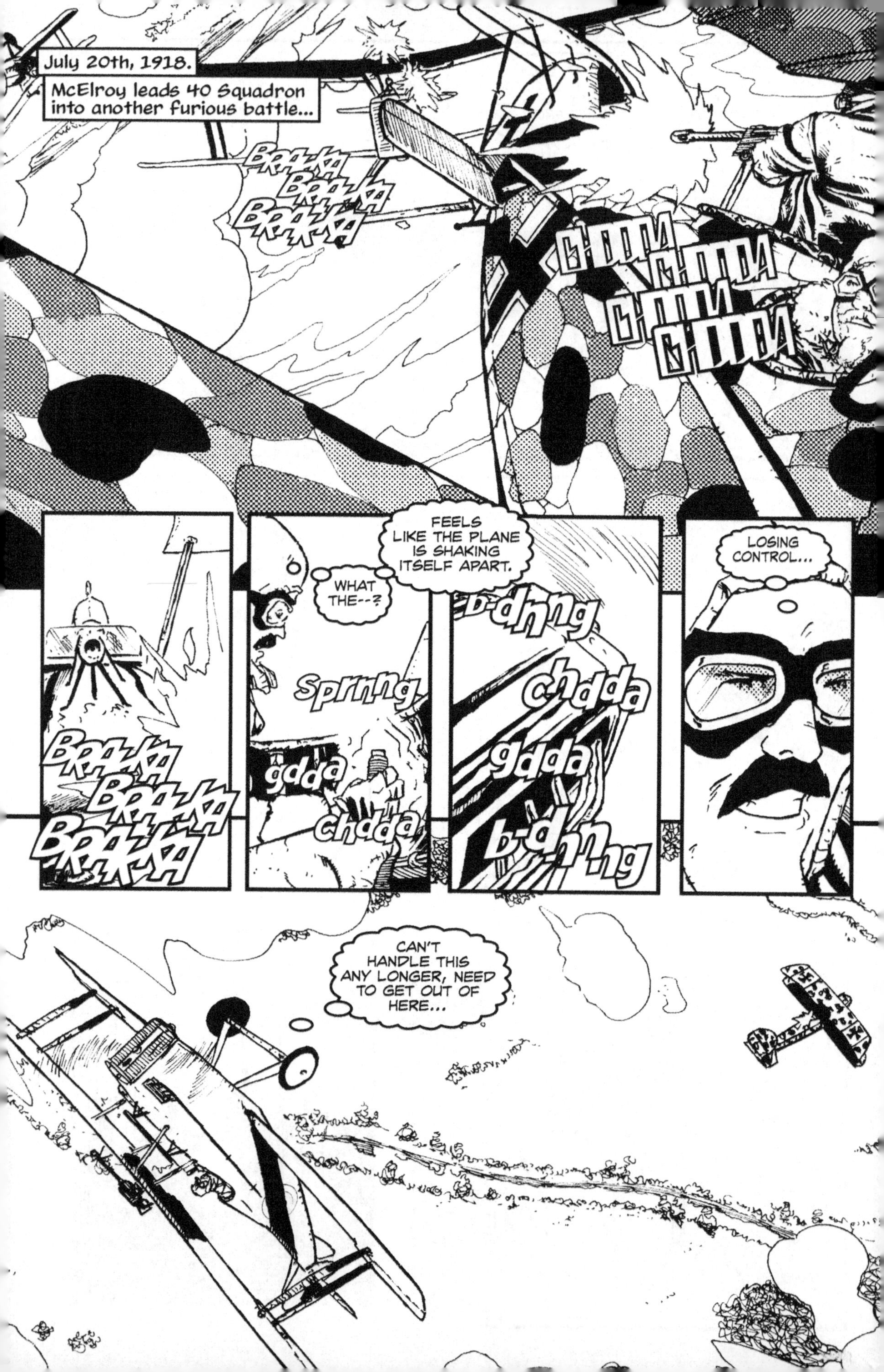
July 20th, 1918.
McElroy leads 40 Squadron into another furious battle...
BRAKKA
BRAKKA
BRAKKA
BRAKKA
BRAKKA
BRAKKA
WHAT THE--?
FEELS LIKE THE PLANE IS SHAKING ITSELF APART.
Sprnng
gdda
chdda
b-dhnng
chdda
gdda
b-dhnnng
LOSING CONTROL...
CAN'T HANDLE THIS ANY LONGER, NEED TO GET OUT OF HERE...

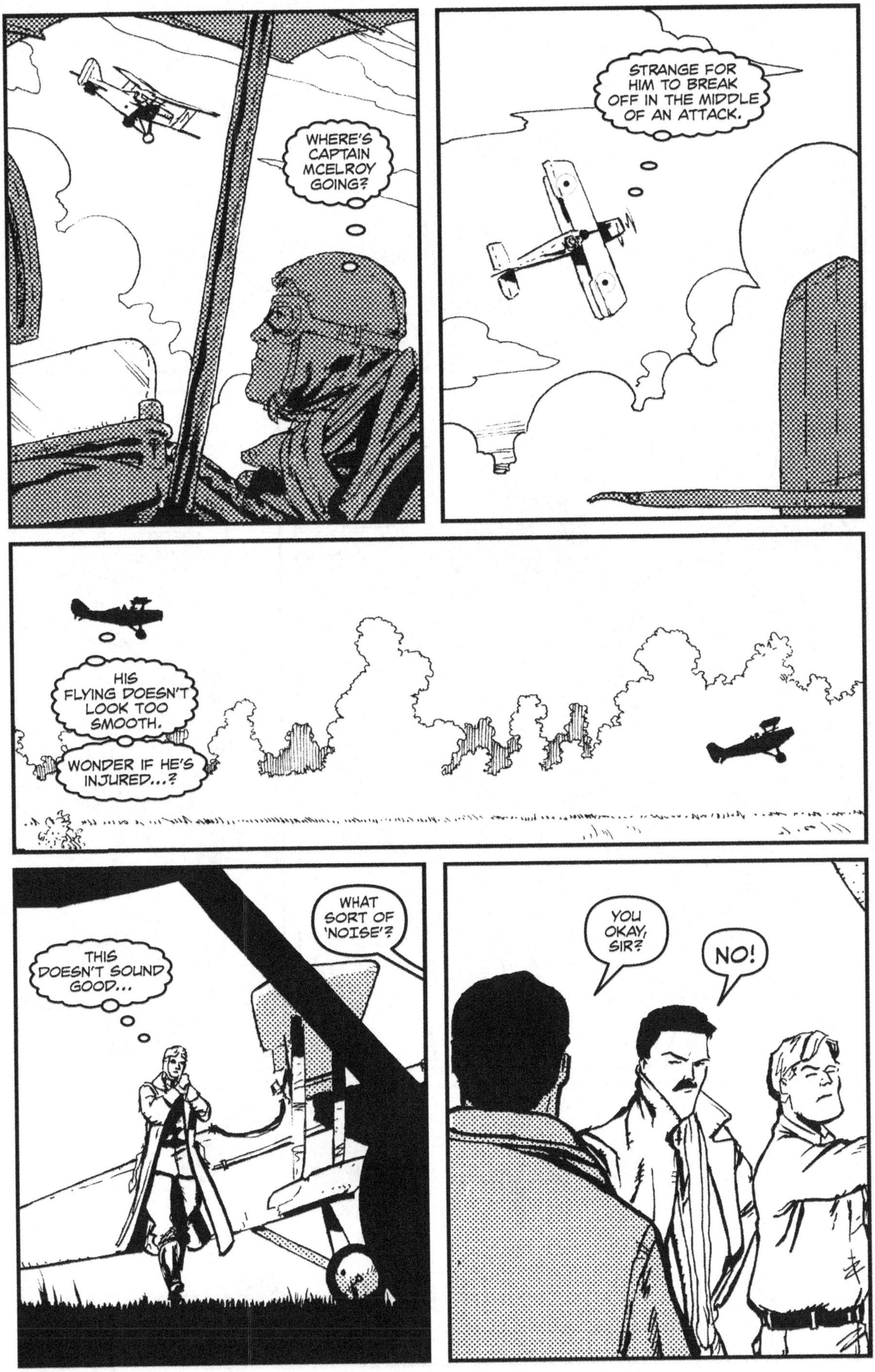
WHERE'S CAPTAIN MCELROY GOING?
STRANGE FOR HIM TO BREAK OFF IN THE MIDDLE OF AN ATTACK.
HIS FLYING DOESN'T LOOK TOO SMOOTH.
WONDER IF HE'S INJURED...?
THIS DOESN'T SOUND GOOD...
WHAT SORT OF 'NOISE'?
YOU OKAY, SIR?
NO!

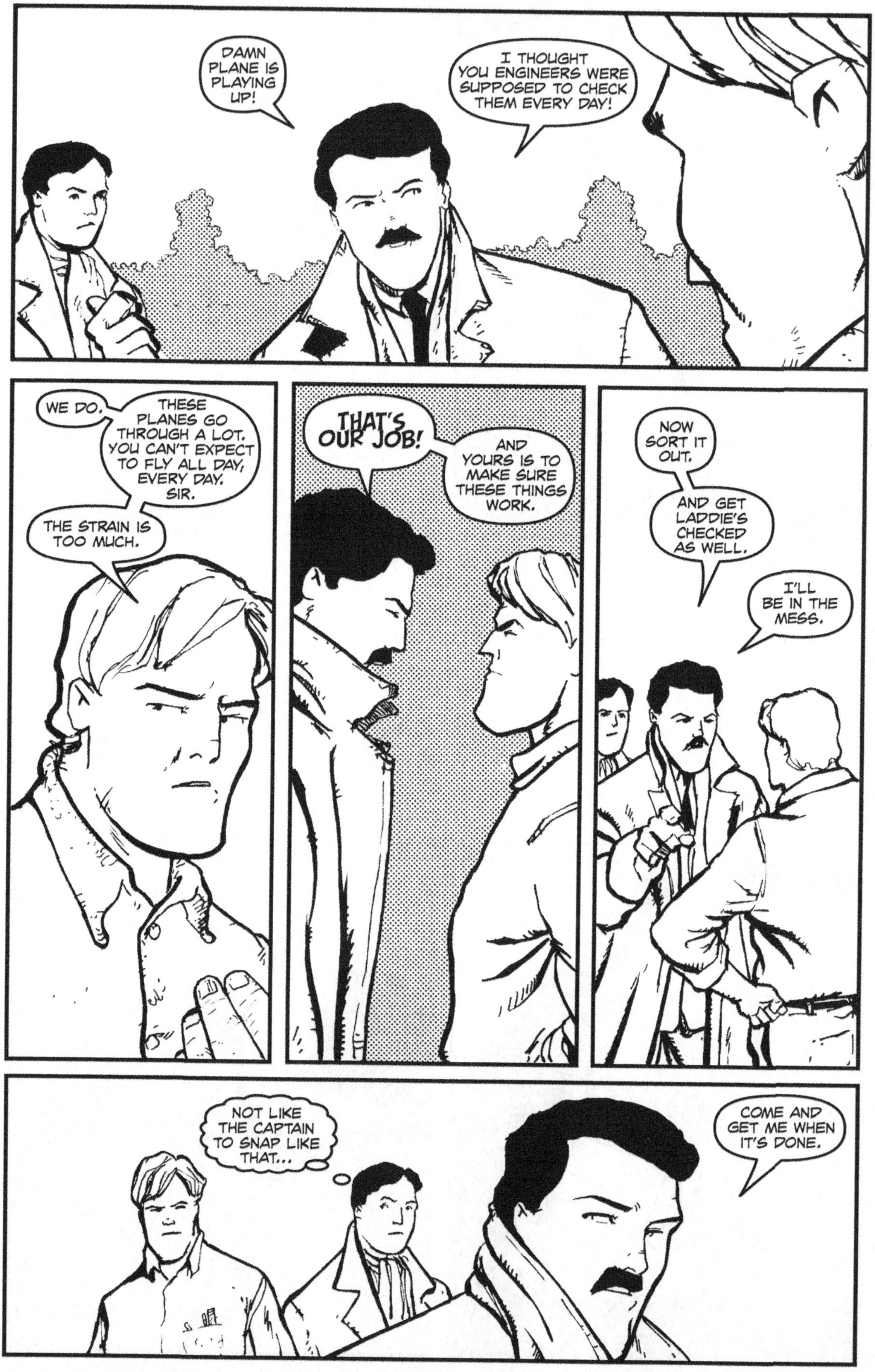
DAMN PLANE IS PLAYING UP!
I THOUGHT YOU ENGINEERS WERE SUPPOSED TO CHECK THEM EVERY DAY!
WE DO.
THESE PLANES GO THROUGH A LOT. YOU CAN'T EXPECT TO FLY ALL DAY, EVERY DAY. SIR.
THE STRAIN IS TOO MUCH.
THAT'S OUR JOB!
AND YOURS IS TO MAKE SURE THESE THINGS WORK.
NOW SORT IT OUT.
AND GET LADDIE'S CHECKED AS WELL.
I'LL BE IN THE MESS.
NOT LIKE THE CAPTAIN TO SNAP LIKE THAT...
COME AND GET ME WHEN IT'S DONE.

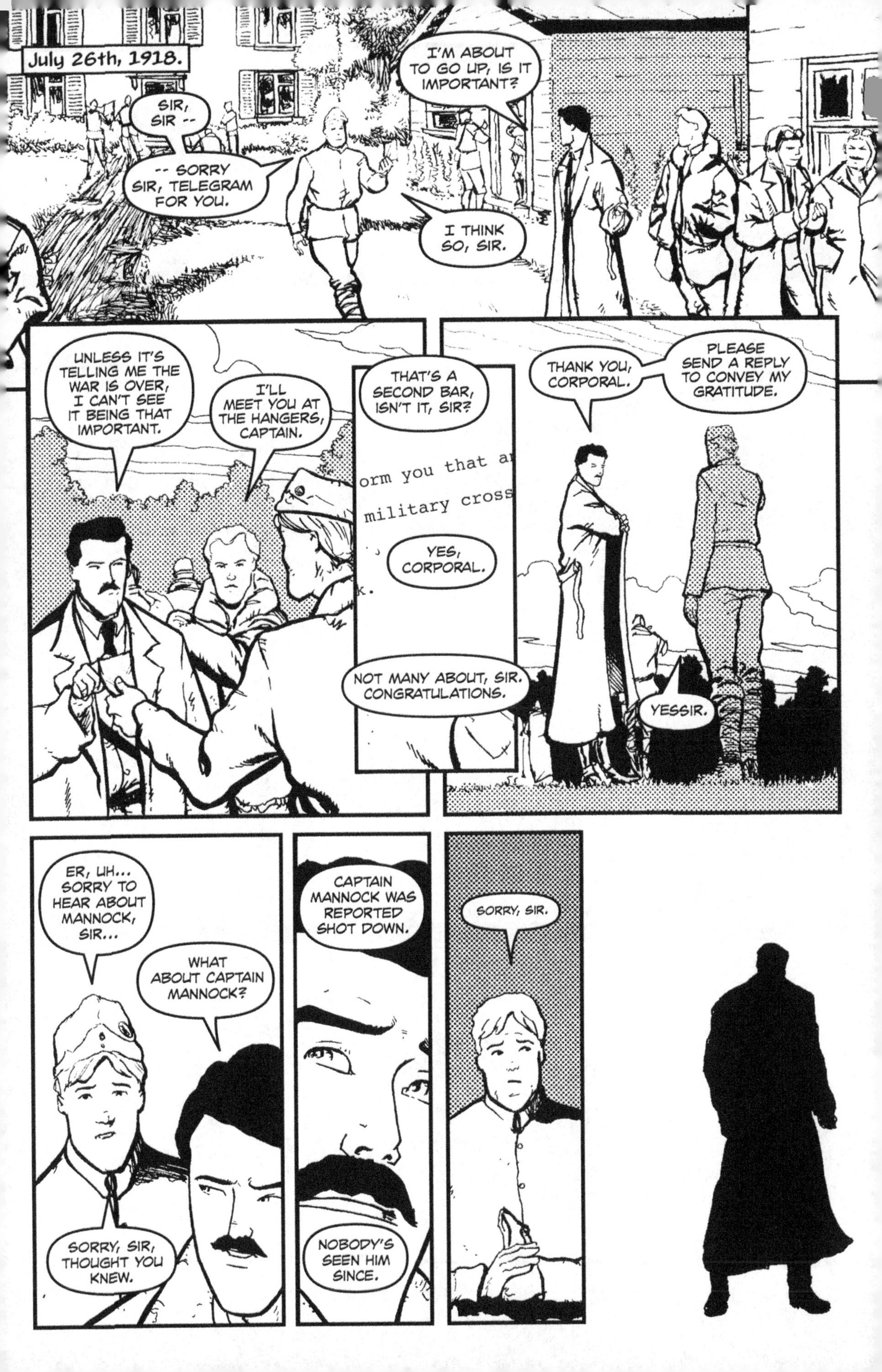
July 26th, 1918.
SIR, SIR --
-- SORRY SIR, TELEGRAM FOR YOU.
I'M ABOUT TO GO UP, IS IT IMPORTANT?
I THINK SO, SIR.
UNLESS IT'S TELLING ME THE WAR IS OVER, I CAN'T SEE IT BEING THAT IMPORTANT.
I'LL MEET YOU AT THE HANGERS, CAPTAIN.
THAT'S A SECOND BAR, ISN'T IT, SIR?
orm you that a
military cross
YES, CORPORAL.
NOT MANY ABOUT, SIR. CONGRATULATIONS.
THANK YOU, CORPORAL.
PLEASE SEND A REPLY TO CONVEY MY GRATITUDE.
YESSIR.
ER, UH... SORRY TO HEAR ABOUT MANNOCK, SIR...
WHAT ABOUT CAPTAIN MANNOCK?
SORRY, SIR, THOUGHT YOU KNEW.
CAPTAIN MANNOCK WAS REPORTED SHOT DOWN.
NOBODY'S SEEN HIM SINCE.
SORRY, SIR.

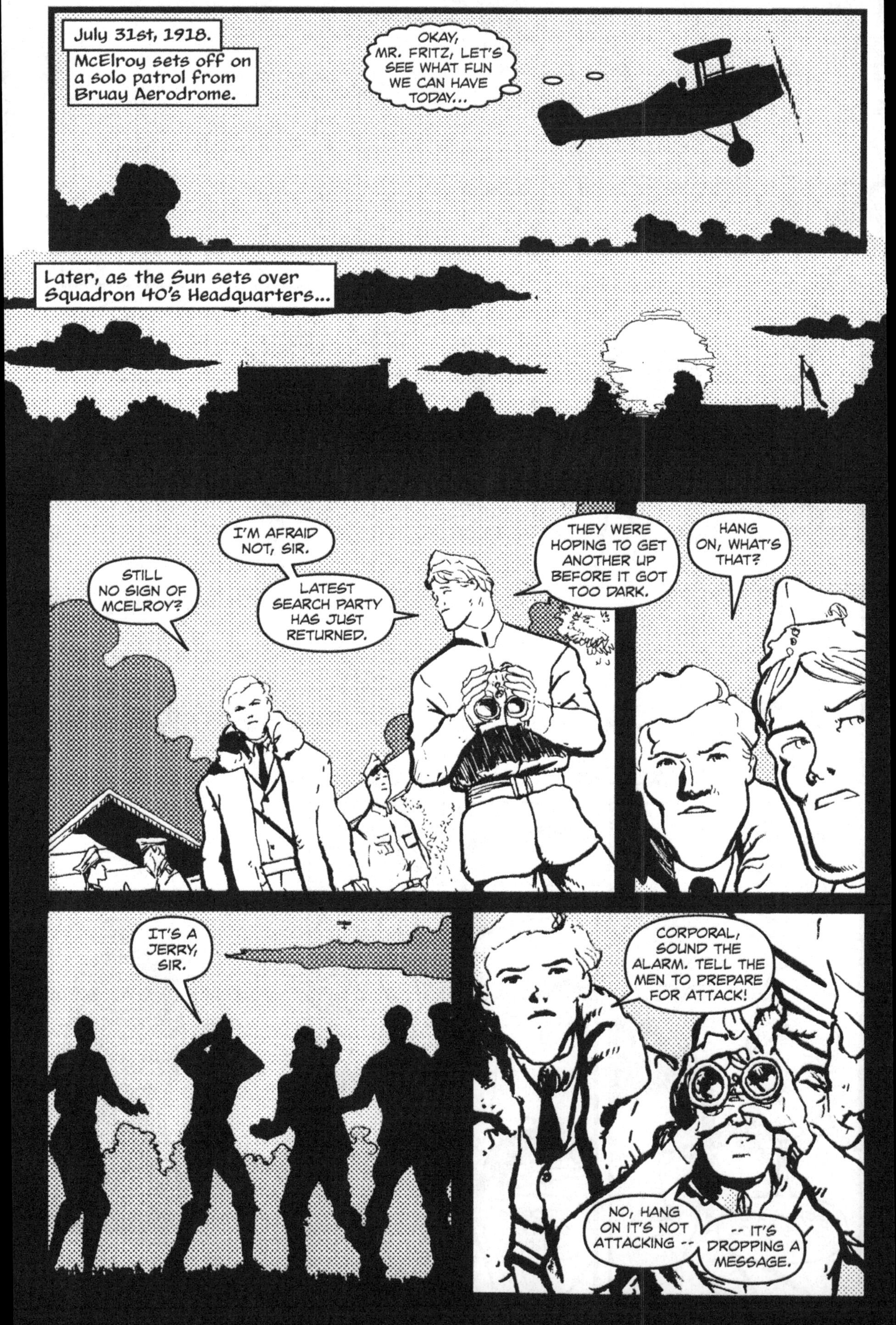
July 31st, 1918.
McElroy sets off on a solo patrol from Bruay Aerodrome.
OKAY, MR. FRITZ, LET'S SEE WHAT FUN WE CAN HAVE TODAY...
Later, as the Sun sets over Squadron 40's Headquarters...
STILL NO SIGN OF MCELROY?
I'M AFRAID NOT, SIR.
LATEST SEARCH PARTY HAS JUST RETURNED.
THEY WERE HOPING TO GET ANOTHER UP BEFORE IT GOT TOO DARK.
HANG ON, WHAT'S THAT?
IT'S A JERRY, SIR.
CORPORAL, SOUND THE ALARM. TELL THE MEN TO PREPARE FOR ATTACK!
NO, HANG ON IT'S NOT ATTACKING --
-- IT'S DROPPING A MESSAGE.

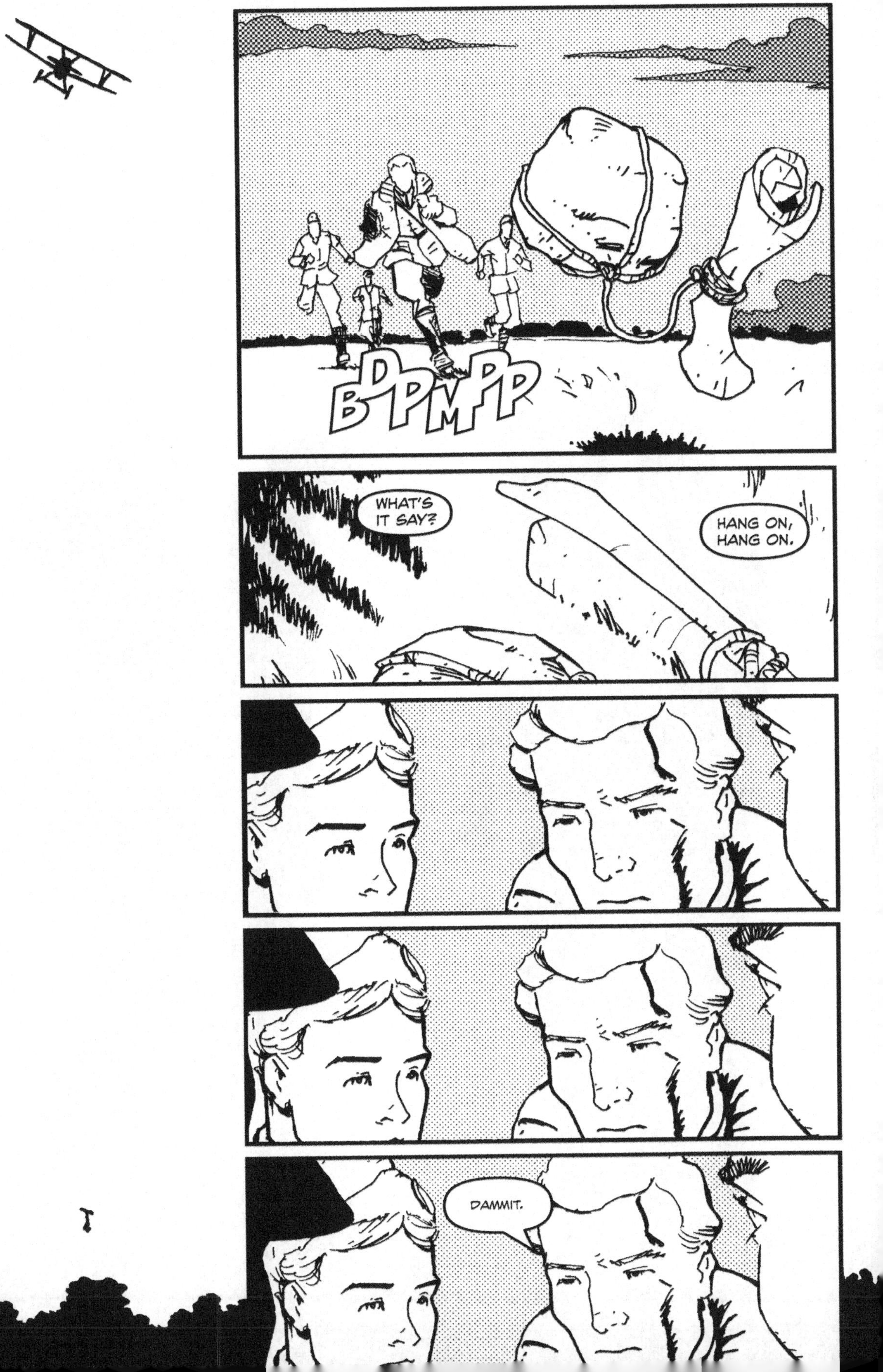
BDPMPP
WHAT'S IT SAY?
HANG ON, HANG ON.
DAMMIT.

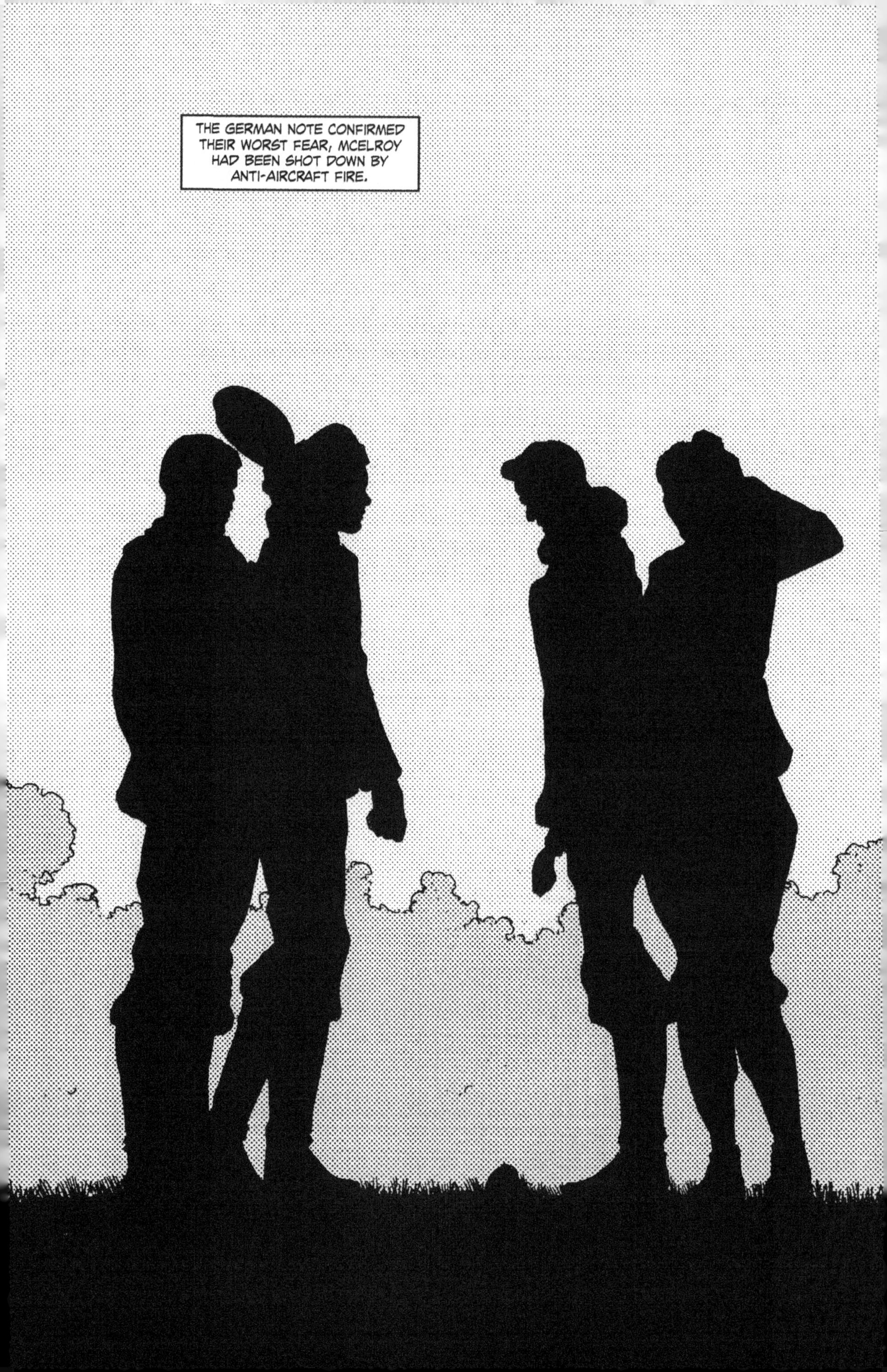
THE GERMAN NOTE CONFIRMED THEIR WORST FEAR, MCELROY HAD BEEN SHOT DOWN BY ANTI-AIRCRAFT FIRE.

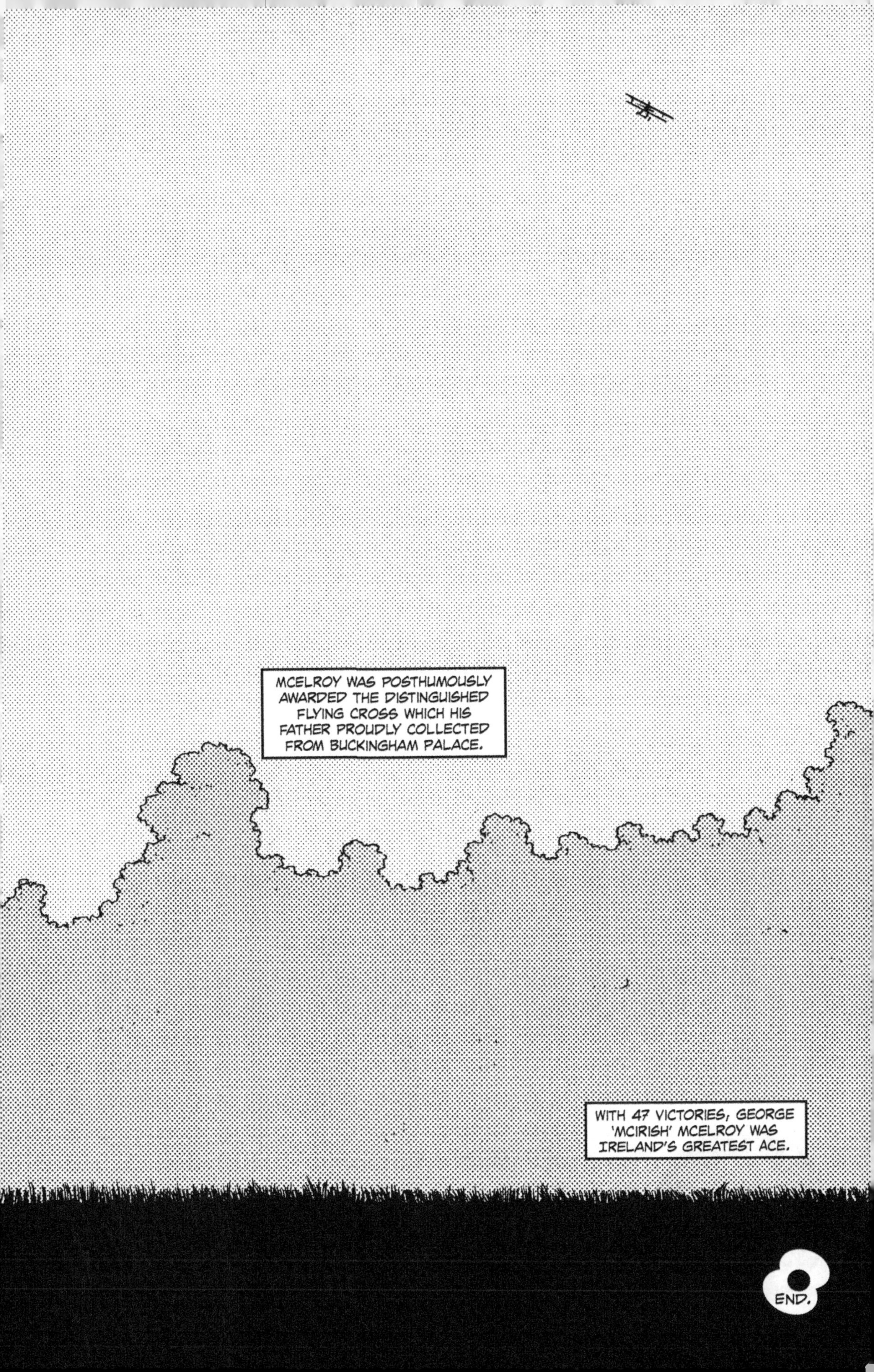
MCELROY WAS POSTHUMOUSLY AWARDED THE DISTINGUISHED FLYING CROSS WHICH HIS FATHER PROUDLY COLLECTED FROM BUCKINGHAM PALACE.
WITH 47 VICTORIES, GEORGE 'MCIRISH' MCELROY WAS IRELAND'S GREATEST ACE.
END.

Edward 'Mick' Mannock
Born in England
Royal Flying Corps/Royal Air Force
61 victories

England

Mannock

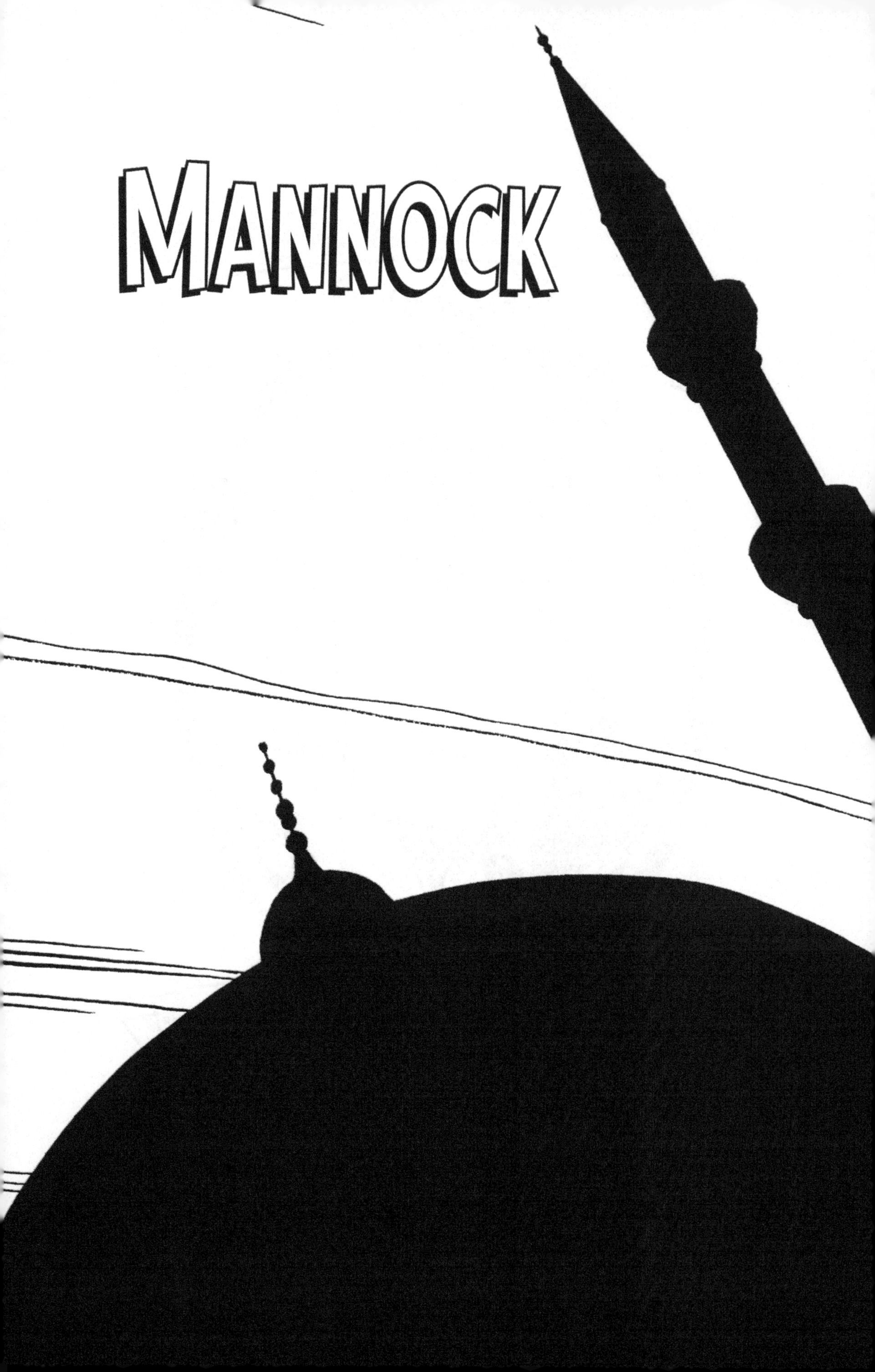
MANNOCK

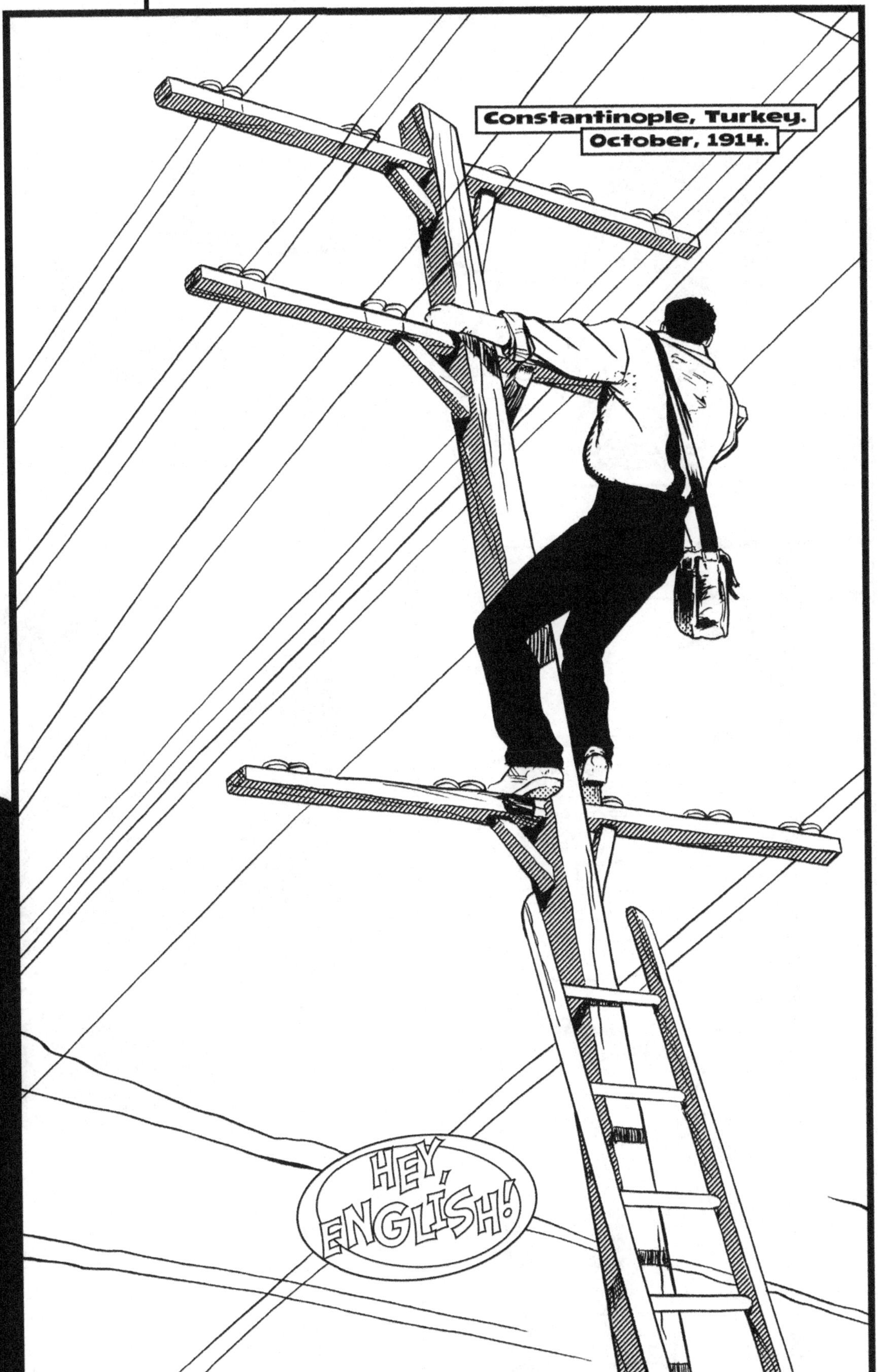
Constantinople, Turkey.
October, 1914.
HEY, ENGLISH!

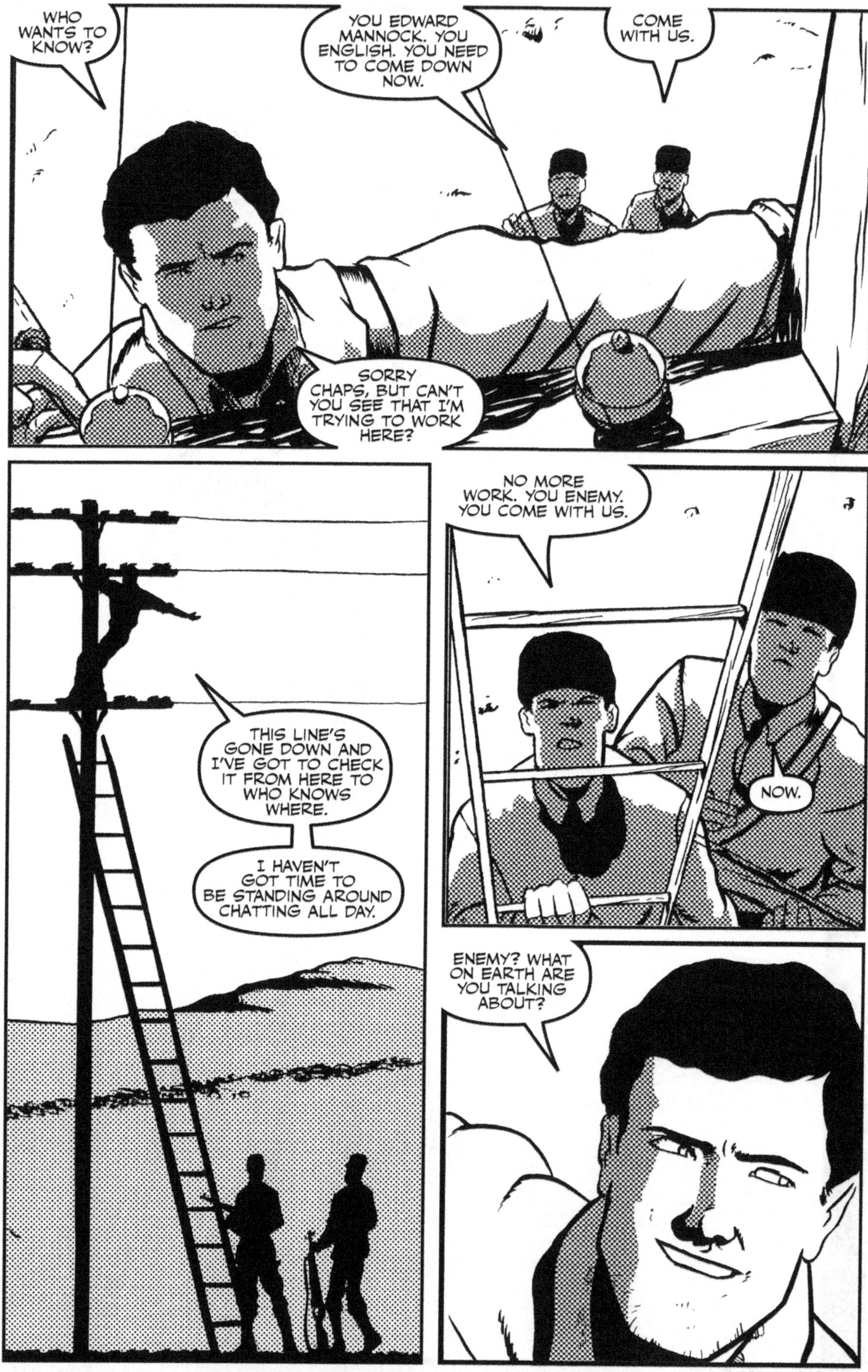
WHO WANTS TO KNOW?
YOU EDWARD MANNOCK. YOU ENGLISH. YOU NEED TO COME DOWN NOW.
COME WITH US.
SORRY CHAPS, BUT CAN'T YOU SEE THAT I'M TRYING TO WORK HERE?
THIS LINE'S GONE DOWN AND I'VE GOT TO CHECK IT FROM HERE TO WHO KNOWS WHERE.
I HAVEN'T GOT TIME TO BE STANDING AROUND CHATTING ALL DAY.
NO MORE WORK. YOU ENEMY. YOU COME WITH US.
NOW.
ENEMY? WHAT ON EARTH ARE YOU TALKING ABOUT?

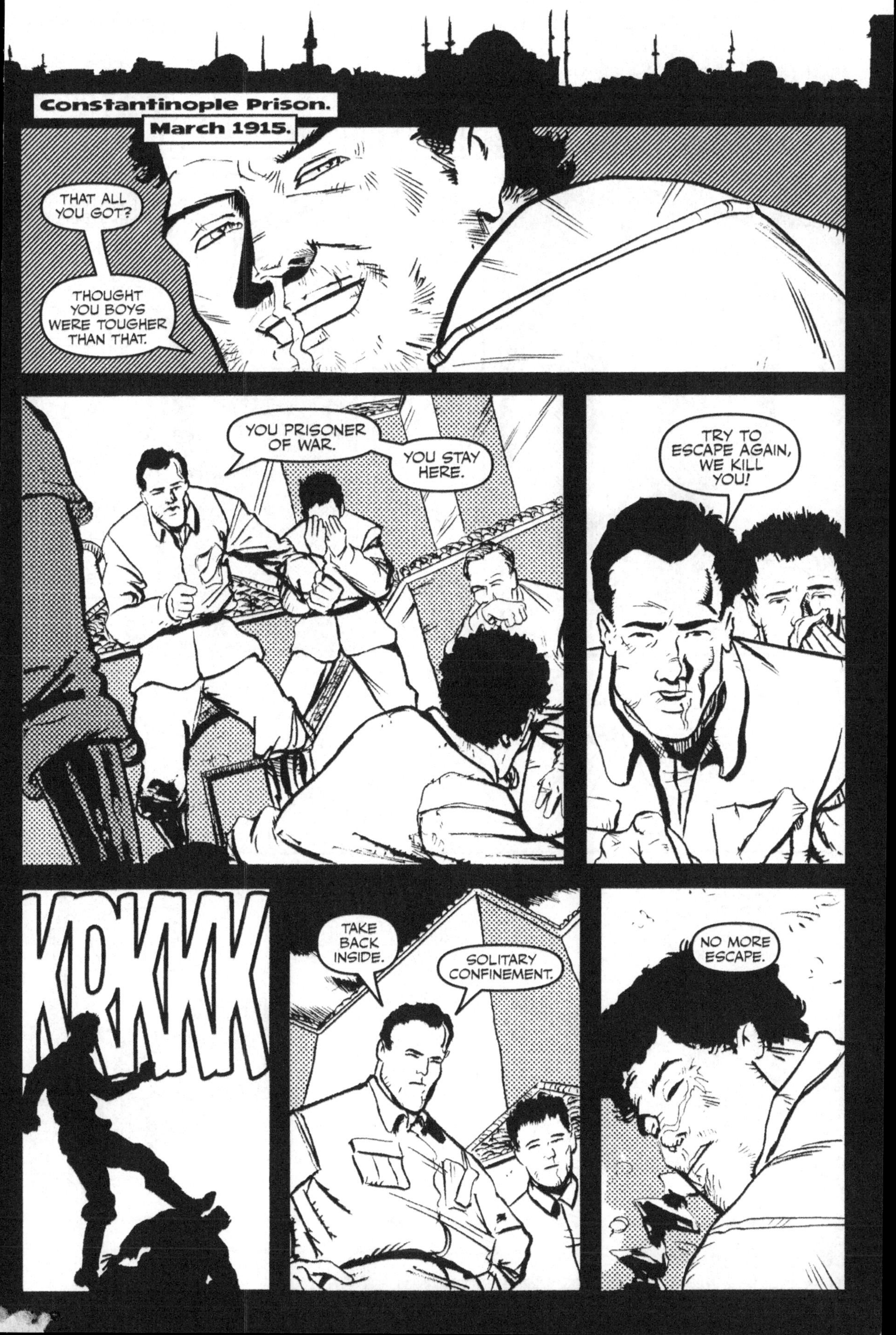
Constantinople Prison.
March 1915.
THAT ALL YOU GOT?
THOUGHT YOU BOYS WERE TOUGHER THAN THAT.
YOU PRISONER OF WAR.
YOU STAY HERE.
TRY TO ESCAPE AGAIN, WE KILL YOU!
TAKE BACK INSIDE.
SOLITARY CONFINEMENT.
NO MORE ESCAPE.

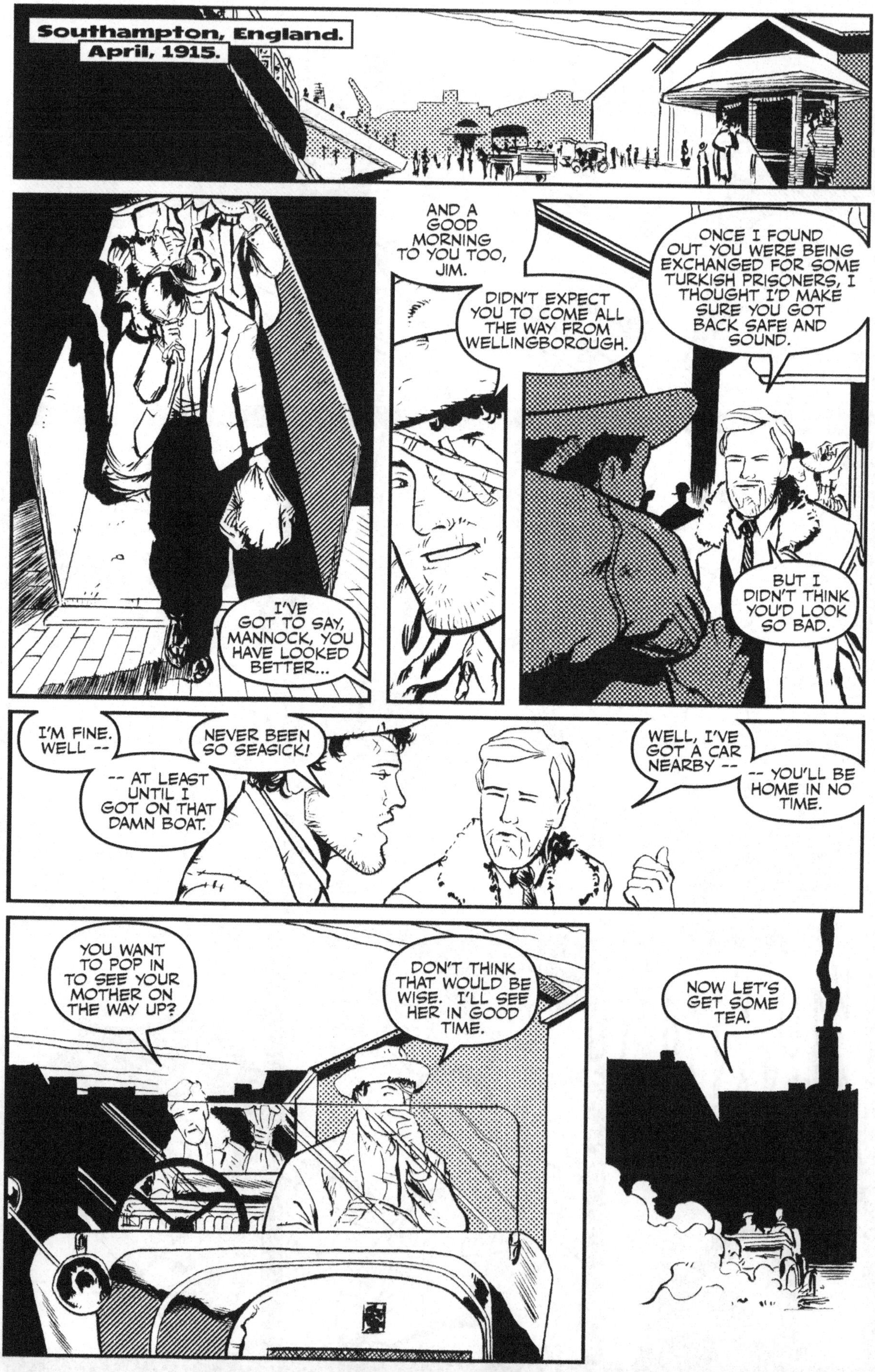
Southampton, England.
April, 1915.
I'VE GOT TO SAY, MANNOCK, YOU HAVE LOOKED BETTER...
AND A GOOD MORNING TO YOU TOO, JIM.
DIDN'T EXPECT YOU TO COME ALL THE WAY FROM WELLINGBOROUGH.
ONCE I FOUND OUT YOU WERE BEING EXCHANGED FOR SOME TURKISH PRISONERS, I THOUGHT I'D MAKE SURE YOU GOT BACK SAFE AND SOUND.
BUT I DIDN'T THINK YOU'D LOOK SO BAD.
I'M FINE. WELL --
-- AT LEAST UNTIL I GOT ON THAT DAMN BOAT.
NEVER BEEN SO SEASICK!
WELL, I'VE GOT A CAR NEARBY --
-- YOU'LL BE HOME IN NO TIME.
YOU WANT TO POP IN TO SEE YOUR MOTHER ON THE WAY UP?
DON'T THINK THAT WOULD BE WISE. I'LL SEE HER IN GOOD TIME.
NOW LET'S GET SOME TEA.

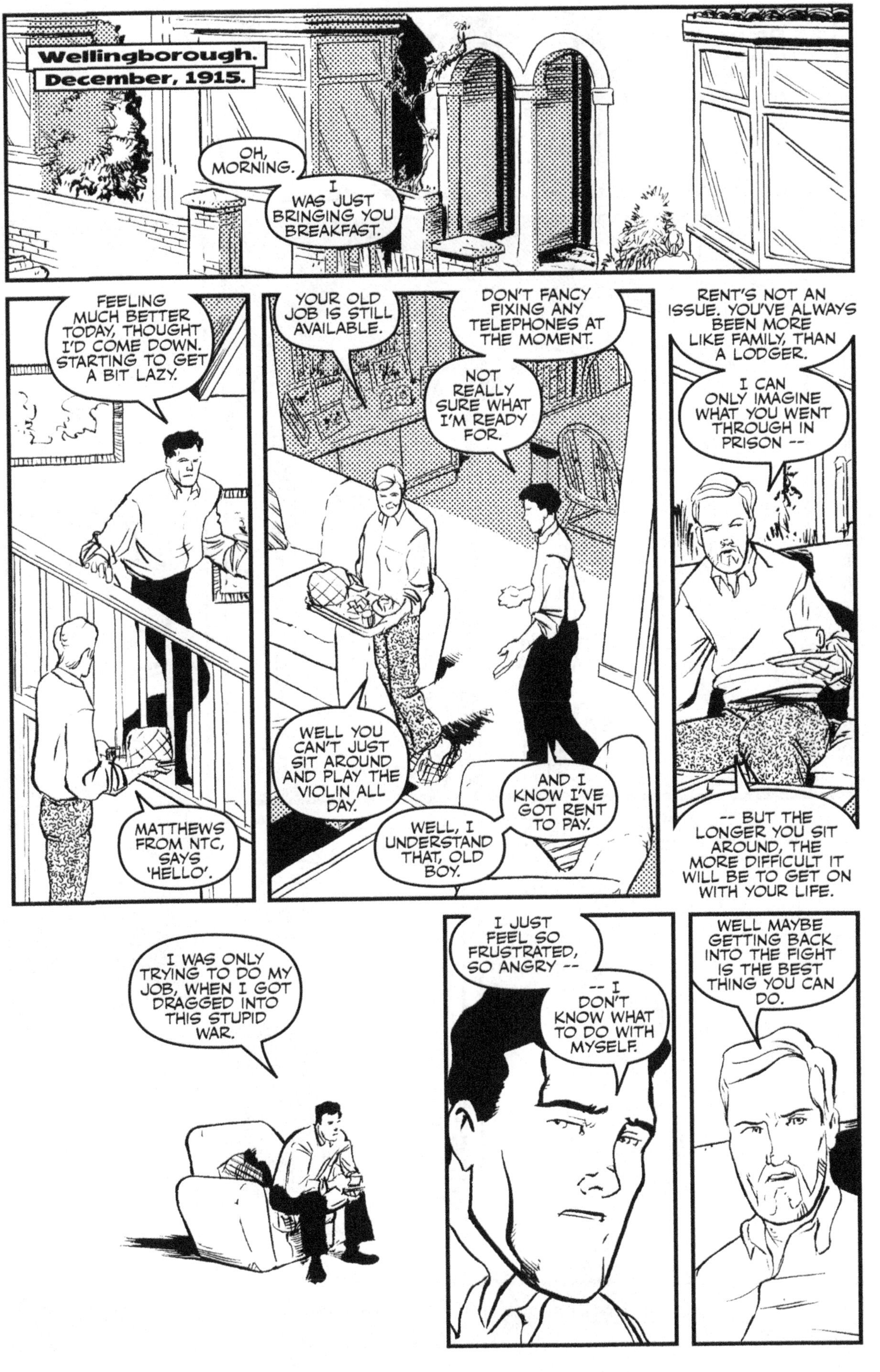

Wellingborough.
December, 1915.
OH, MORNING.
I WAS JUST BRINGING YOU BREAKFAST.
FEELING MUCH BETTER TODAY, THOUGHT I'D COME DOWN. STARTING TO GET A BIT LAZY.
MATTHEWS FROM NTC, SAYS 'HELLO'.
YOUR OLD JOB IS STILL AVAILABLE.
DON'T FANCY FIXING ANY TELEPHONES AT THE MOMENT.
NOT REALLY SURE WHAT I'M READY FOR.
WELL YOU CAN'T JUST SIT AROUND AND PLAY THE VIOLIN ALL DAY.
AND I KNOW I'VE GOT RENT TO PAY.
WELL, I UNDERSTAND THAT, OLD BOY.
RENT'S NOT AN ISSUE. YOU'VE ALWAYS BEEN MORE LIKE FAMILY, THAN A LODGER.
I CAN ONLY IMAGINE WHAT YOU WENT THROUGH IN PRISON --
-- BUT THE LONGER YOU SIT AROUND, THE MORE DIFFICULT IT WILL BE TO GET ON WITH YOUR LIFE.
I WAS ONLY TRYING TO DO MY JOB, WHEN I GOT DRAGGED INTO THIS STUPID WAR.
I JUST FEEL SO FRUSTRATED, SO ANGRY --
-- I DON'T KNOW WHAT TO DO WITH MYSELF.
WELL MAYBE GETTING BACK INTO THE FIGHT IS THE BEST THING YOU CAN DO.

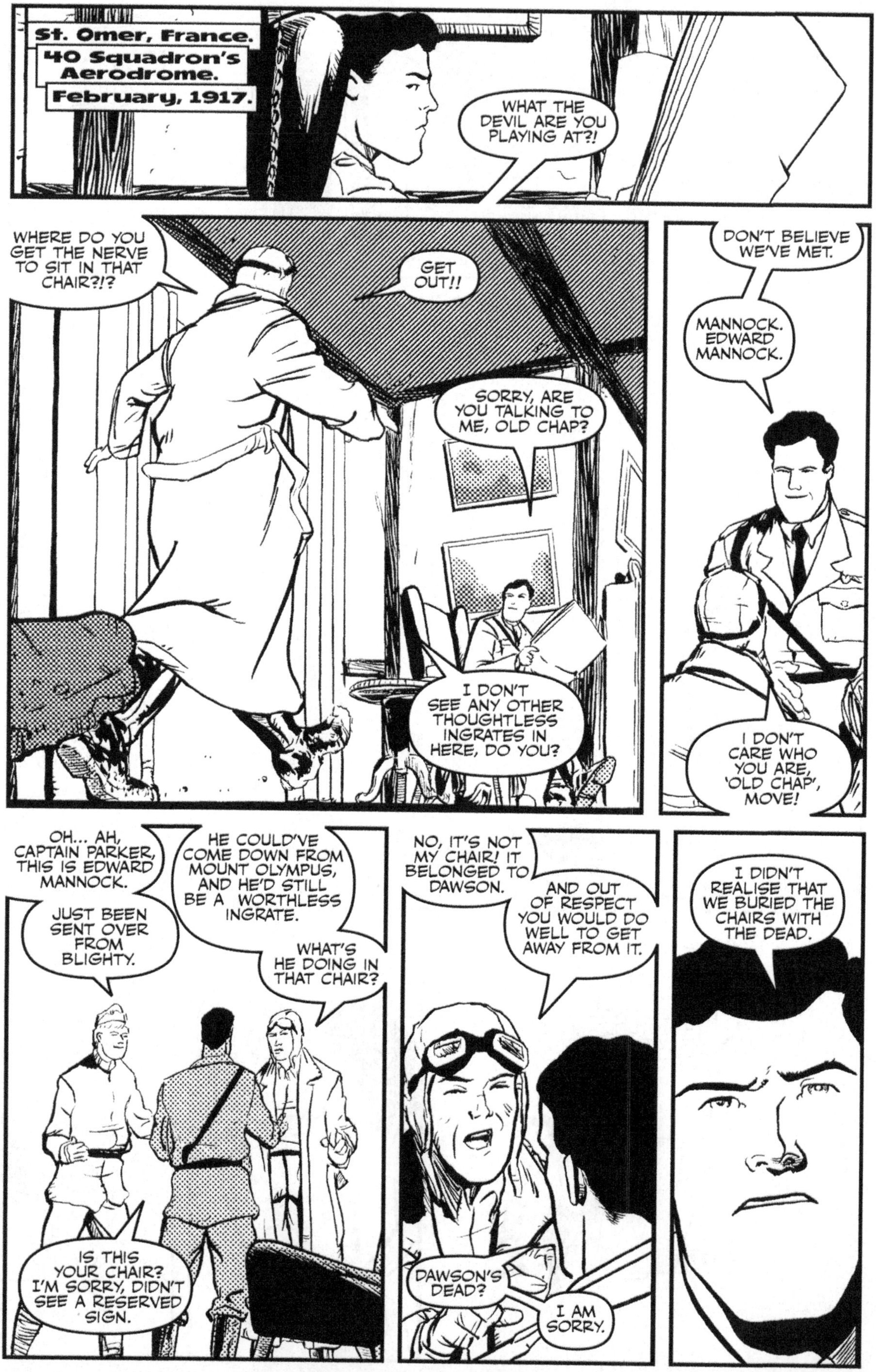
St. Omer, France.
40 Squadron's Aerodrome.
February, 1917.
WHAT THE DEVIL ARE YOU PLAYING AT?!
WHERE DO YOU GET THE NERVE TO SIT IN THAT CHAIR?!?
GET OUT!!
SORRY, ARE YOU TALKING TO ME, OLD CHAP?
I DON'T SEE ANY OTHER THOUGHTLESS INGRATES IN HERE, DO YOU?
DON'T BELIEVE WE'VE MET.
MANNOCK. EDWARD MANNOCK.
I DON'T CARE WHO YOU ARE, 'OLD CHAP', MOVE!
OH... AH, CAPTAIN PARKER, THIS IS EDWARD MANNOCK.
JUST BEEN SENT OVER FROM BLIGHTY.
HE COULD'VE COME DOWN FROM MOUNT OLYMPUS, AND HE'D STILL BE A WORTHLESS INGRATE.
WHAT'S HE DOING IN THAT CHAIR?
IS THIS YOUR CHAIR? I'M SORRY, DIDN'T SEE A RESERVED SIGN.
NO, IT'S NOT MY CHAIR! IT BELONGED TO DAWSON.
AND OUT OF RESPECT YOU WOULD DO WELL TO GET AWAY FROM IT.
DAWSON'S DEAD?
I AM SORRY.
I DIDN'T REALISE THAT WE BURIED THE CHAIRS WITH THE DEAD.

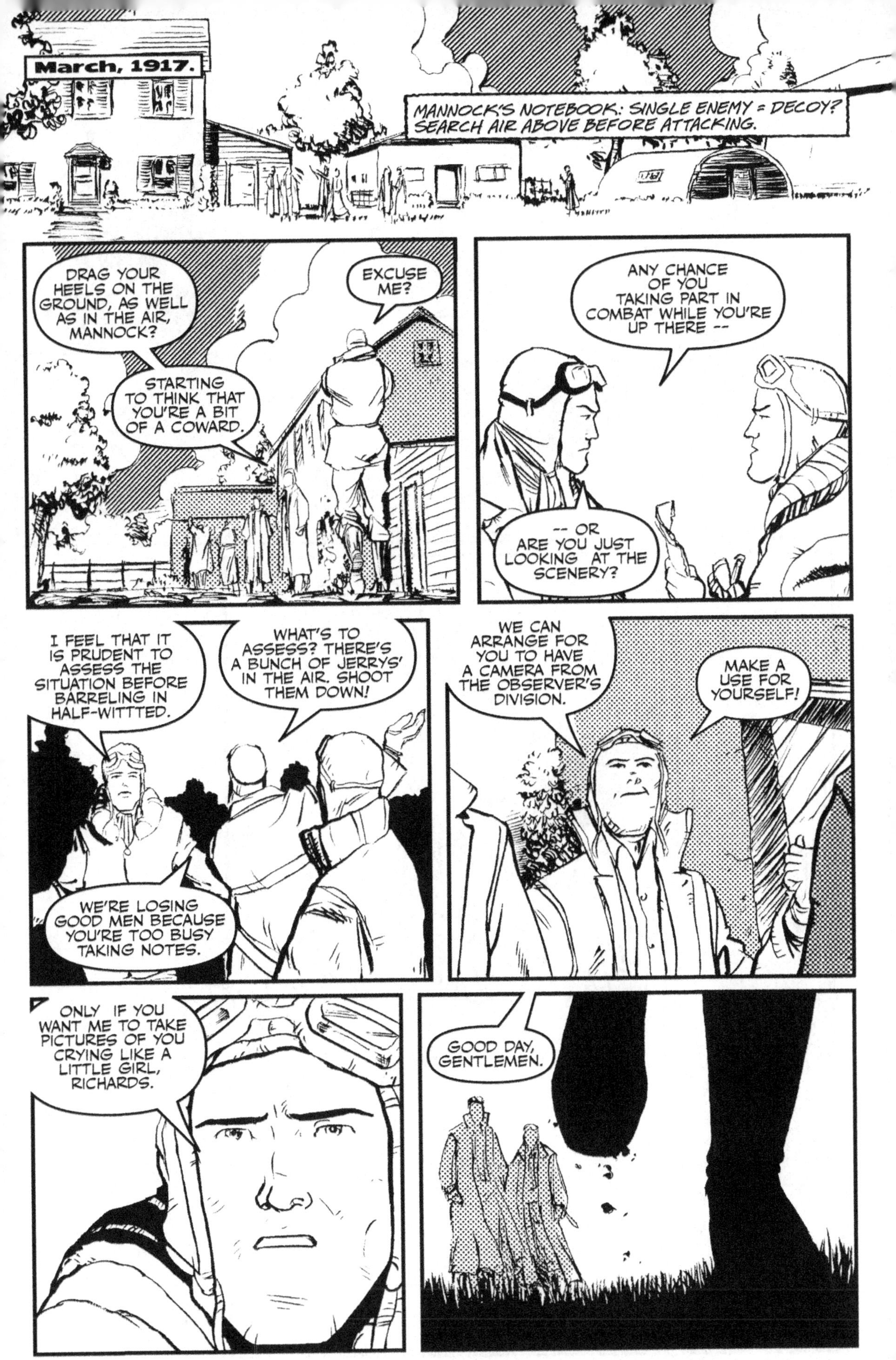
March, 1917.
MANNOCK'S NOTEBOOK: SINGLE ENEMY = DECOY? SEARCH AIR ABOVE BEFORE ATTACKING.
DRAG YOUR HEELS ON THE GROUND, AS WELL AS IN THE AIR, MANNOCK?
STARTING TO THINK THAT YOU'RE A BIT OF A COWARD.
EXCUSE ME?
ANY CHANCE OF YOU TAKING PART IN COMBAT WHILE YOU'RE UP THERE --
-- OR ARE YOU JUST LOOKING AT THE SCENERY?
I FEEL THAT IT IS PRUDENT TO ASSESS THE SITUATION BEFORE BARRELING IN HALF-WITTTED.
WHAT'S TO ASSESS? THERE'S A BUNCH OF JERRYS' IN THE AIR. SHOOT THEM DOWN!
WE'RE LOSING GOOD MEN BECAUSE YOU'RE TOO BUSY TAKING NOTES.
WE CAN ARRANGE FOR YOU TO HAVE A CAMERA FROM THE OBSERVER'S DIVISION.
MAKE A USE FOR YOURSELF!
ONLY IF YOU WANT ME TO TAKE PICTURES OF YOU CRYING LIKE A LITTLE GIRL, RICHARDS.
GOOD DAY, GENTLEMEN.

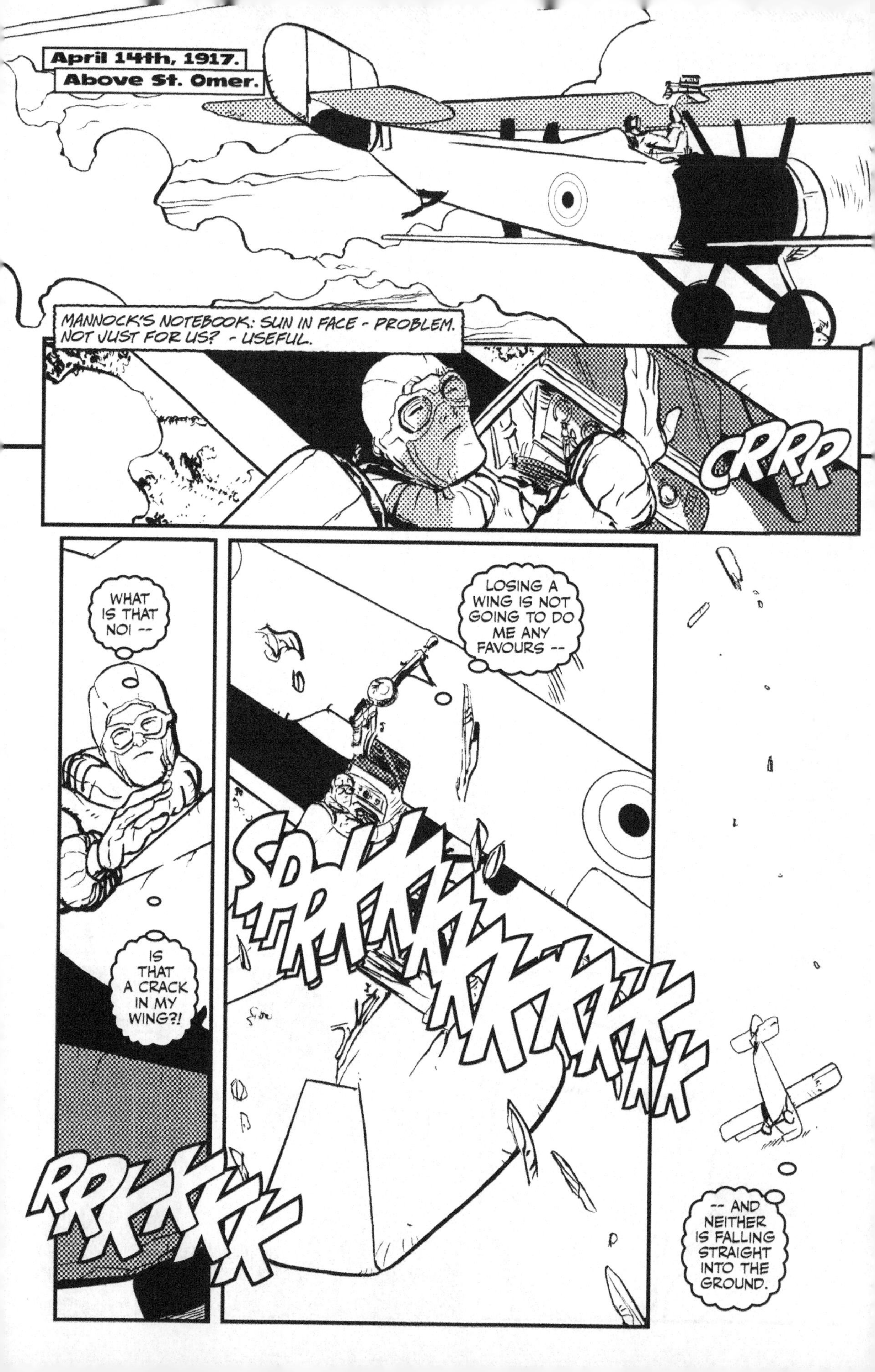
April 14th, 1917.
Above St. Omer.
MANNOCK'S NOTEBOOK: SUN IN FACE - PROBLEM. NOT JUST FOR US? - USEFUL.
CRRR
WHAT IS THAT NOI --
IS THAT A CRACK IN MY WING?!
RRKKKK
LOSING A WING IS NOT GOING TO DO ME ANY FAVOURS --
SPRAKKKKKKKKKKK
-- AND NEITHER IS FALLING STRAIGHT INTO THE GROUND.

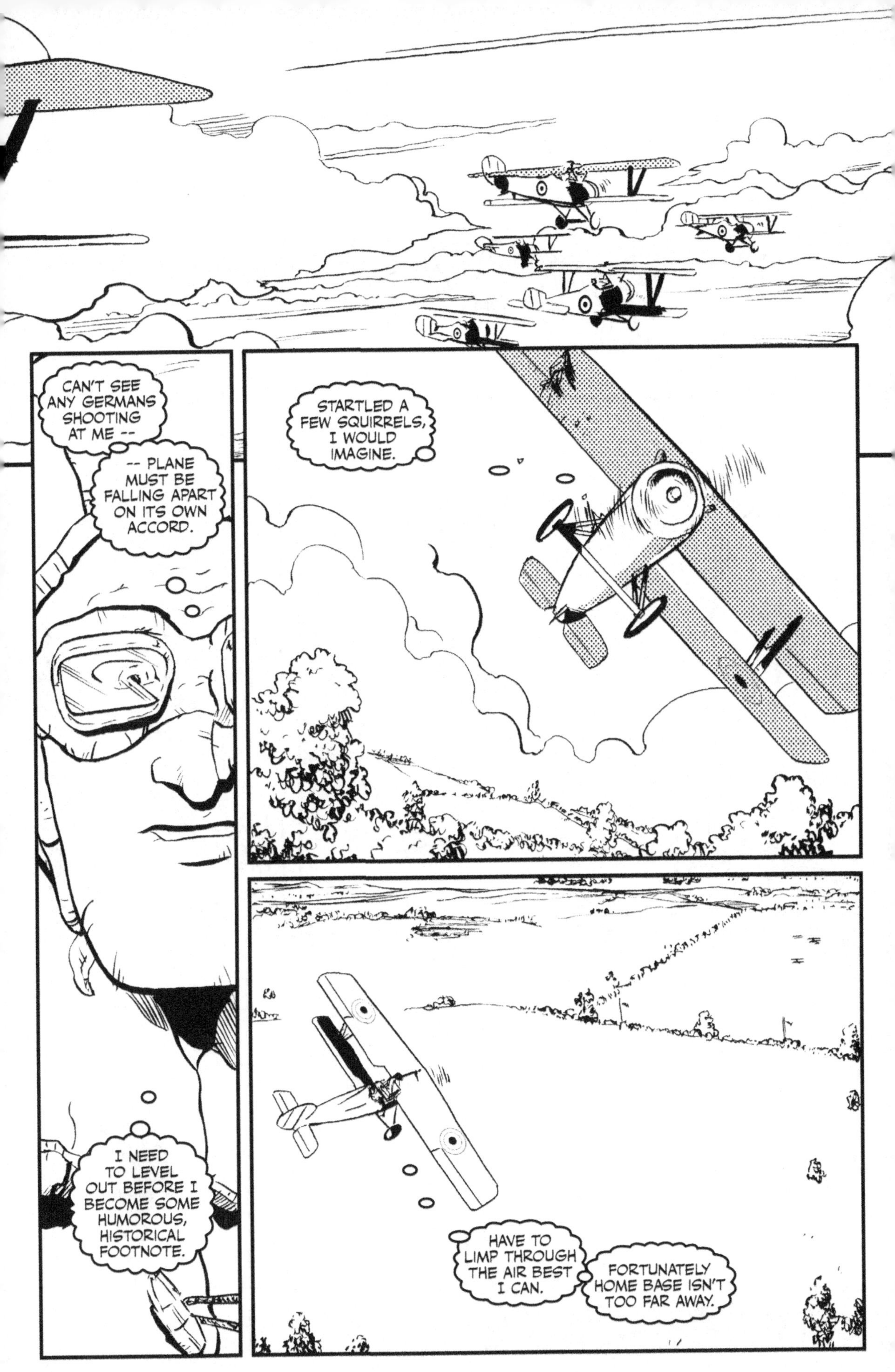

CAN'T SEE ANY GERMANS SHOOTING AT ME --
-- PLANE MUST BE FALLING APART ON ITS OWN ACCORD.
I NEED TO LEVEL OUT BEFORE I BECOME SOME HUMOROUS, HISTORICAL FOOTNOTE.
STARTLED A FEW SQUIRRELS, I WOULD IMAGINE.
HAVE TO LIMP THROUGH THE AIR BEST I CAN.
FORTUNATELY HOME BASE ISN'T TOO FAR AWAY.

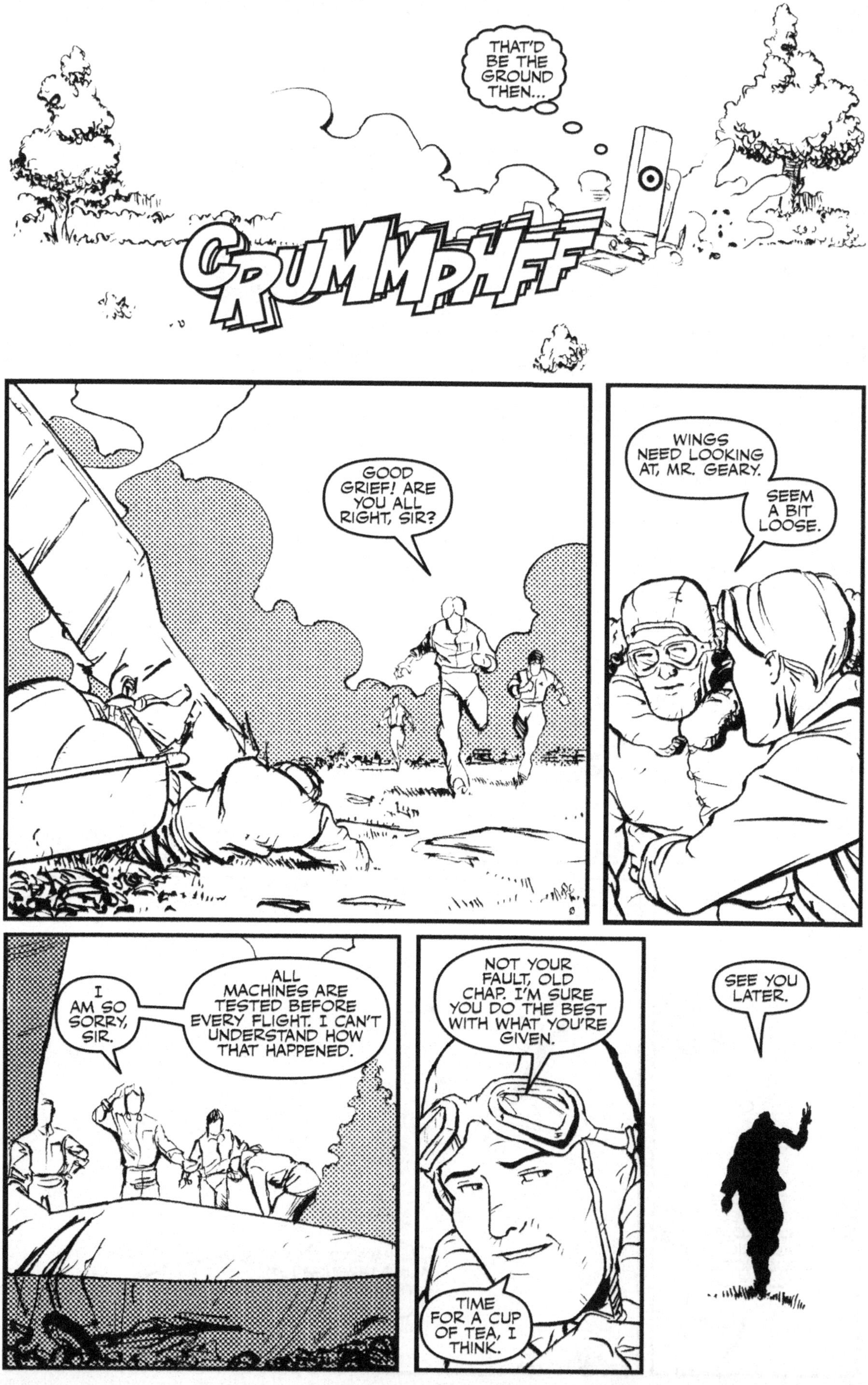
THAT'D BE THE GROUND THEN...
CRUMMPHFF
GOOD GRIEF! ARE YOU ALL RIGHT, SIR?
WINGS NEED LOOKING AT, MR. GEARY.
SEEM A BIT LOOSE.
I AM SO SORRY, SIR.
ALL MACHINES ARE TESTED BEFORE EVERY FLIGHT. I CAN'T UNDERSTAND HOW THAT HAPPENED.
NOT YOUR FAULT, OLD CHAP. I'M SURE YOU DO THE BEST WITH WHAT YOU'RE GIVEN.
TIME FOR A CUP OF TEA, I THINK.
SEE YOU LATER.

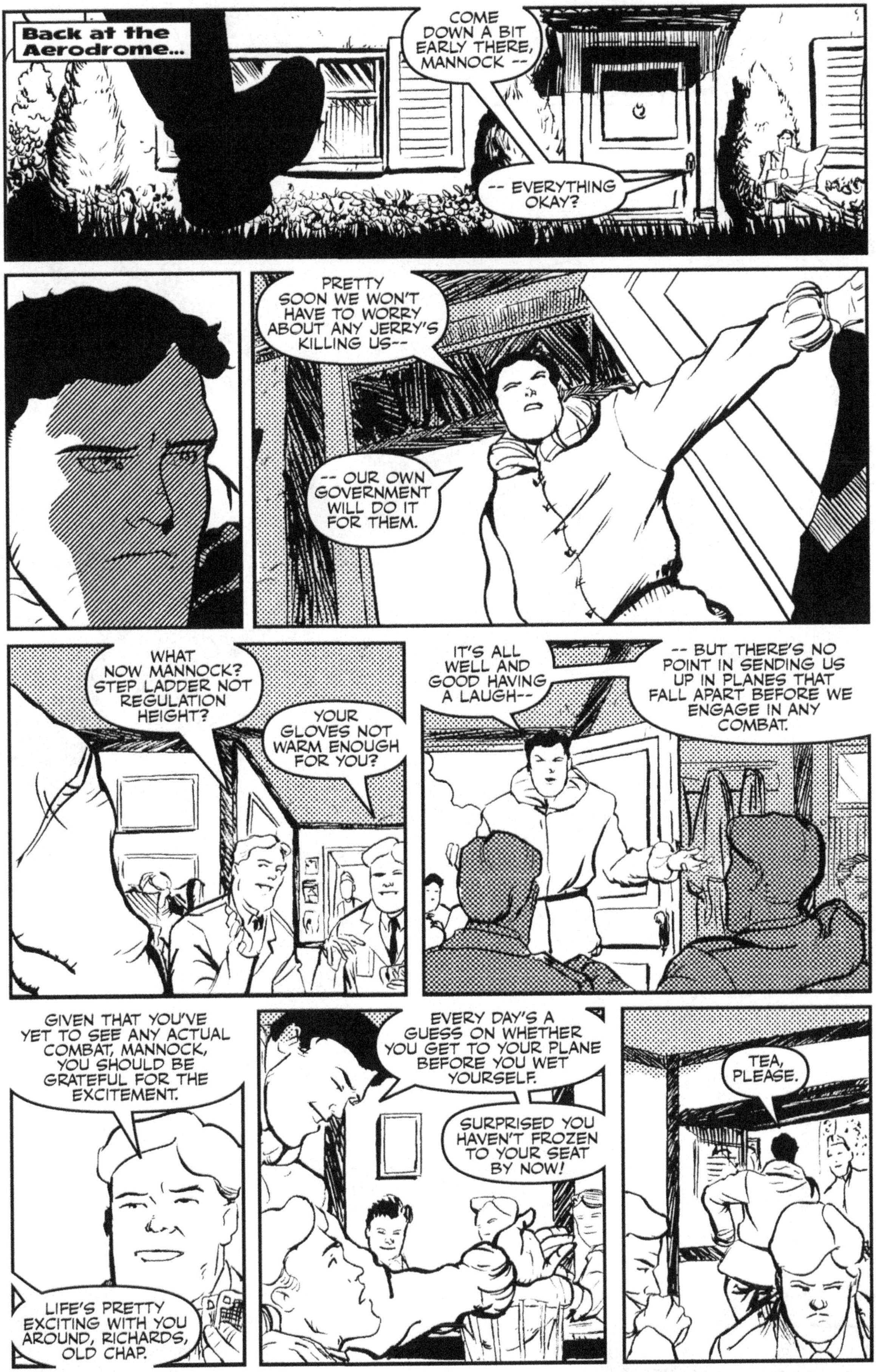
Back at the Aerodrome...
COME DOWN A BIT EARLY THERE, MANNOCK --
-- EVERYTHING OKAY?
PRETTY SOON WE WON'T HAVE TO WORRY ABOUT ANY JERRY'S KILLING US--
-- OUR OWN GOVERNMENT WILL DO IT FOR THEM.
WHAT NOW MANNOCK? STEP LADDER NOT REGULATION HEIGHT?
YOUR GLOVES NOT WARM ENOUGH FOR YOU?
IT'S ALL WELL AND GOOD HAVING A LAUGH--
-- BUT THERE'S NO POINT IN SENDING US UP IN PLANES THAT FALL APART BEFORE WE ENGAGE IN ANY COMBAT.
GIVEN THAT YOU'VE YET TO SEE ANY ACTUAL COMBAT, MANNOCK, YOU SHOULD BE GRATEFUL FOR THE EXCITEMENT.
LIFE'S PRETTY EXCITING WITH YOU AROUND, RICHARDS, OLD CHAP.
EVERY DAY'S A GUESS ON WHETHER YOU GET TO YOUR PLANE BEFORE YOU WET YOURSELF.
SURPRISED YOU HAVEN'T FROZEN TO YOUR SEAT BY NOW!
TEA, PLEASE.

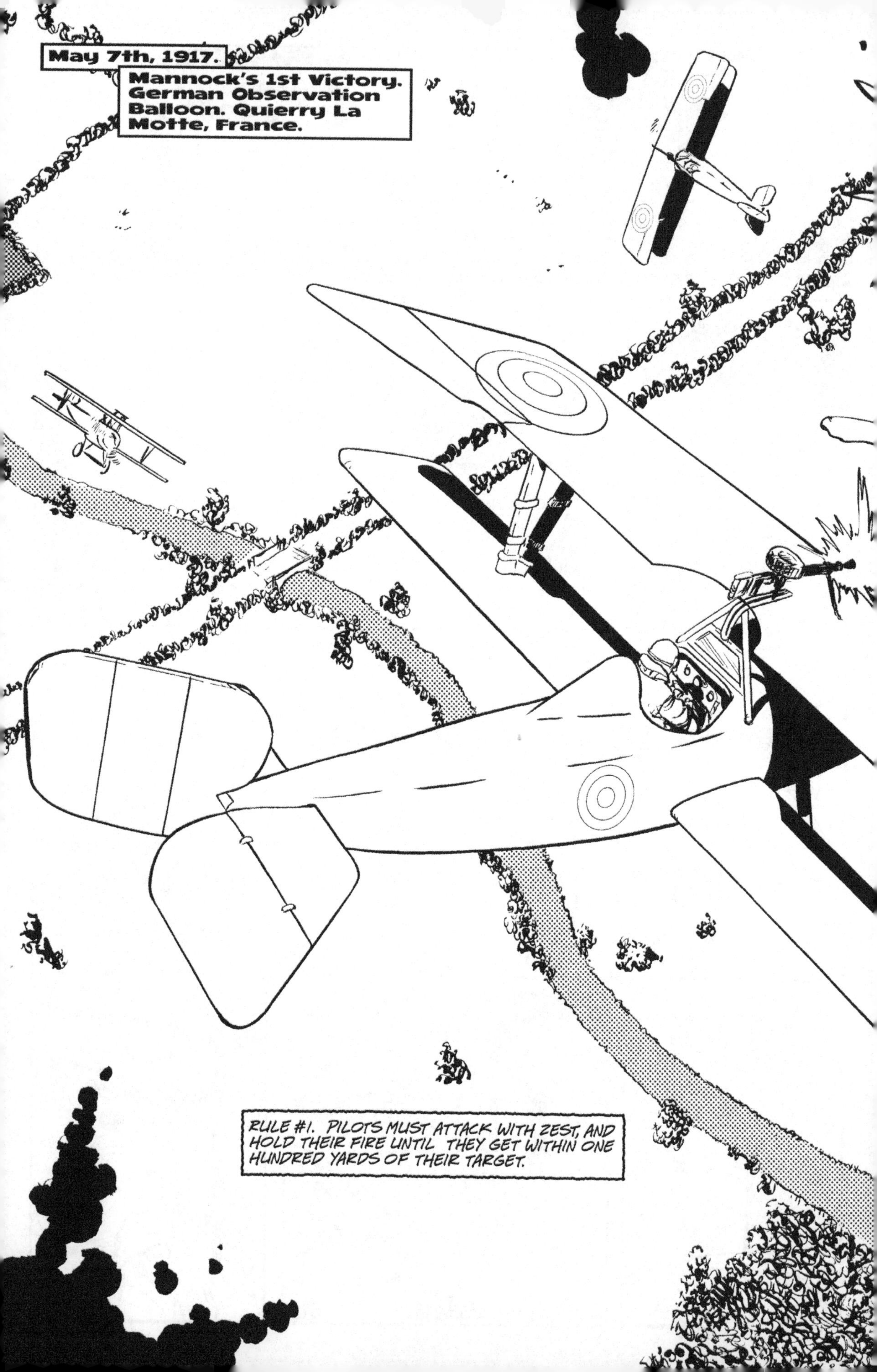
May 7th, 1917.
Mannock's 1st Victory. German Observation Balloon. Quierry La Motte, France.
RULE #1. PILOTS MUST ATTACK WITH ZEST, AND HOLD THEIR FIRE UNTIL THEY GET WITHIN ONE HUNDRED YARDS OF THEIR TARGET.

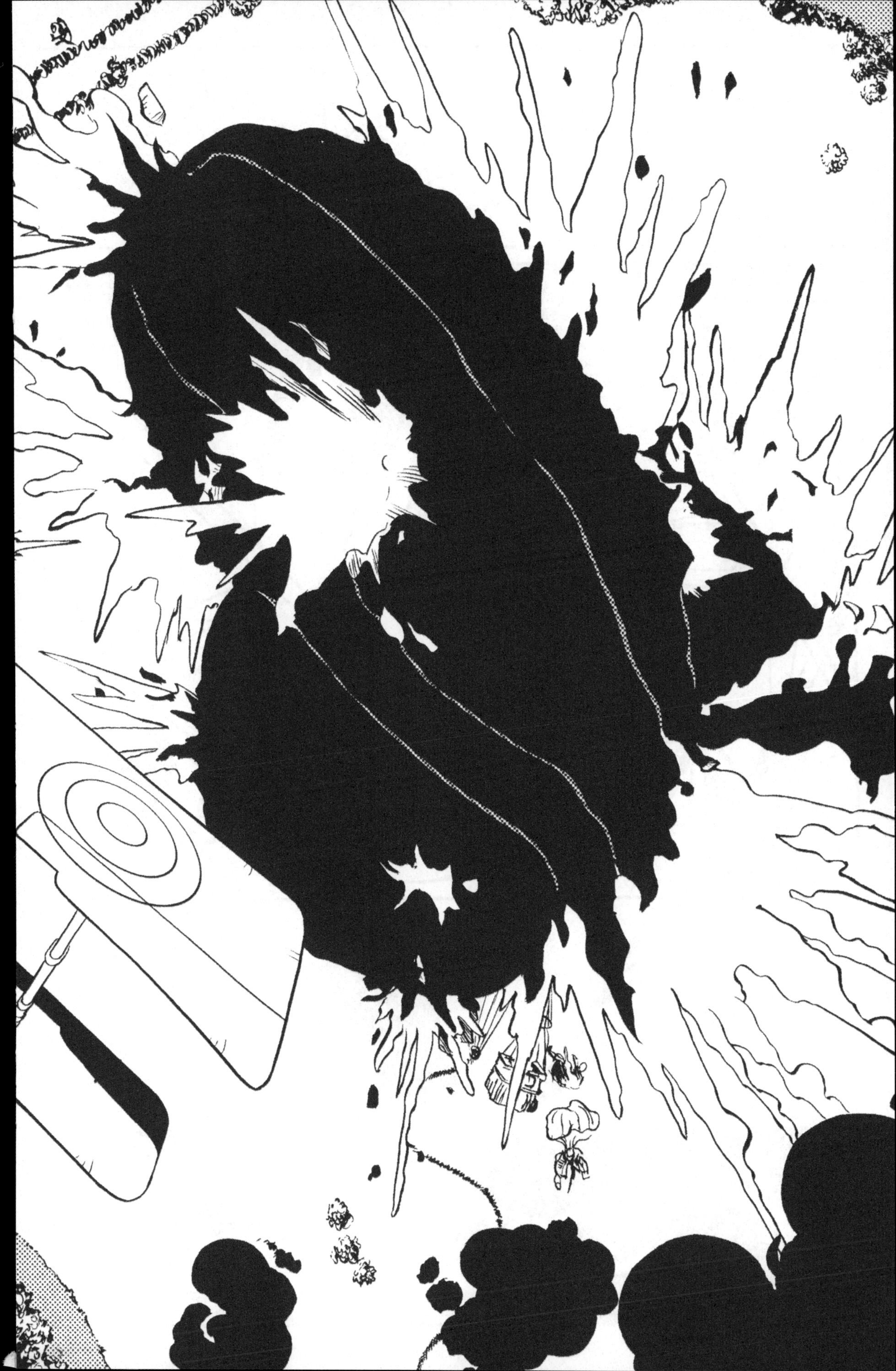

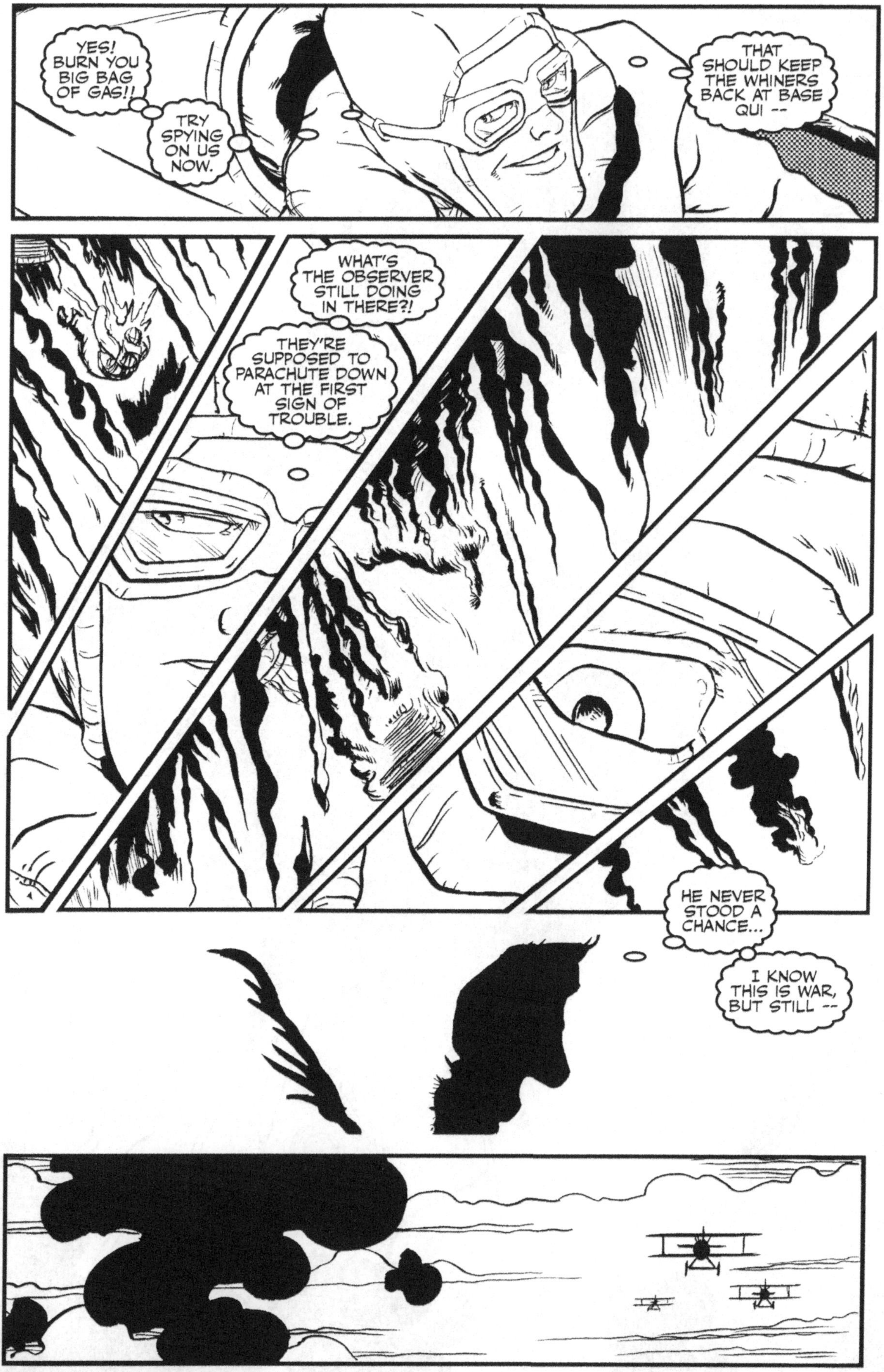
YES! BURN YOU BIG BAG OF GAS!!
TRY SPYING ON US NOW.
THAT SHOULD KEEP THE WHINERS BACK AT BASE QUI --
WHAT'S THE OBSERVER STILL DOING IN THERE?!
THEY'RE SUPPOSED TO PARACHUTE DOWN AT THE FIRST SIGN OF TROUBLE.
HE NEVER STOOD A CHANCE...
I KNOW THIS IS WAR, BUT STILL --

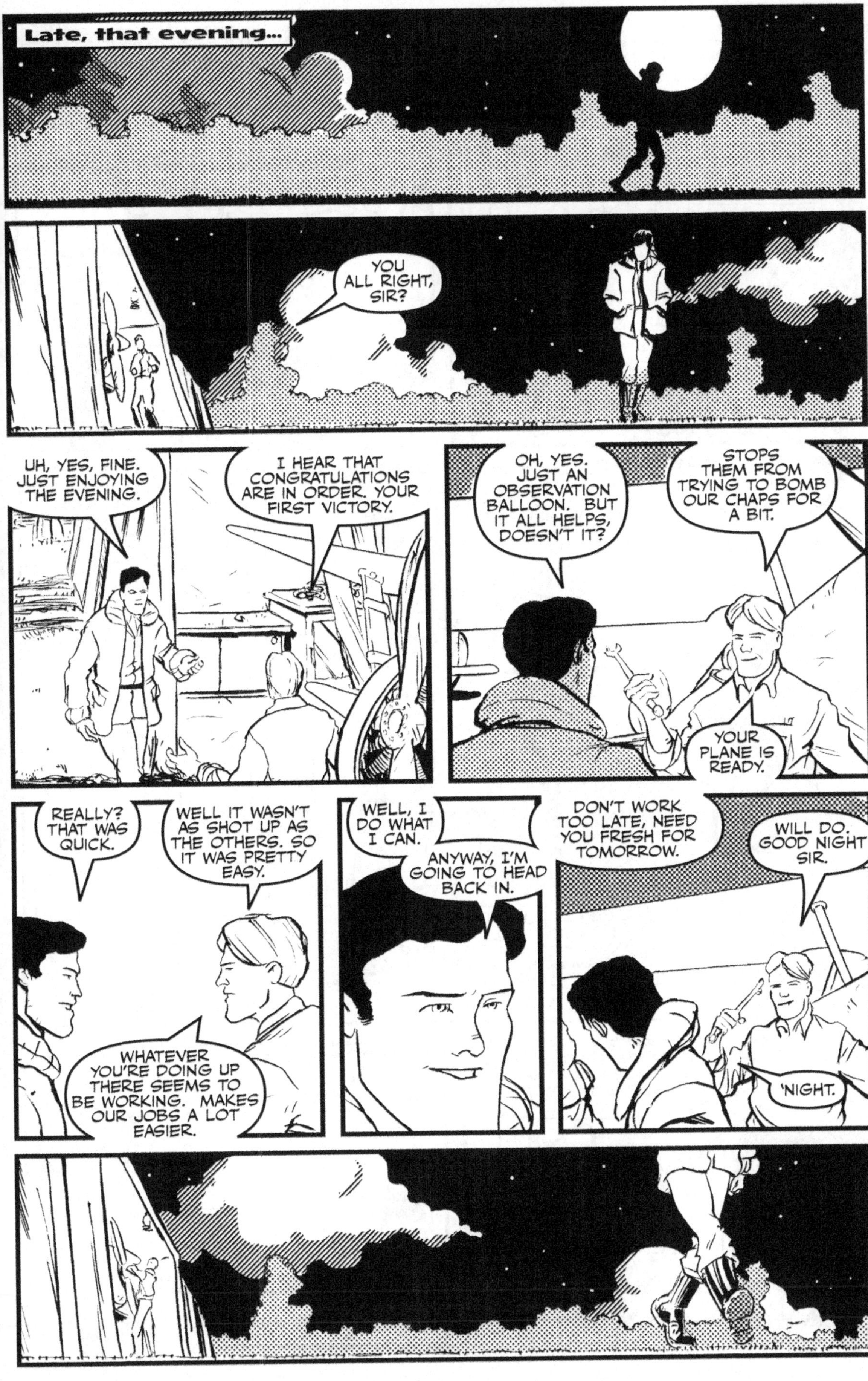
Late, that evening...
YOU ALL RIGHT, SIR?
UH, YES, FINE. JUST ENJOYING THE EVENING.
I HEAR THAT CONGRATULATIONS ARE IN ORDER. YOUR FIRST VICTORY.
OH, YES. JUST AN OBSERVATION BALLOON. BUT IT ALL HELPS, DOESN'T IT?
STOPS THEM FROM TRYING TO BOMB OUR CHAPS FOR A BIT.
YOUR PLANE IS READY.
REALLY? THAT WAS QUICK.
WELL IT WASN'T AS SHOT UP AS THE OTHERS. SO IT WAS PRETTY EASY.
WHATEVER YOU'RE DOING UP THERE SEEMS TO BE WORKING. MAKES OUR JOBS A LOT EASIER.
WELL, I DO WHAT I CAN.
ANYWAY, I'M GOING TO HEAD BACK IN.
DON'T WORK TOO LATE, NEED YOU FRESH FOR TOMORROW.
WILL DO. GOOD NIGHT SIR.
'NIGHT.

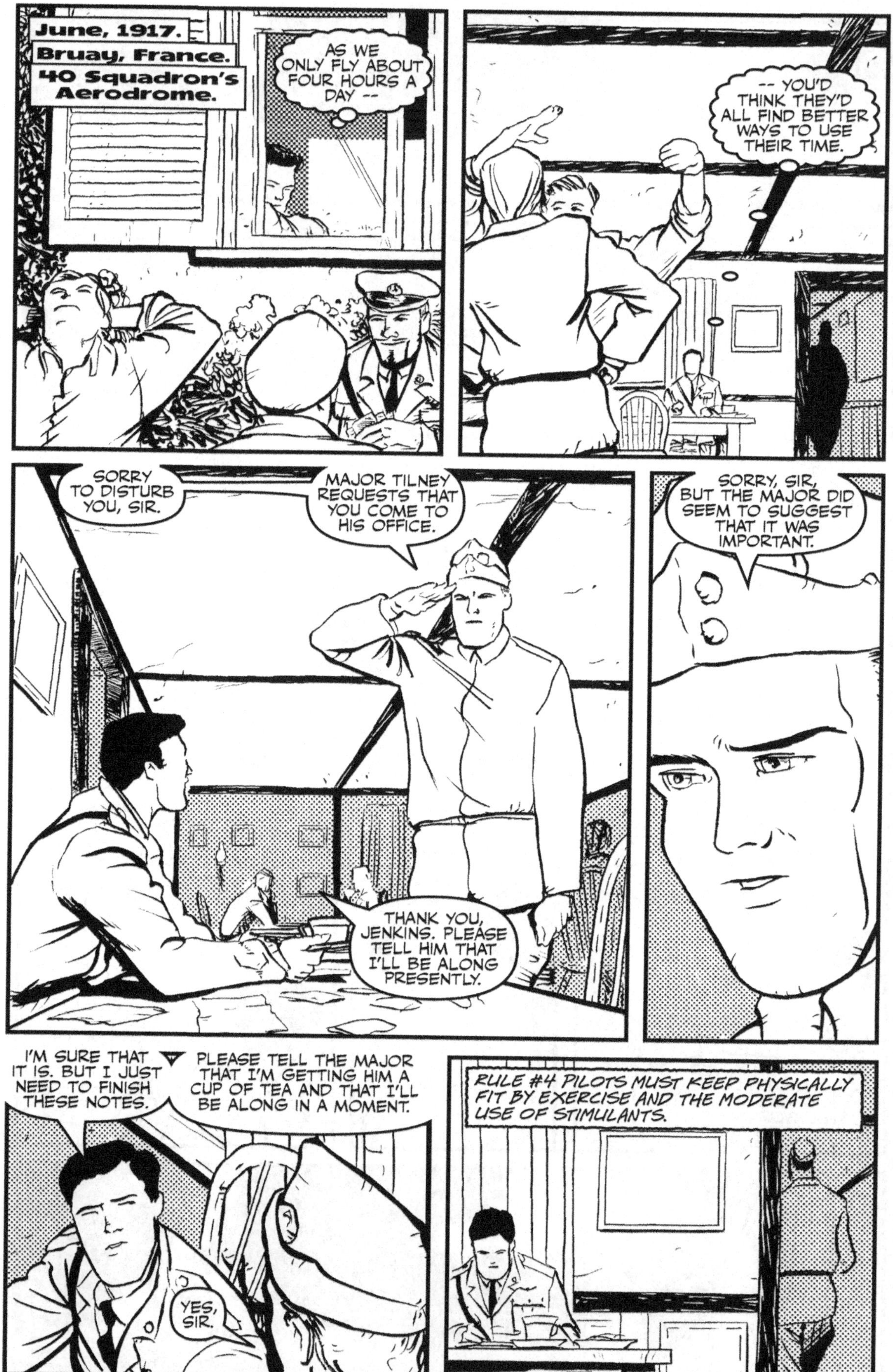
June, 1917.
Bruay, France.
40 Squadron's Aerodrome.
AS WE ONLY FLY ABOUT FOUR HOURS A DAY --
-- YOU'D THINK THEY'D ALL FIND BETTER WAYS TO USE THEIR TIME.
SORRY TO DISTURB YOU, SIR.
MAJOR TILNEY REQUESTS THAT YOU COME TO HIS OFFICE.
THANK YOU, JENKINS. PLEASE TELL HIM THAT I'LL BE ALONG PRESENTLY.
SORRY, SIR, BUT THE MAJOR DID SEEM TO SUGGEST THAT IT WAS IMPORTANT.
I'M SURE THAT IT IS. BUT I JUST NEED TO FINISH THESE NOTES.
PLEASE TELL THE MAJOR THAT I'M GETTING HIM A CUP OF TEA AND THAT I'LL BE ALONG IN A MOMENT.
YES, SIR.
RULE #4 PILOTS MUST KEEP PHYSICALLY FIT BY EXERCISE AND THE MODERATE USE OF STIMULANTS.

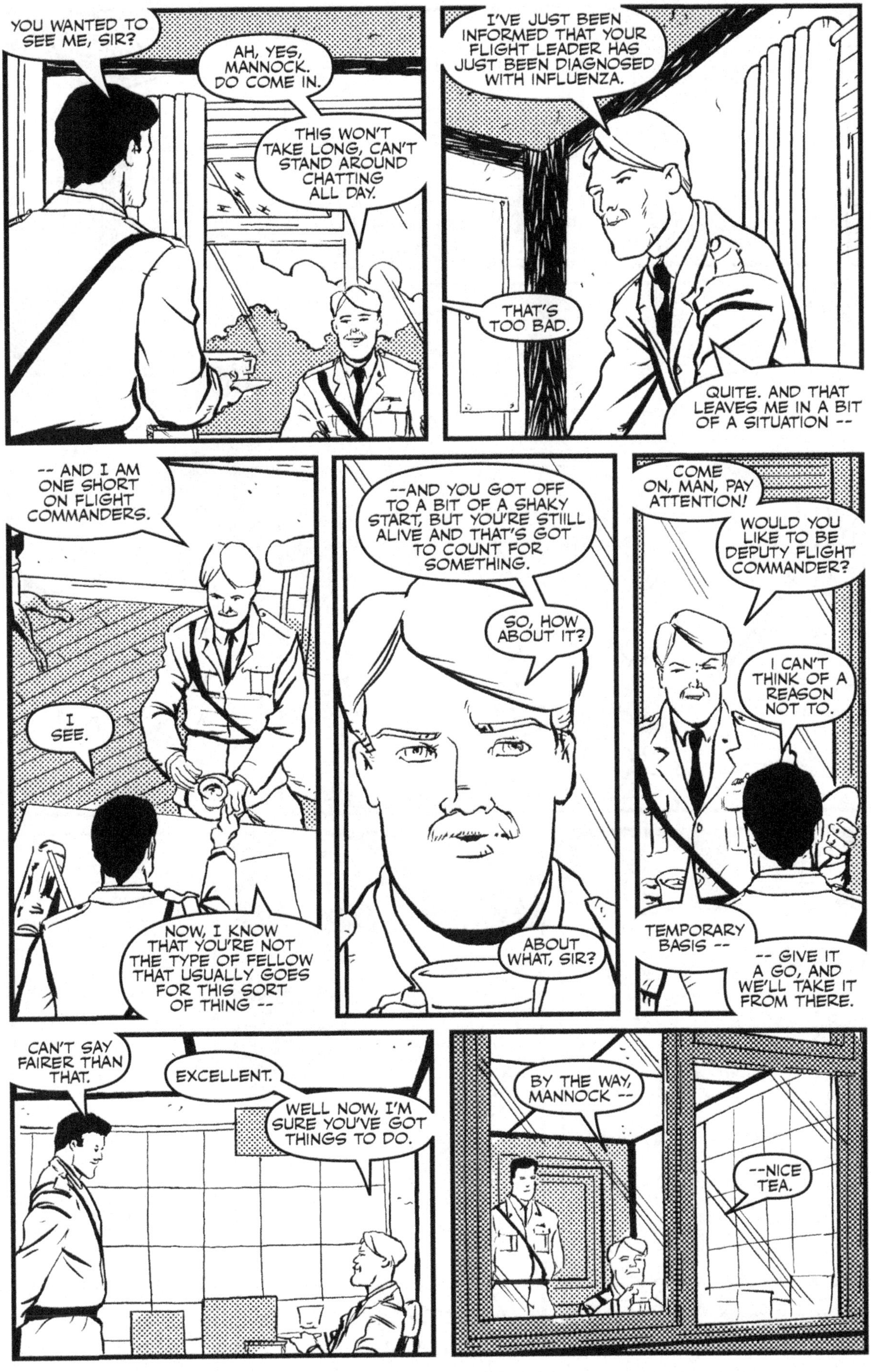
YOU WANTED TO SEE ME, SIR?
AH, YES, MANNOCK. DO COME IN.
THIS WON'T TAKE LONG, CAN'T STAND AROUND CHATTING ALL DAY.
I'VE JUST BEEN INFORMED THAT YOUR FLIGHT LEADER HAS JUST BEEN DIAGNOSED WITH INFLUENZA.
THAT'S TOO BAD.
QUITE. AND THAT LEAVES ME IN A BIT OF A SITUATION --
-- AND I AM ONE SHORT ON FLIGHT COMMANDERS.
I SEE.
NOW, I KNOW THAT YOU'RE NOT THE TYPE OF FELLOW THAT USUALLY GOES FOR THIS SORT OF THING --
--AND YOU GOT OFF TO A BIT OF A SHAKY START, BUT YOU'RE STIILL ALIVE AND THAT'S GOT TO COUNT FOR SOMETHING.
SO, HOW ABOUT IT?
ABOUT WHAT, SIR?
COME ON, MAN, PAY ATTENTION!
WOULD YOU LIKE TO BE DEPUTY FLIGHT COMMANDER?
I CAN'T THINK OF A REASON NOT TO.
TEMPORARY BASIS --
-- GIVE IT A GO, AND WE'LL TAKE IT FROM THERE.
CAN'T SAY FAIRER THAN THAT.
EXCELLENT.
WELL NOW, I'M SURE YOU'VE GOT THINGS TO DO.
BY THE WAY, MANNOCK --
--NICE TEA.

Later...

I SAY, IS GEARY ABOUT?

AT THE BACK, SIR, JUST REPAIRING THAT ENGINE.

GEARY, OLD CHAP, HOW YOU DOING?

VERY GOOD, SIR. YOURSELF?

THE USUAL. DON'T KNOW HOW YOU LIKE YOUR TEA, SO I WENT WITH TRADITIONAL.

THANK YOU VERY MUCH, SIR.

NOW THAT I'VE GOT YOUR ATTENTION, CAN I BORROW YOU FOR A MINUTE?

NO PROBLEM, HOW CAN I HELP?

HAVE A LOOK AT THIS, SEE WHAT YOU THINK.

I'M NO ARTIST, BUT I THINK YOU GET THE IDEA.

I SEE EXACTLY WHAT YOU MEAN.

YOU THINK IT WILL WORK?

DON'T SEE WHY NOT. I'D HAVE TO LOOK AT THE ANGLE.

YOU GOT PERMISSION TO DO THIS?

I'VE NOT BEEN TOLD I CAN'T DO IT.

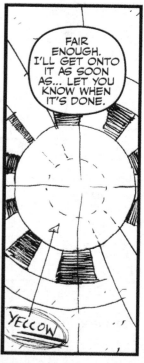

FAIR ENOUGH. I'LL GET ONTO IT AS SOON AS... LET YOU KNOW WHEN IT'S DONE.

YELLOW

The next day...

FANTASTIC JOB, GEARY. YOUR MOTHER WOULD BE PROUD.

THANK YOU, SIR. HOPE IT DOES THE JOB.

BUT WHY HAVE YOU GOT A YELLOW CONE STUCK ON THE FRONT OF YOUR PLANE, SIR?

IT'S CALLED A 'SPINNER', BRIDGEMAN.

IS IT INSTEAD OF PUTTING STREAMERS ON THE WING STRUTS LIKE THE OTHER FLIGHT COMMANDERS, SIR?

IT'S NOT TO SHOW WHO'S IN CHARGE, OLD CHAP --

-- IT'S TO MAKE THE PLANE FLY BETTER.

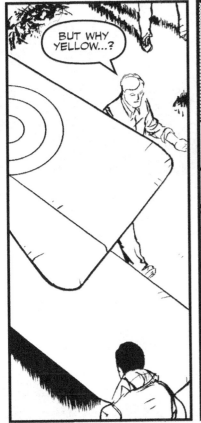

BUT WHY YELLOW...?

EXTRA RATION OF CHOCOLATE FOR ANYONE THAT CAN FIGURE THAT OUT...

NOW, STAND CLEAR SO I CAN GIVE IT A WHIRL!

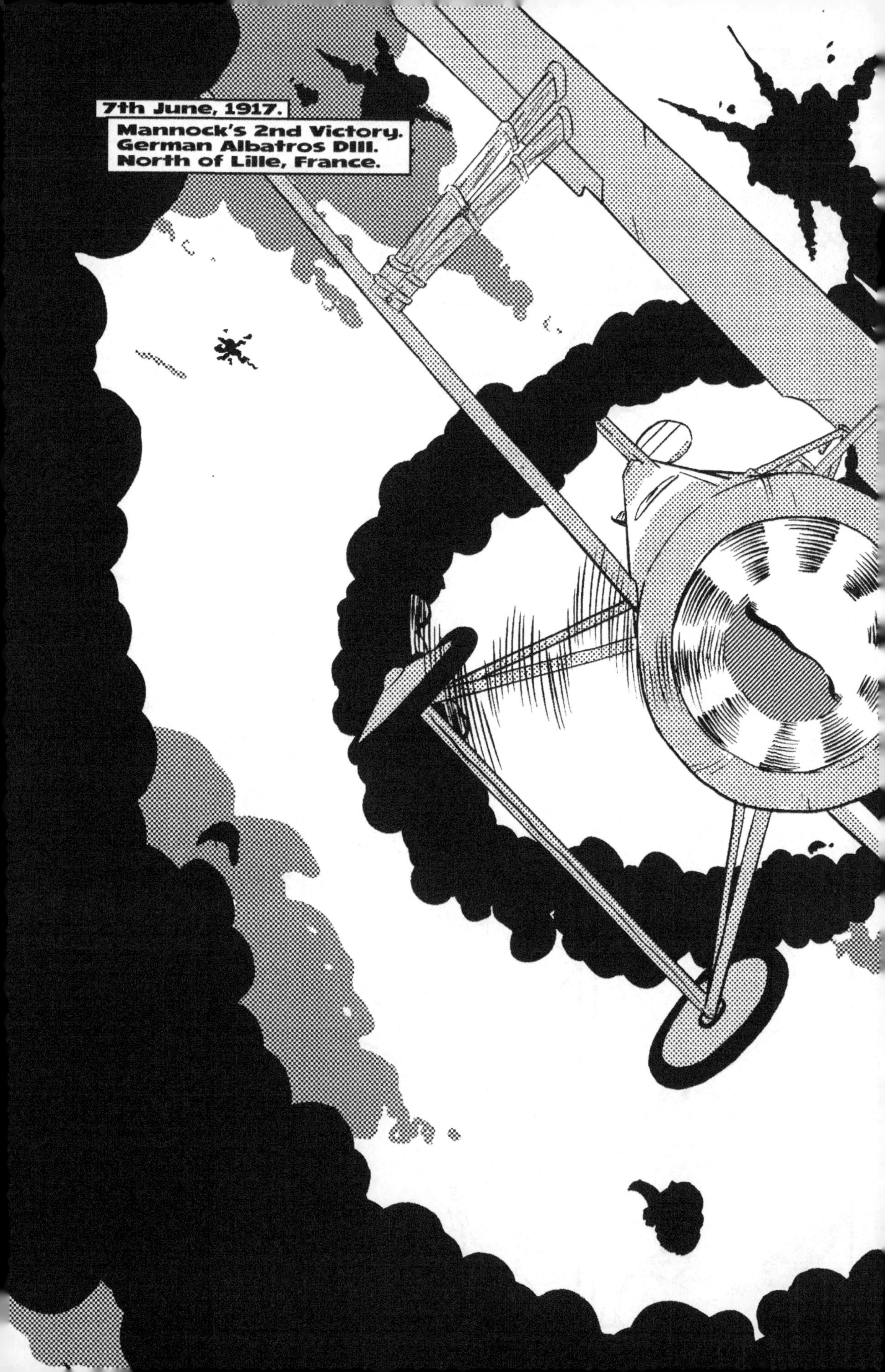
7th June, 1917.
Mannock's 2nd Victory.
German Albatros DIII.
North of Lille, France.

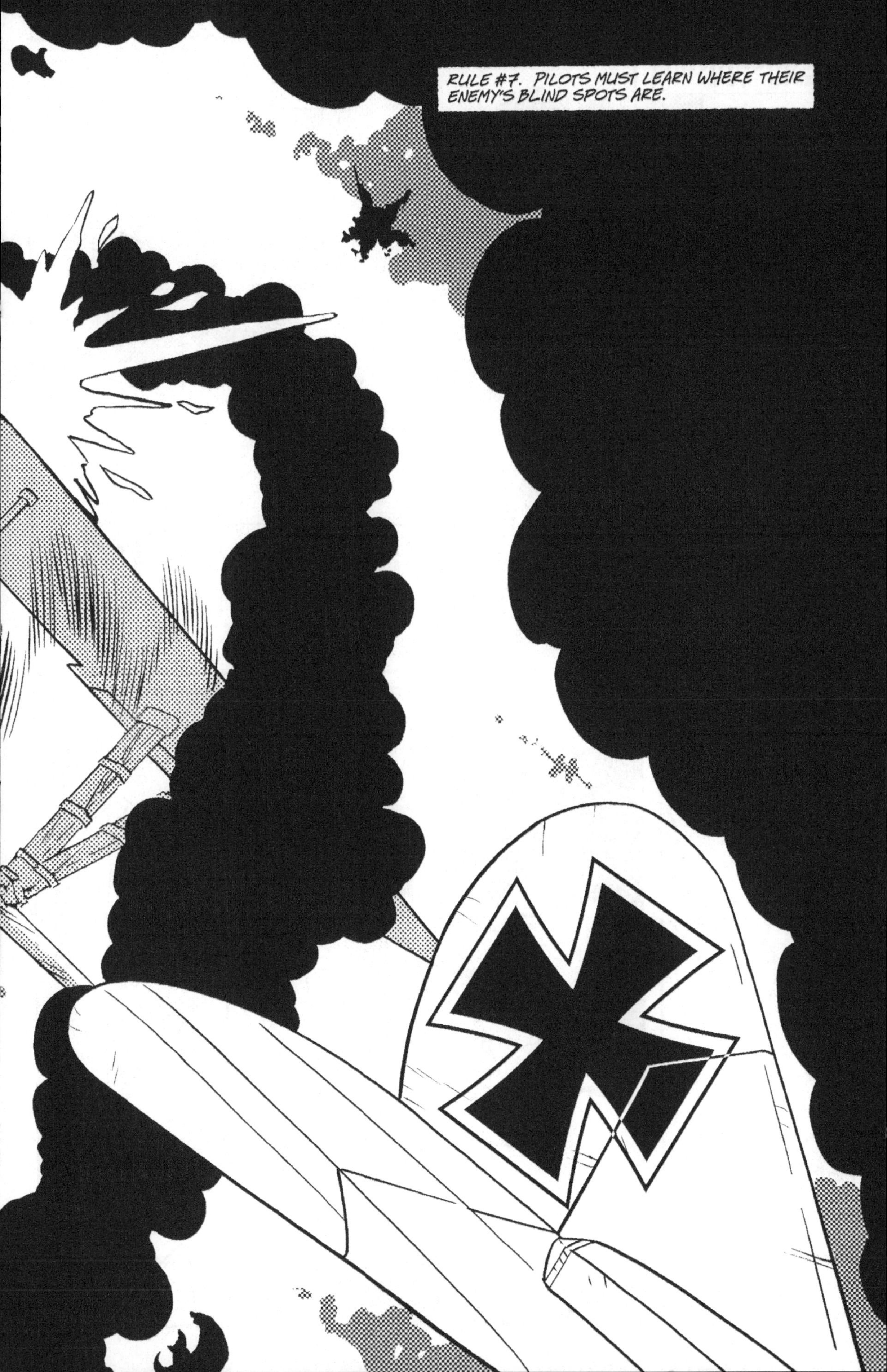
RULE #7. PILOTS MUST LEARN WHERE THEIR ENEMY'S BLIND SPOTS ARE.

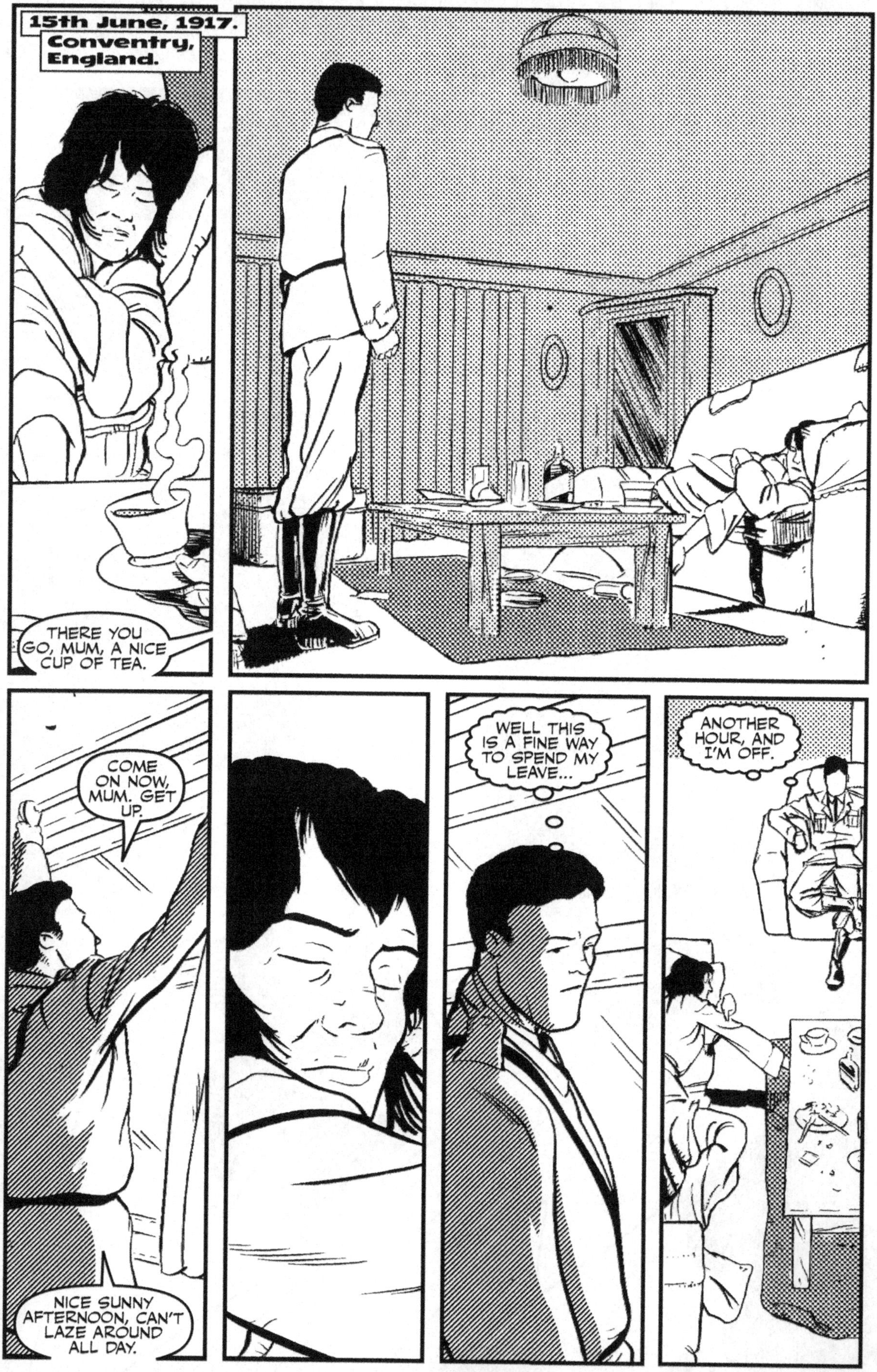
15th June, 1917.
Conventry, England.
THERE YOU GO, MUM, A NICE CUP OF TEA.
COME ON NOW, MUM. GET UP.
NICE SUNNY AFTERNOON, CAN'T LAZE AROUND ALL DAY.
WELL THIS IS A FINE WAY TO SPEND MY LEAVE...
ANOTHER HOUR, AND I'M OFF.

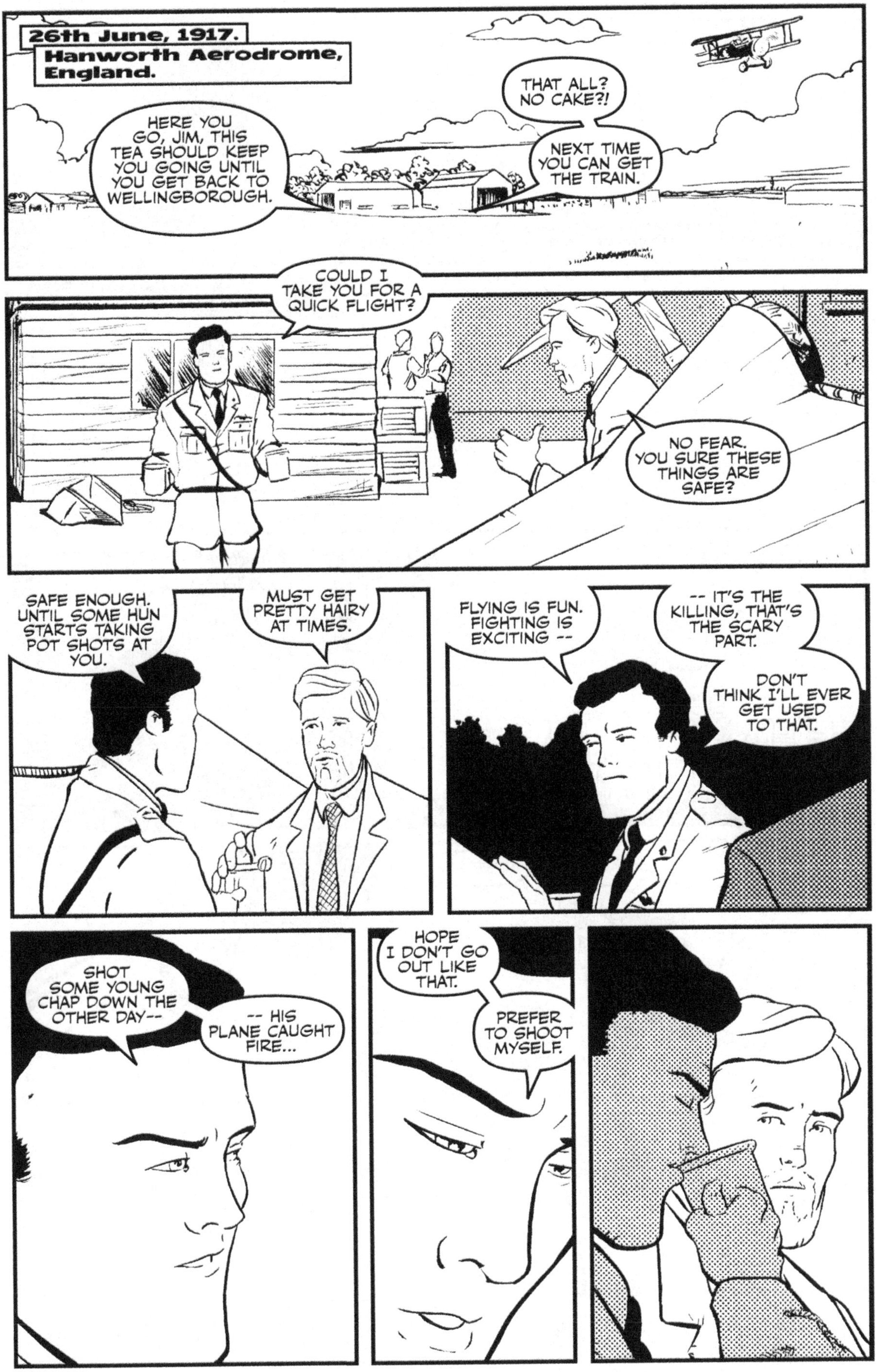
26th June, 1917.
Hanworth Aerodrome, England.
HERE YOU GO, JIM, THIS TEA SHOULD KEEP YOU GOING UNTIL YOU GET BACK TO WELLINGBOROUGH.
THAT ALL? NO CAKE?!
NEXT TIME YOU CAN GET THE TRAIN.
COULD I TAKE YOU FOR A QUICK FLIGHT?
NO FEAR. YOU SURE THESE THINGS ARE SAFE?
SAFE ENOUGH. UNTIL SOME HUN STARTS TAKING POT SHOTS AT YOU.
MUST GET PRETTY HAIRY AT TIMES.
FLYING IS FUN. FIGHTING IS EXCITING --
-- IT'S THE KILLING, THAT'S THE SCARY PART.
DON'T THINK I'LL EVER GET USED TO THAT.
SHOT SOME YOUNG CHAP DOWN THE OTHER DAY--
-- HIS PLANE CAUGHT FIRE...
HOPE I DON'T GO OUT LIKE THAT.
PREFER TO SHOOT MYSELF.

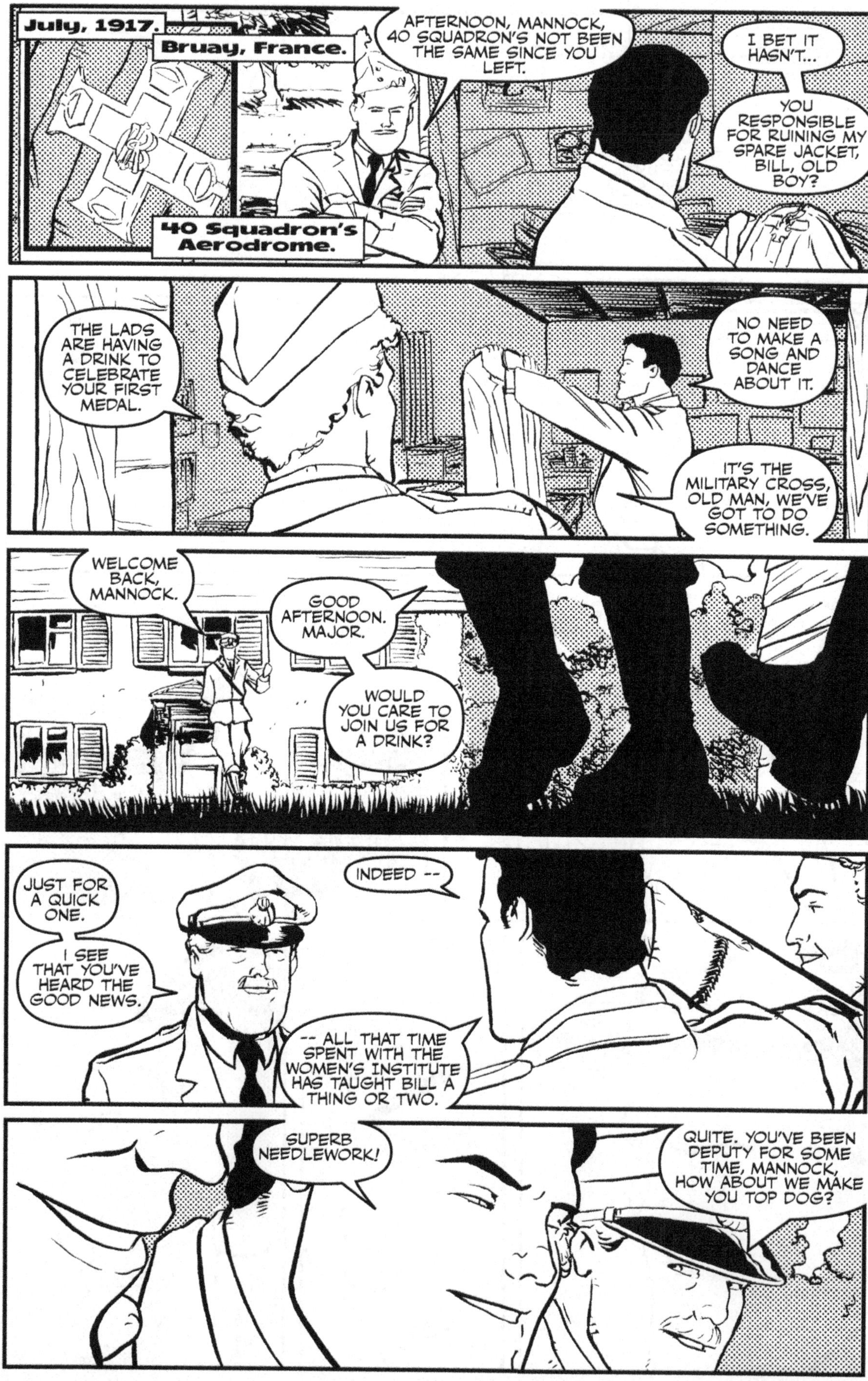
July, 1917.
Bruay, France.
40 Squadron's Aerodrome.
AFTERNOON, MANNOCK, 40 SQUADRON'S NOT BEEN THE SAME SINCE YOU LEFT.
I BET IT HASN'T...
YOU RESPONSIBLE FOR RUINING MY SPARE JACKET, BILL, OLD BOY?
THE LADS ARE HAVING A DRINK TO CELEBRATE YOUR FIRST MEDAL.
NO NEED TO MAKE A SONG AND DANCE ABOUT IT.
IT'S THE MILITARY CROSS, OLD MAN, WE'VE GOT TO DO SOMETHING.
WELCOME BACK, MANNOCK.
GOOD AFTERNOON. MAJOR.
WOULD YOU CARE TO JOIN US FOR A DRINK?
JUST FOR A QUICK ONE.
I SEE THAT YOU'VE HEARD THE GOOD NEWS.
INDEED --
-- ALL THAT TIME SPENT WITH THE WOMEN'S INSTITUTE HAS TAUGHT BILL A THING OR TWO.
SUPERB NEEDLEWORK!
QUITE. YOU'VE BEEN DEPUTY FOR SOME TIME, MANNOCK, HOW ABOUT WE MAKE YOU TOP DOG?

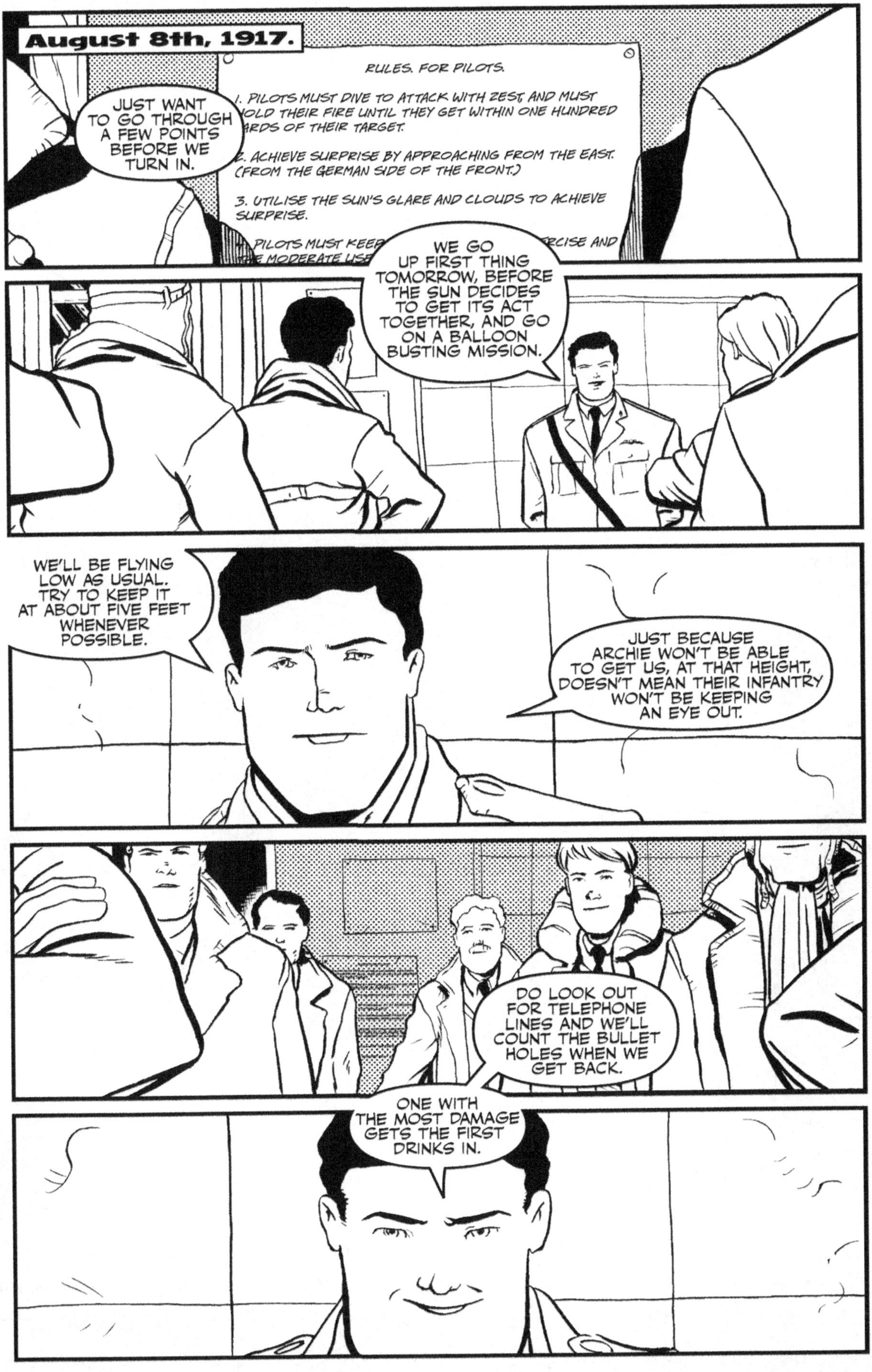
August 8th, 1917.
RULES. FOR PILOTS.
1. PILOTS MUST DIVE TO ATTACK WITH ZEST, AND MUST HOLD THEIR FIRE UNTIL THEY GET WITHIN ONE HUNDRED YARDS OF THEIR TARGET.
2. ACHIEVE SURPRISE BY APPROACHING FROM THE EAST. (FROM THE GERMAN SIDE OF THE FRONT.)
3. UTILISE THE SUN'S GLARE AND CLOUDS TO ACHIEVE SURPRISE.
JUST WANT TO GO THROUGH A FEW POINTS BEFORE WE TURN IN.
WE GO UP FIRST THING TOMORROW, BEFORE THE SUN DECIDES TO GET ITS ACT TOGETHER, AND GO ON A BALLOON BUSTING MISSION.
WE'LL BE FLYING LOW AS USUAL. TRY TO KEEP IT AT ABOUT FIVE FEET WHENEVER POSSIBLE.
JUST BECAUSE ARCHIE WON'T BE ABLE TO GET US, AT THAT HEIGHT, DOESN'T MEAN THEIR INFANTRY WON'T BE KEEPING AN EYE OUT.
DO LOOK OUT FOR TELEPHONE LINES AND WE'LL COUNT THE BULLET HOLES WHEN WE GET BACK.
ONE WITH THE MOST DAMAGE GETS THE FIRST DRINKS IN.

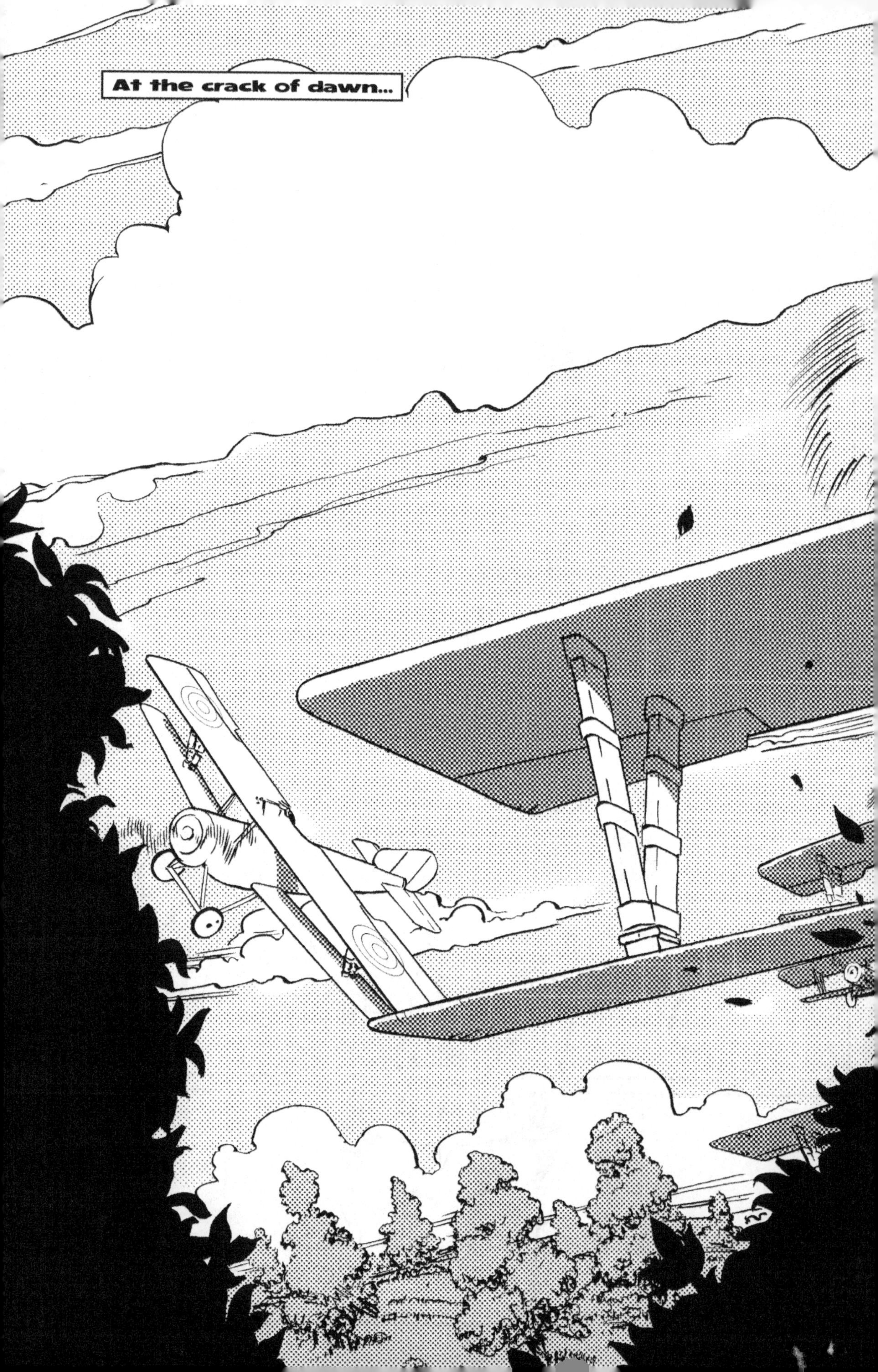
At the crack of dawn...

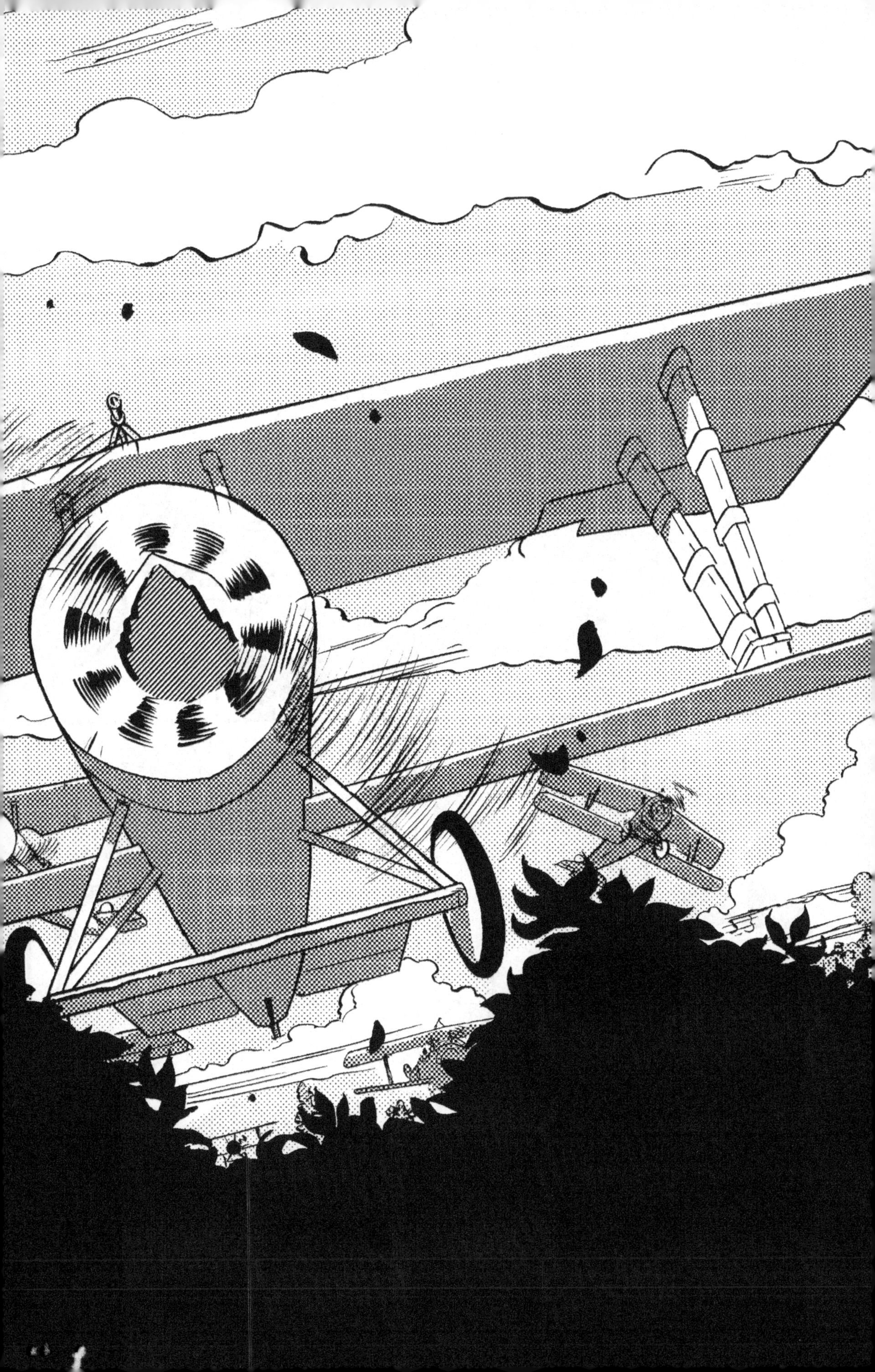

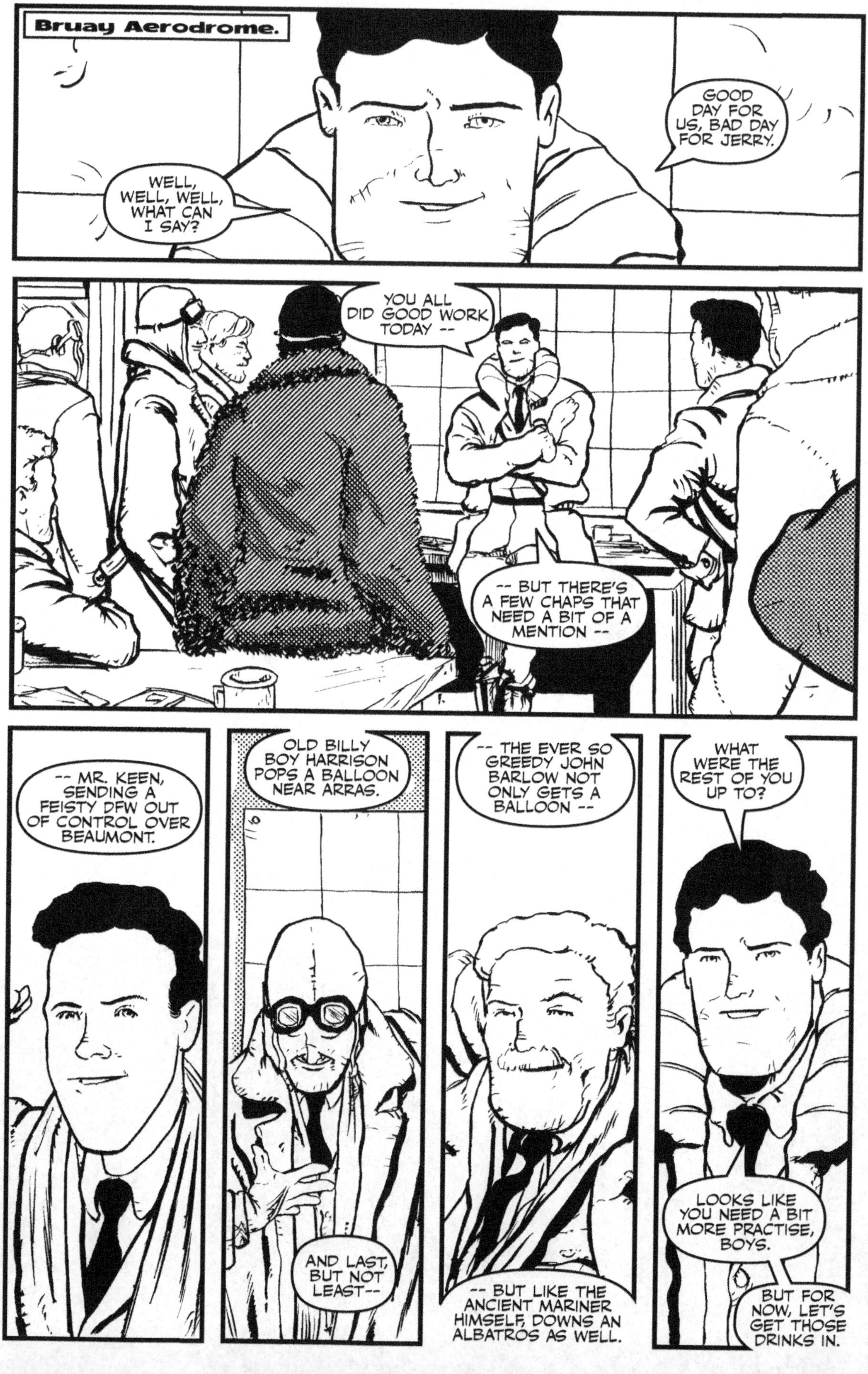
Bruay Aerodrome.
WELL, WELL, WELL, WHAT CAN I SAY?
GOOD DAY FOR US, BAD DAY FOR JERRY.
YOU ALL DID GOOD WORK TODAY --
-- BUT THERE'S A FEW CHAPS THAT NEED A BIT OF A MENTION --
-- MR. KEEN, SENDING A FEISTY DFW OUT OF CONTROL OVER BEAUMONT.
OLD BILLY BOY HARRISON POPS A BALLOON NEAR ARRAS.
AND LAST, BUT NOT LEAST--
-- THE EVER SO GREEDY JOHN BARLOW NOT ONLY GETS A BALLOON --
-- BUT LIKE THE ANCIENT MARINER HIMSELF, DOWNS AN ALBATROS AS WELL.
WHAT WERE THE REST OF YOU UP TO?
LOOKS LIKE YOU NEED A BIT MORE PRACTISE, BOYS.
BUT FOR NOW, LET'S GET THOSE DRINKS IN.

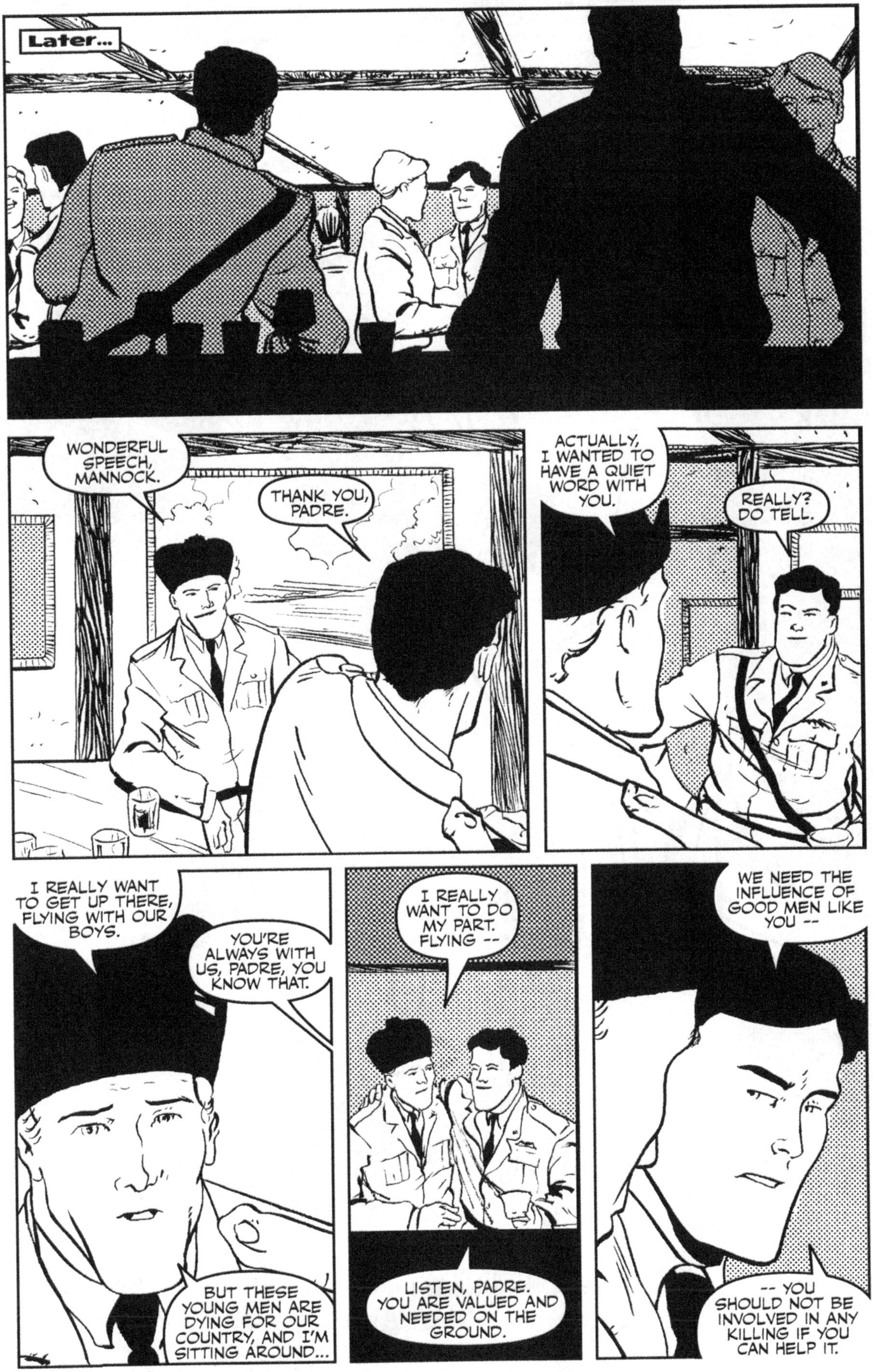
Later...
WONDERFUL SPEECH, MANNOCK.
THANK YOU, PADRE.
ACTUALLY, I WANTED TO HAVE A QUIET WORD WITH YOU.
REALLY? DO TELL.
I REALLY WANT TO GET UP THERE, FLYING WITH OUR BOYS.
YOU'RE ALWAYS WITH US, PADRE, YOU KNOW THAT.
BUT THESE YOUNG MEN ARE DYING FOR OUR COUNTRY, AND I'M SITTING AROUND...
I REALLY WANT TO DO MY PART. FLYING --
LISTEN, PADRE. YOU ARE VALUED AND NEEDED ON THE GROUND.
WE NEED THE INFLUENCE OF GOOD MEN LIKE YOU --
-- YOU SHOULD NOT BE INVOLVED IN ANY KILLING IF YOU CAN HELP IT.

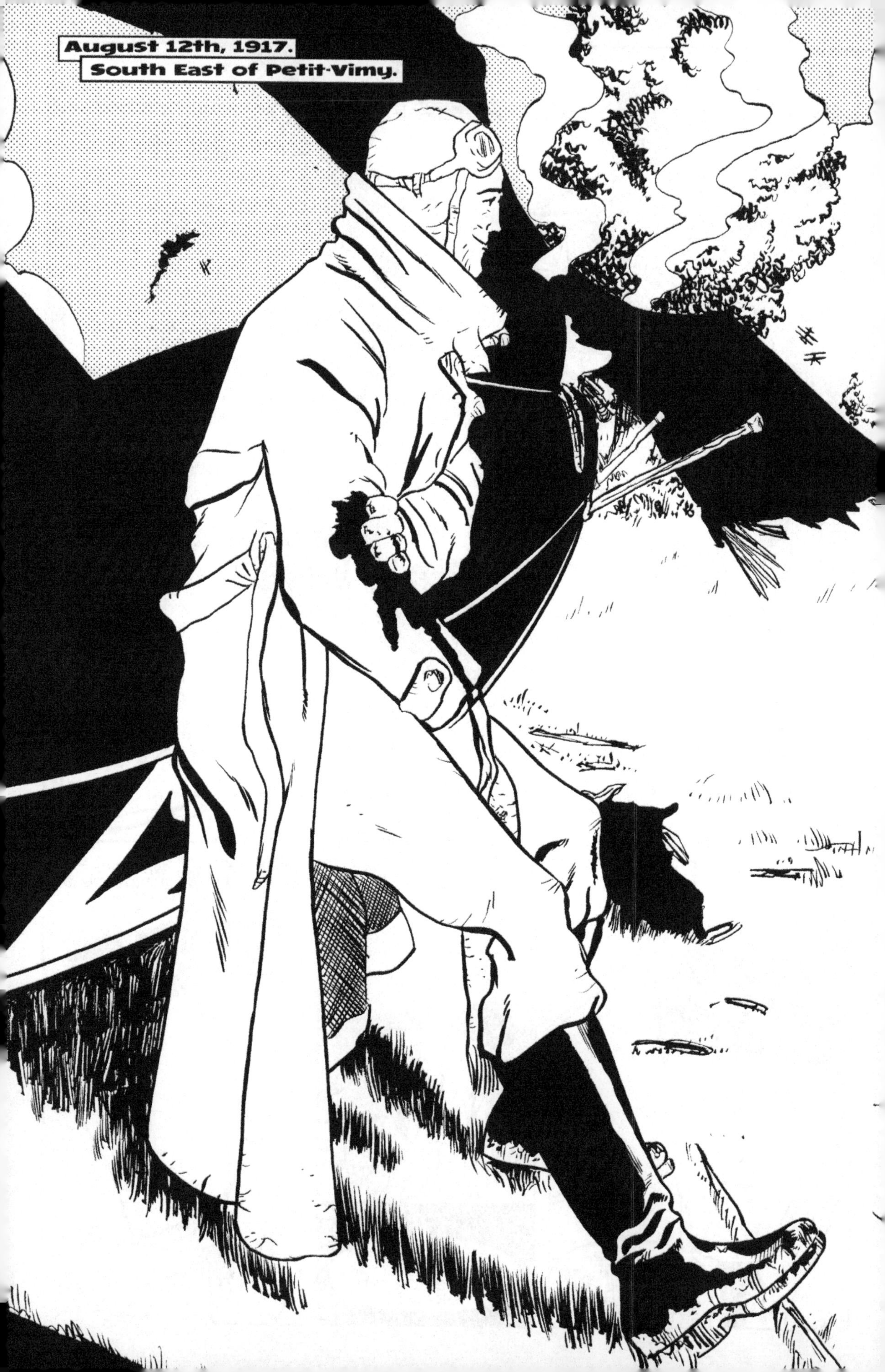
August 12th, 1917.
South East of Petit-Vimy.

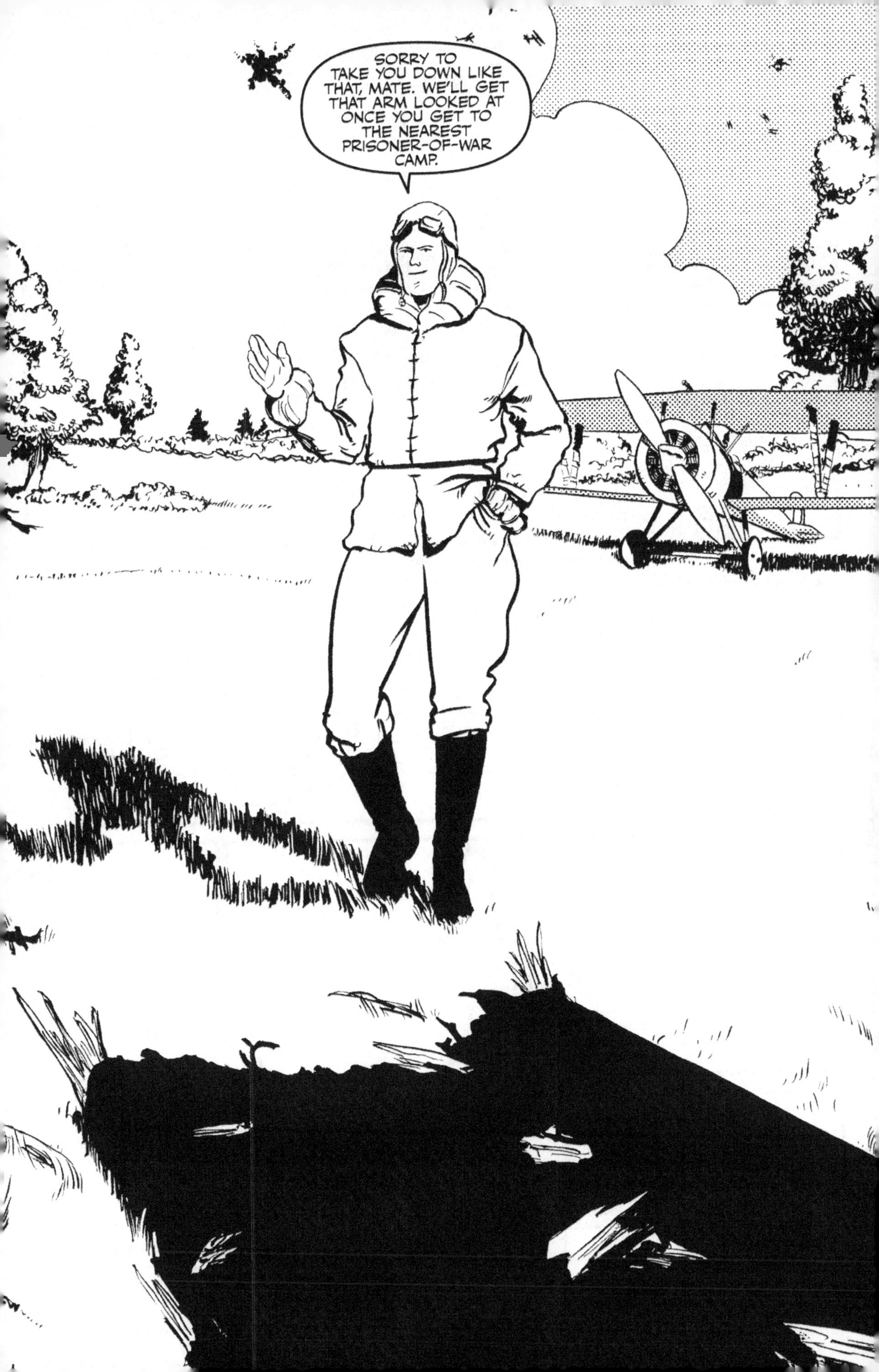
SORRY TO TAKE YOU DOWN LIKE THAT, MATE. WE'LL GET THAT ARM LOOKED AT ONCE YOU GET TO THE NEAREST PRISONER-OF-WAR CAMP.

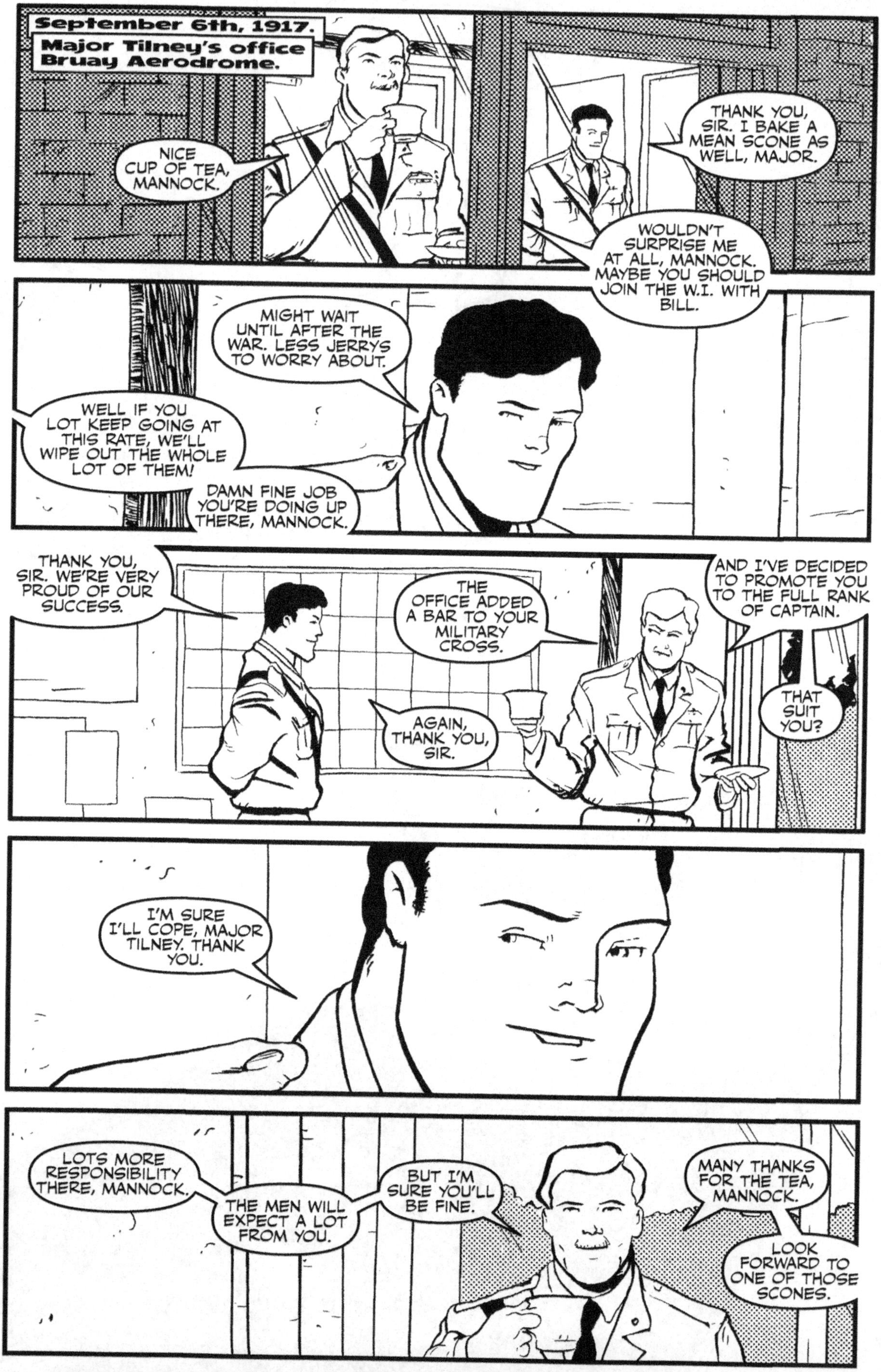
September 6th, 1917.
Major Tilney's office
Bruay Aerodrome.
NICE CUP OF TEA, MANNOCK.
THANK YOU, SIR. I BAKE A MEAN SCONE AS WELL, MAJOR.
WOULDN'T SURPRISE ME AT ALL, MANNOCK. MAYBE YOU SHOULD JOIN THE W.I. WITH BILL.
MIGHT WAIT UNTIL AFTER THE WAR. LESS JERRYS TO WORRY ABOUT.
WELL IF YOU LOT KEEP GOING AT THIS RATE, WE'LL WIPE OUT THE WHOLE LOT OF THEM!
DAMN FINE JOB YOU'RE DOING UP THERE, MANNOCK.
THANK YOU, SIR. WE'RE VERY PROUD OF OUR SUCCESS.
THE OFFICE ADDED A BAR TO YOUR MILITARY CROSS.
AND I'VE DECIDED TO PROMOTE YOU TO THE FULL RANK OF CAPTAIN.
AGAIN, THANK YOU, SIR.
THAT SUIT YOU?
I'M SURE I'LL COPE, MAJOR TILNEY. THANK YOU.
LOTS MORE RESPONSIBILITY THERE, MANNOCK.
THE MEN WILL EXPECT A LOT FROM YOU.
BUT I'M SURE YOU'LL BE FINE.
MANY THANKS FOR THE TEA, MANNOCK.
LOOK FORWARD TO ONE OF THOSE SCONES.

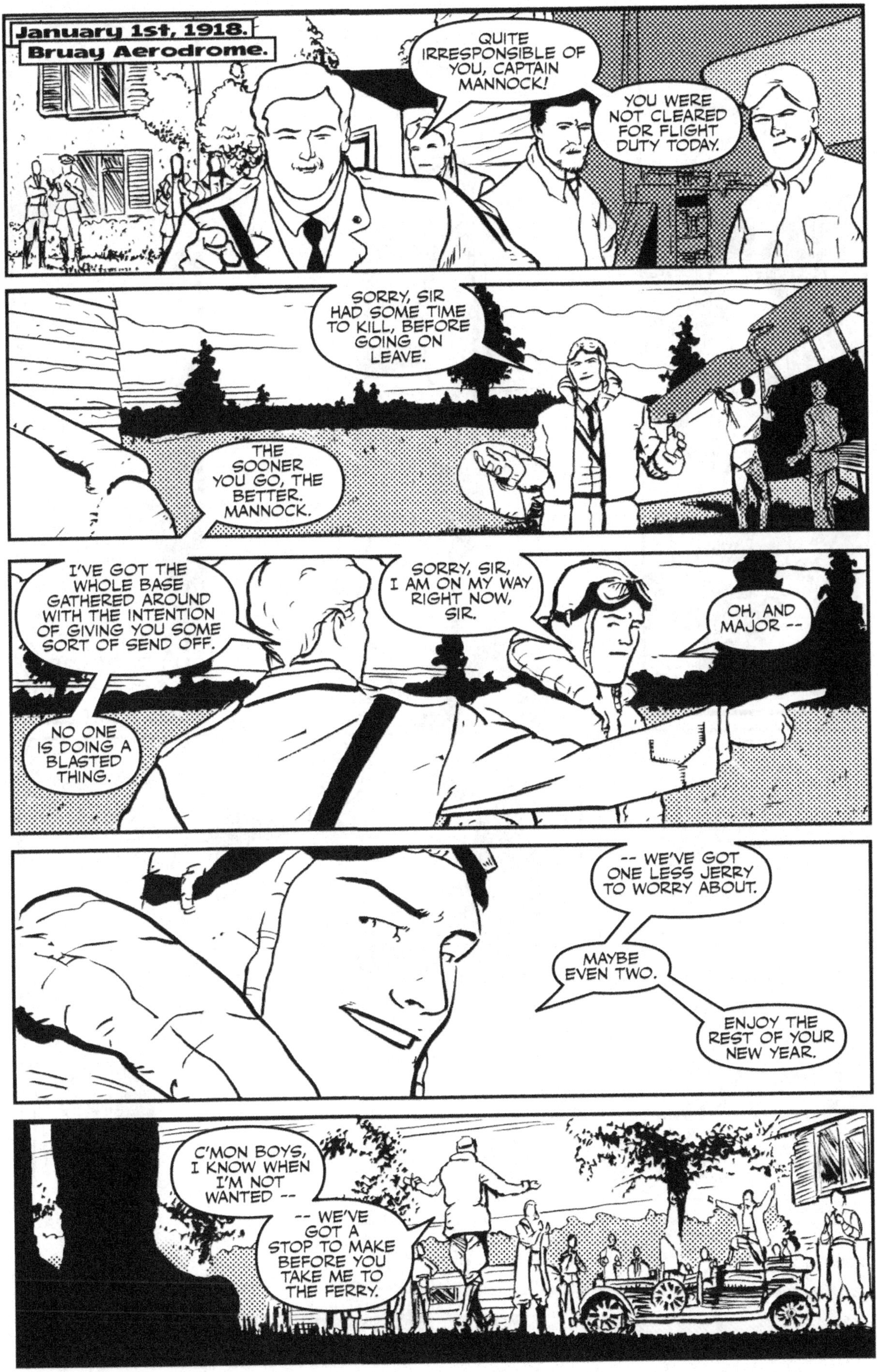
January 1st, 1918.
Bruay Aerodrome.
QUITE IRRESPONSIBLE OF YOU, CAPTAIN MANNOCK!
YOU WERE NOT CLEARED FOR FLIGHT DUTY TODAY.
SORRY, SIR HAD SOME TIME TO KILL, BEFORE GOING ON LEAVE.
THE SOONER YOU GO, THE BETTER. MANNOCK.
I'VE GOT THE WHOLE BASE GATHERED AROUND WITH THE INTENTION OF GIVING YOU SOME SORT OF SEND OFF.
NO ONE IS DOING A BLASTED THING.
SORRY, SIR, I AM ON MY WAY RIGHT NOW, SIR.
OH, AND MAJOR --
-- WE'VE GOT ONE LESS JERRY TO WORRY ABOUT.
MAYBE EVEN TWO.
ENJOY THE REST OF YOUR NEW YEAR.
C'MON BOYS, I KNOW WHEN I'M NOT WANTED --
-- WE'VE GOT A STOP TO MAKE BEFORE YOU TAKE ME TO THE FERRY.

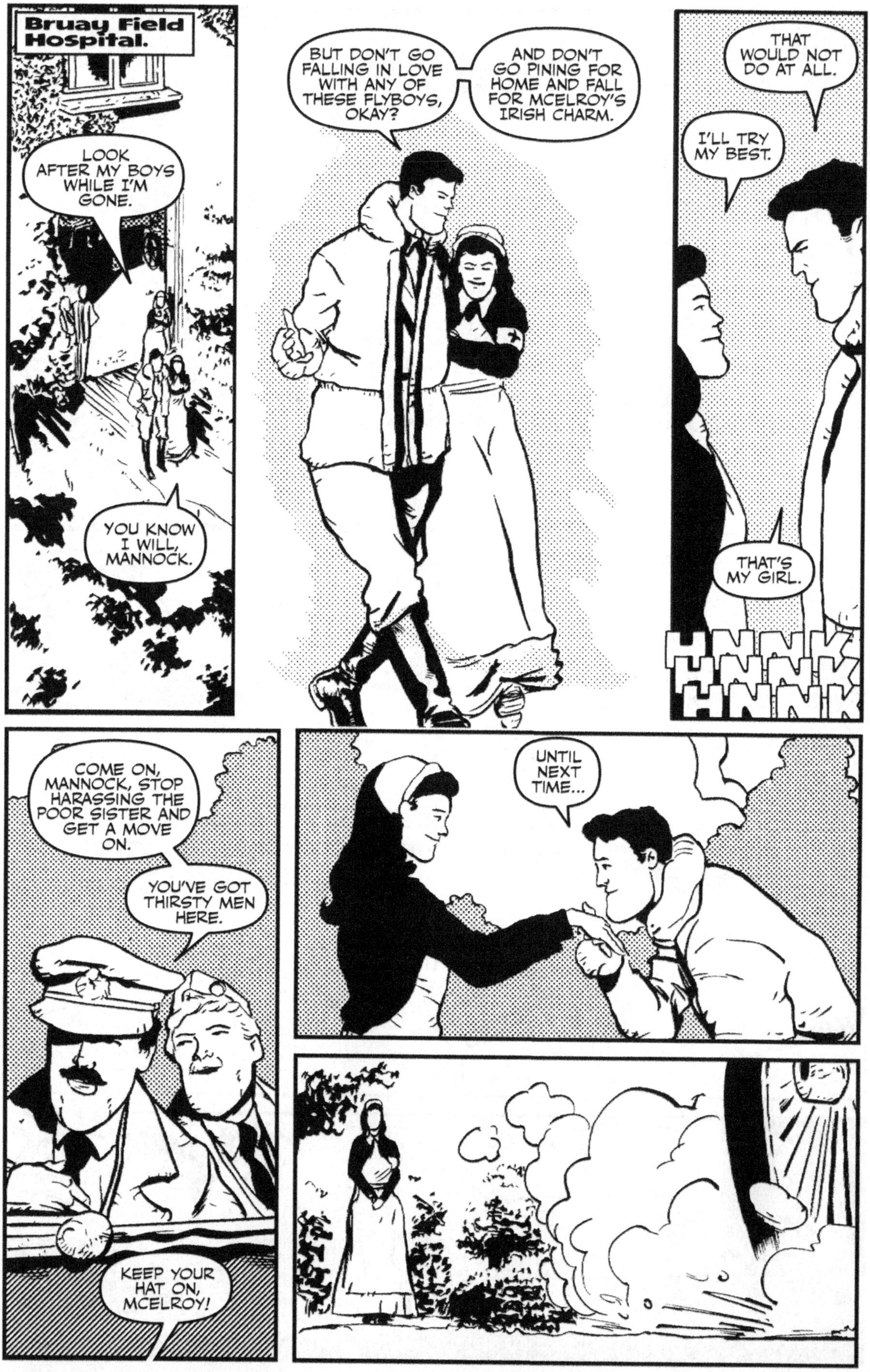
Bruay Field Hospital.
LOOK AFTER MY BOYS WHILE I'M GONE.
YOU KNOW I WILL, MANNOCK.
BUT DON'T GO FALLING IN LOVE WITH ANY OF THESE FLYBOYS, OKAY?
AND DON'T GO PINING FOR HOME AND FALL FOR MCELROY'S IRISH CHARM.
THAT WOULD NOT DO AT ALL.
I'LL TRY MY BEST.
THAT'S MY GIRL.
HNNK HNNK HNNK
COME ON, MANNOCK, STOP HARASSING THE POOR SISTER AND GET A MOVE ON.
YOU'VE GOT THIRSTY MEN HERE.
KEEP YOUR HAT ON, MCELROY!
UNTIL NEXT TIME...

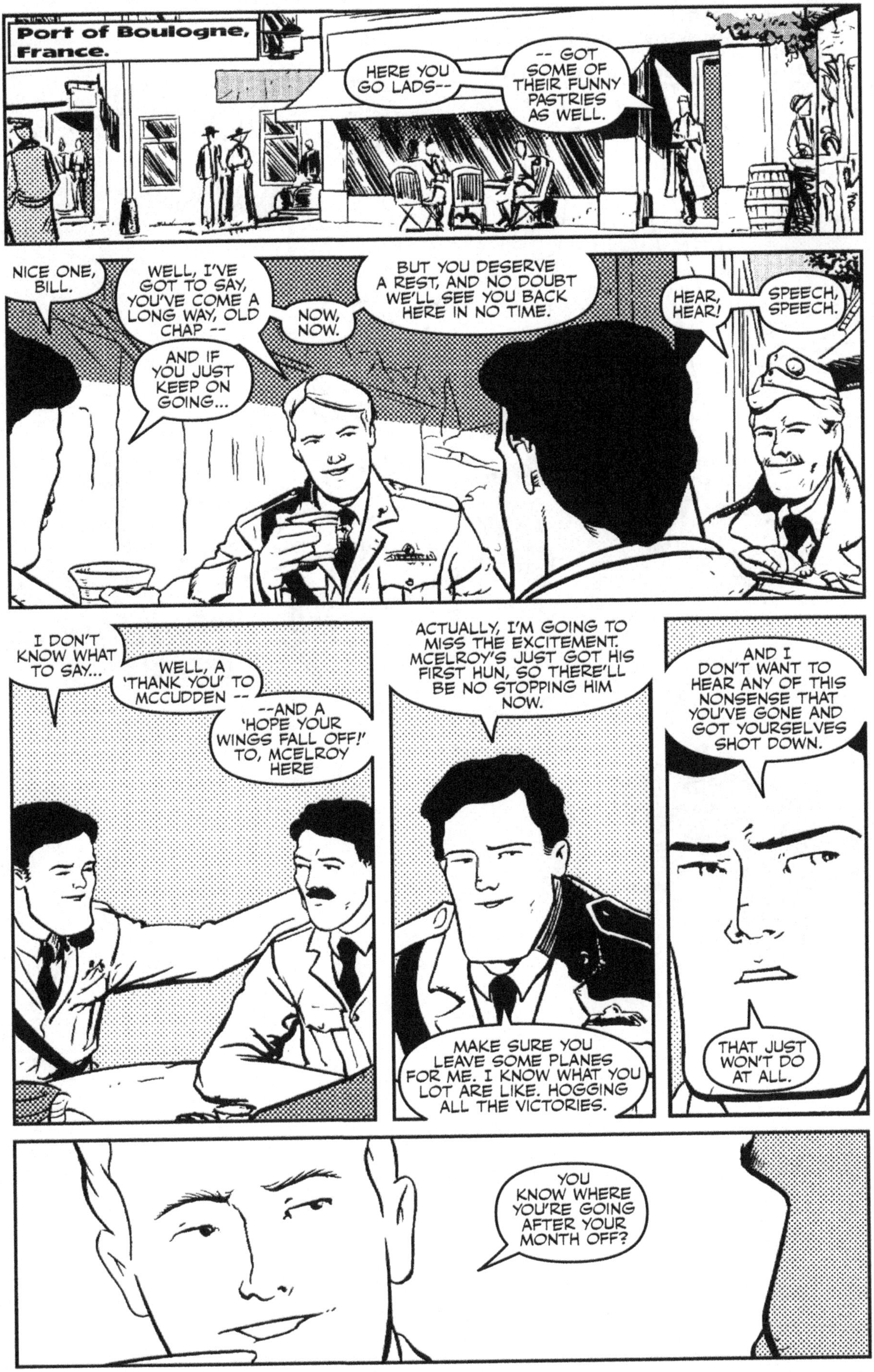
Port of Boulogne, France.
HERE YOU GO LADS--
-- GOT SOME OF THEIR FUNNY PASTRIES AS WELL.
NICE ONE, BILL.
WELL, I'VE GOT TO SAY, YOU'VE COME A LONG WAY, OLD CHAP --
AND IF YOU JUST KEEP ON GOING...
NOW, NOW.
BUT YOU DESERVE A REST, AND NO DOUBT WE'LL SEE YOU BACK HERE IN NO TIME.
HEAR, HEAR!
SPEECH, SPEECH.
I DON'T KNOW WHAT TO SAY...
WELL, A 'THANK YOU' TO MCCUDDEN --
--AND A 'HOPE YOUR WINGS FALL OFF!' TO, MCELROY HERE
ACTUALLY, I'M GOING TO MISS THE EXCITEMENT. MCELROY'S JUST GOT HIS FIRST HUN, SO THERE'LL BE NO STOPPING HIM NOW.
MAKE SURE YOU LEAVE SOME PLANES FOR ME. I KNOW WHAT YOU LOT ARE LIKE. HOGGING ALL THE VICTORIES.
AND I DON'T WANT TO HEAR ANY OF THIS NONSENSE THAT YOU'VE GONE AND GOT YOURSELVES SHOT DOWN.
THAT JUST WON'T DO AT ALL.
YOU KNOW WHERE YOU'RE GOING AFTER YOUR MONTH OFF?

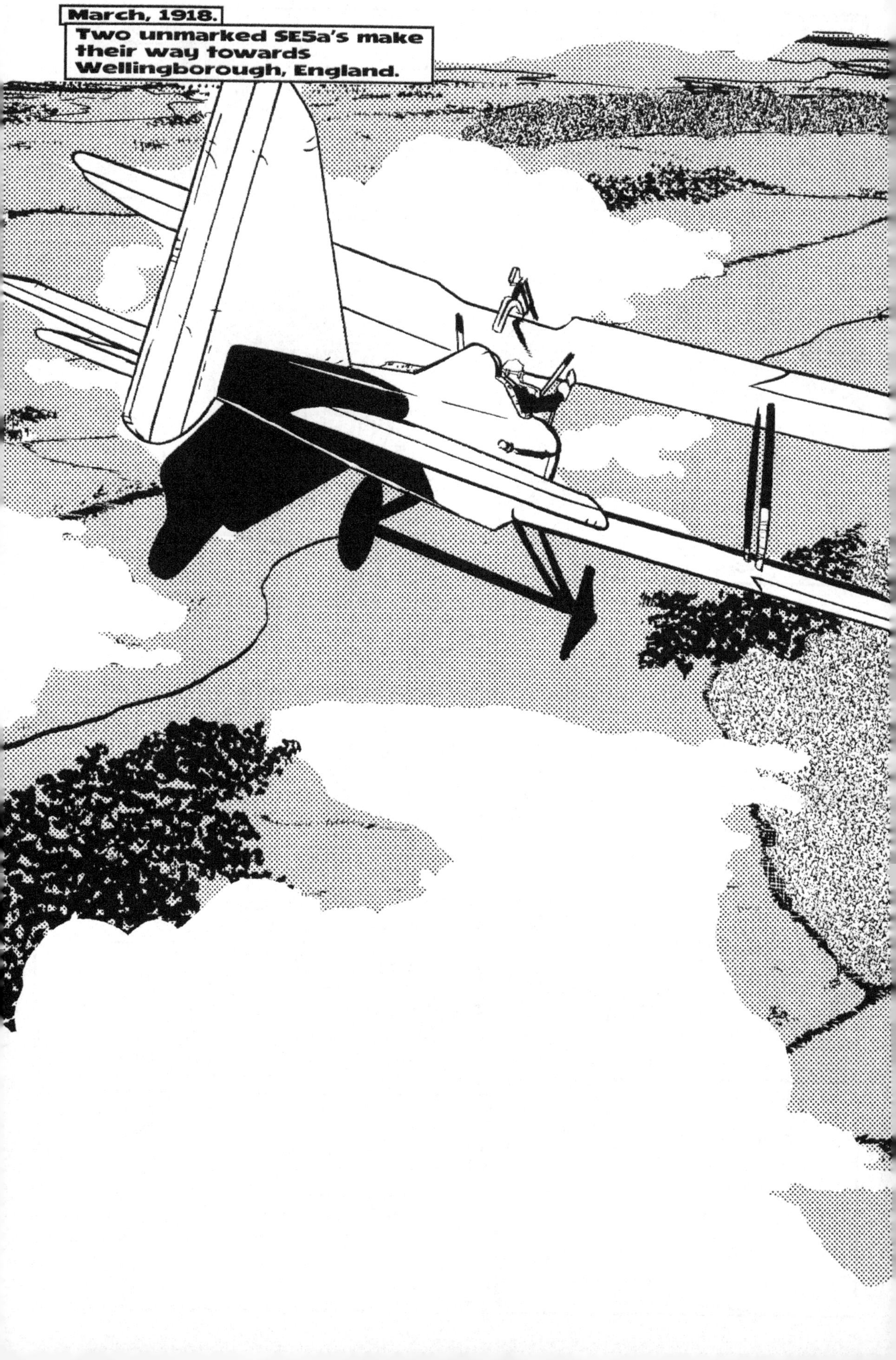
March, 1918.
Two unmarked SE5a's make their way towards Wellingborough, England.

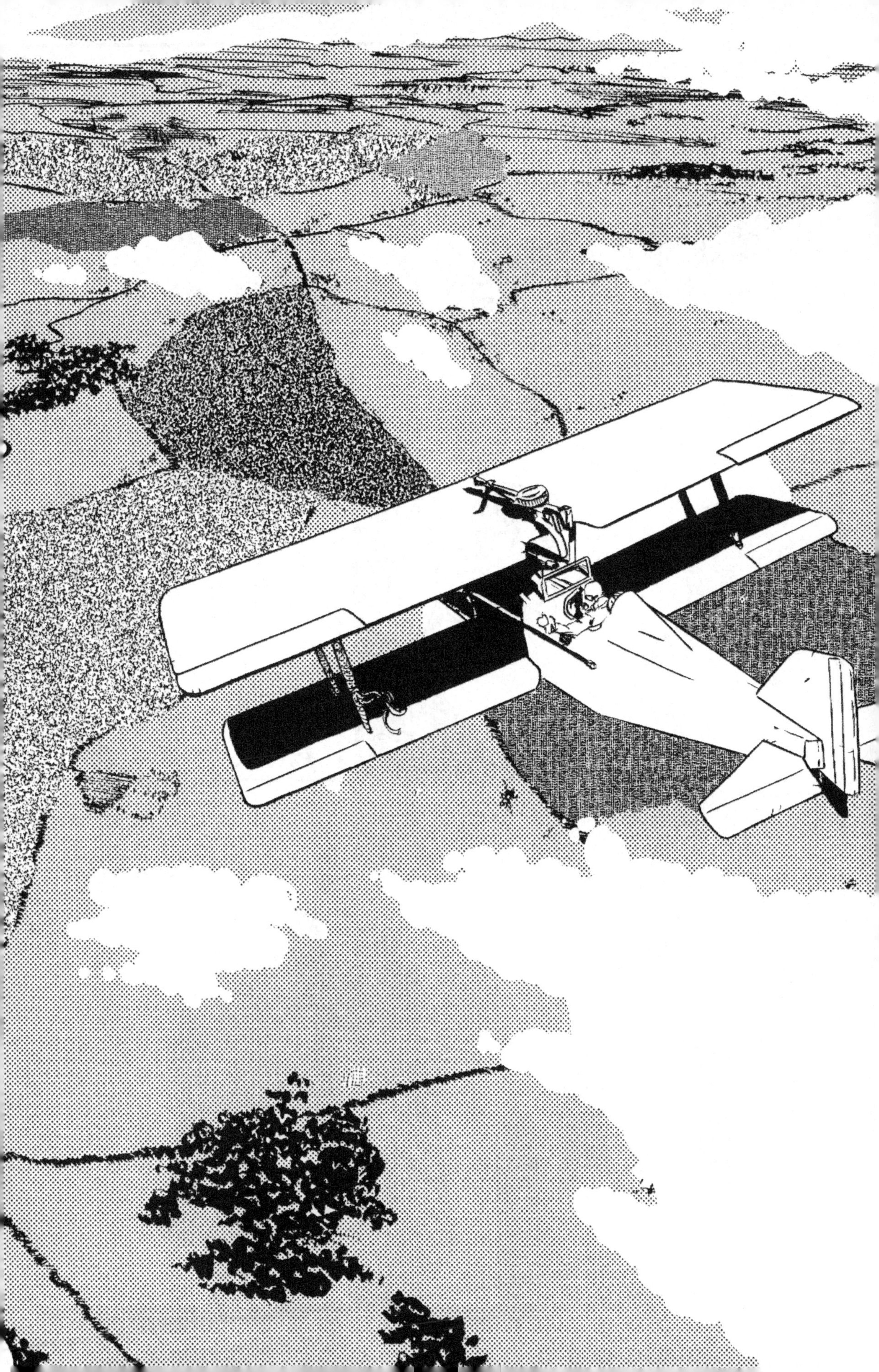

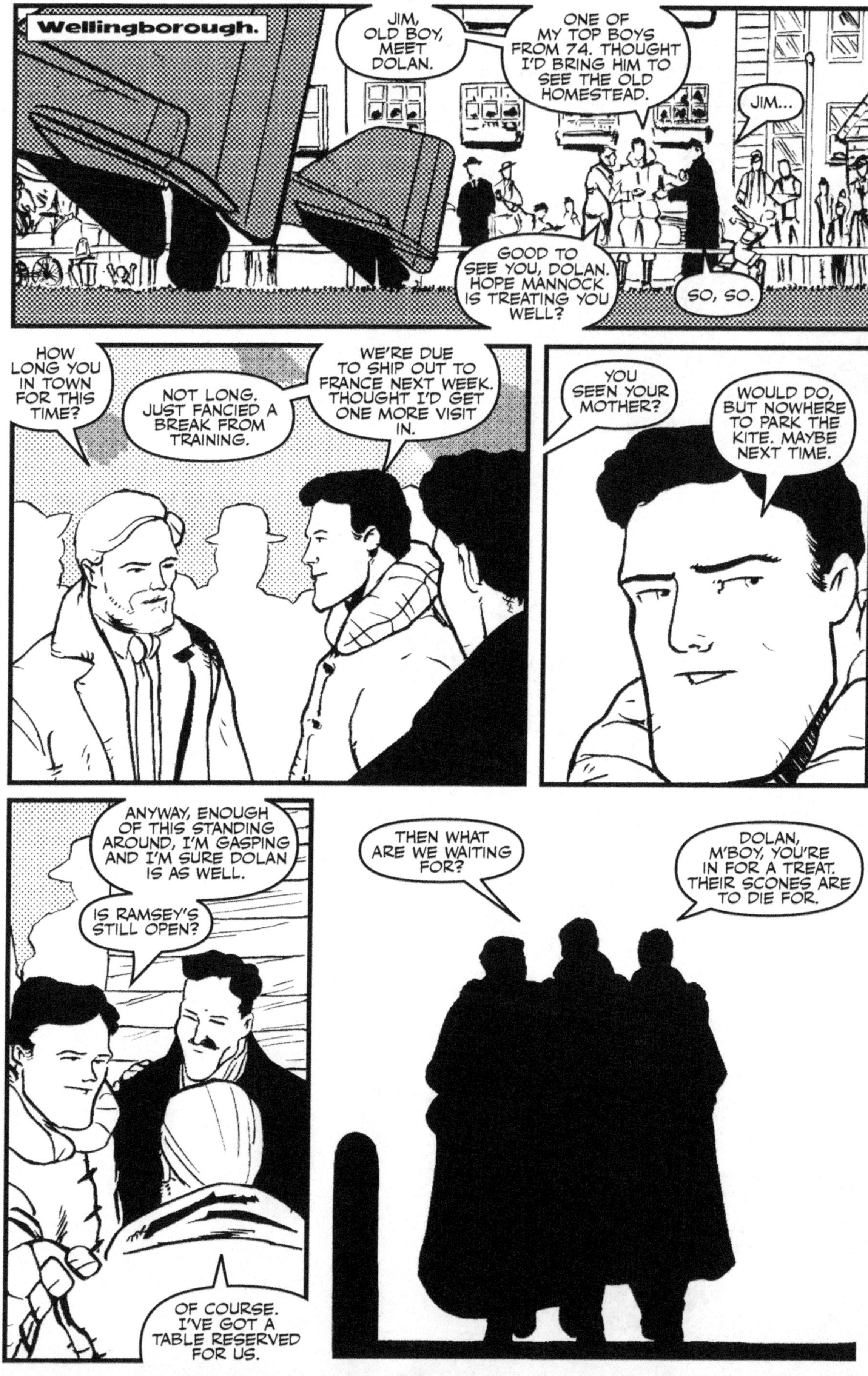
Wellingborough.
JIM, OLD BOY, MEET DOLAN.
ONE OF MY TOP BOYS FROM 74. THOUGHT I'D BRING HIM TO SEE THE OLD HOMESTEAD.
JIM...
GOOD TO SEE YOU, DOLAN. HOPE MANNOCK IS TREATING YOU WELL?
SO, SO.
HOW LONG YOU IN TOWN FOR THIS TIME?
NOT LONG. JUST FANCIED A BREAK FROM TRAINING.
WE'RE DUE TO SHIP OUT TO FRANCE NEXT WEEK. THOUGHT I'D GET ONE MORE VISIT IN.
YOU SEEN YOUR MOTHER?
WOULD DO, BUT NOWHERE TO PARK THE KITE. MAYBE NEXT TIME.
ANYWAY, ENOUGH OF THIS STANDING AROUND, I'M GASPING AND I'M SURE DOLAN IS AS WELL.
IS RAMSEY'S STILL OPEN?
OF COURSE. I'VE GOT A TABLE RESERVED FOR US.
THEN WHAT ARE WE WAITING FOR?
DOLAN, M'BOY, YOU'RE IN FOR A TREAT. THEIR SCONES ARE TO DIE FOR.

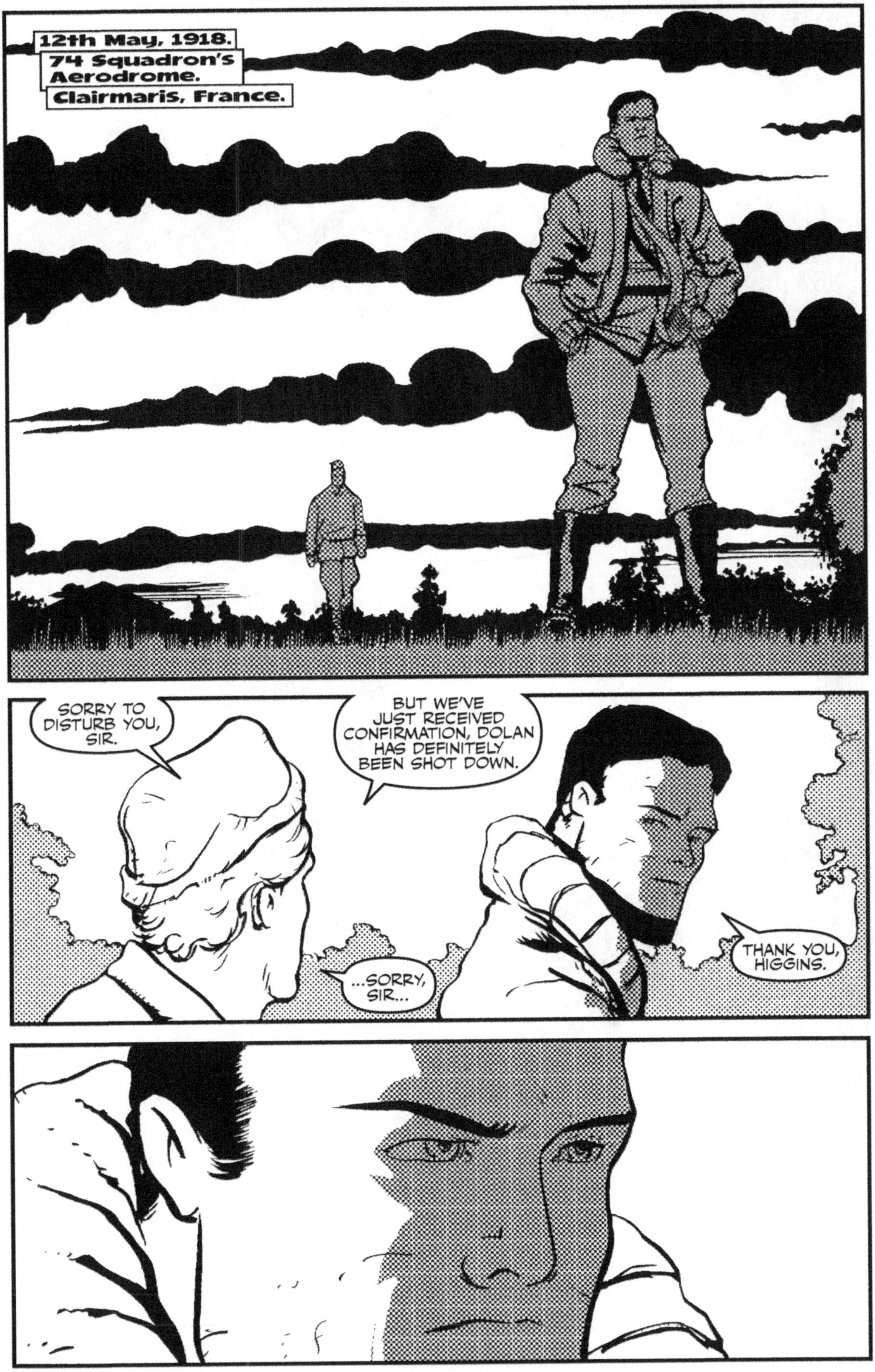
12th May, 1918.
74 Squadron's Aerodrome.
Clairmaris, France.
SORRY TO DISTURB YOU, SIR.
BUT WE'VE JUST RECEIVED CONFIRMATION, DOLAN HAS DEFINITELY BEEN SHOT DOWN.
...SORRY, SIR...
THANK YOU, HIGGINS.

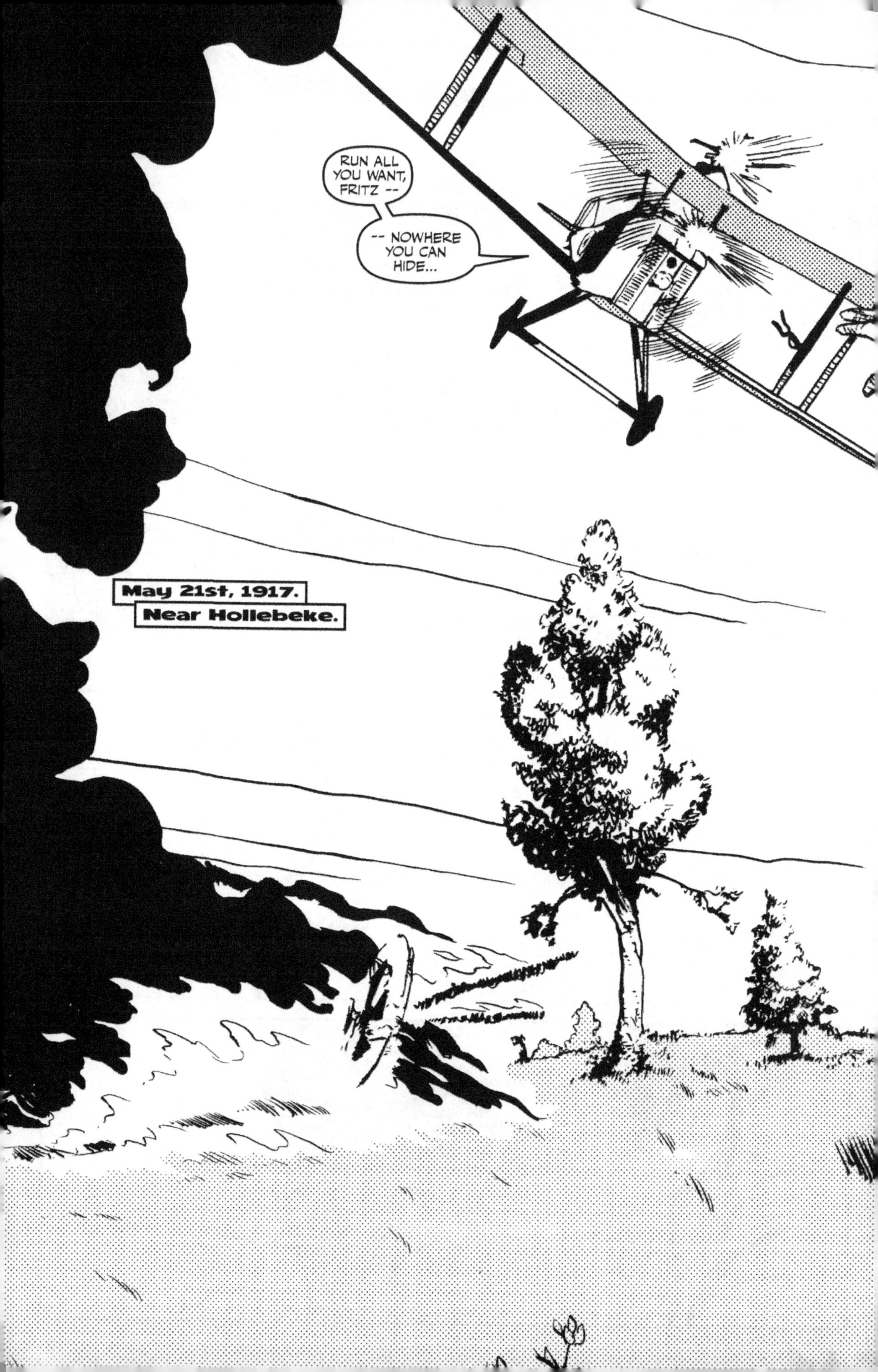
RUN ALL YOU WANT, FRITZ --
-- NOWHERE YOU CAN HIDE...
May 21st, 1917.
Near Hollebeke.

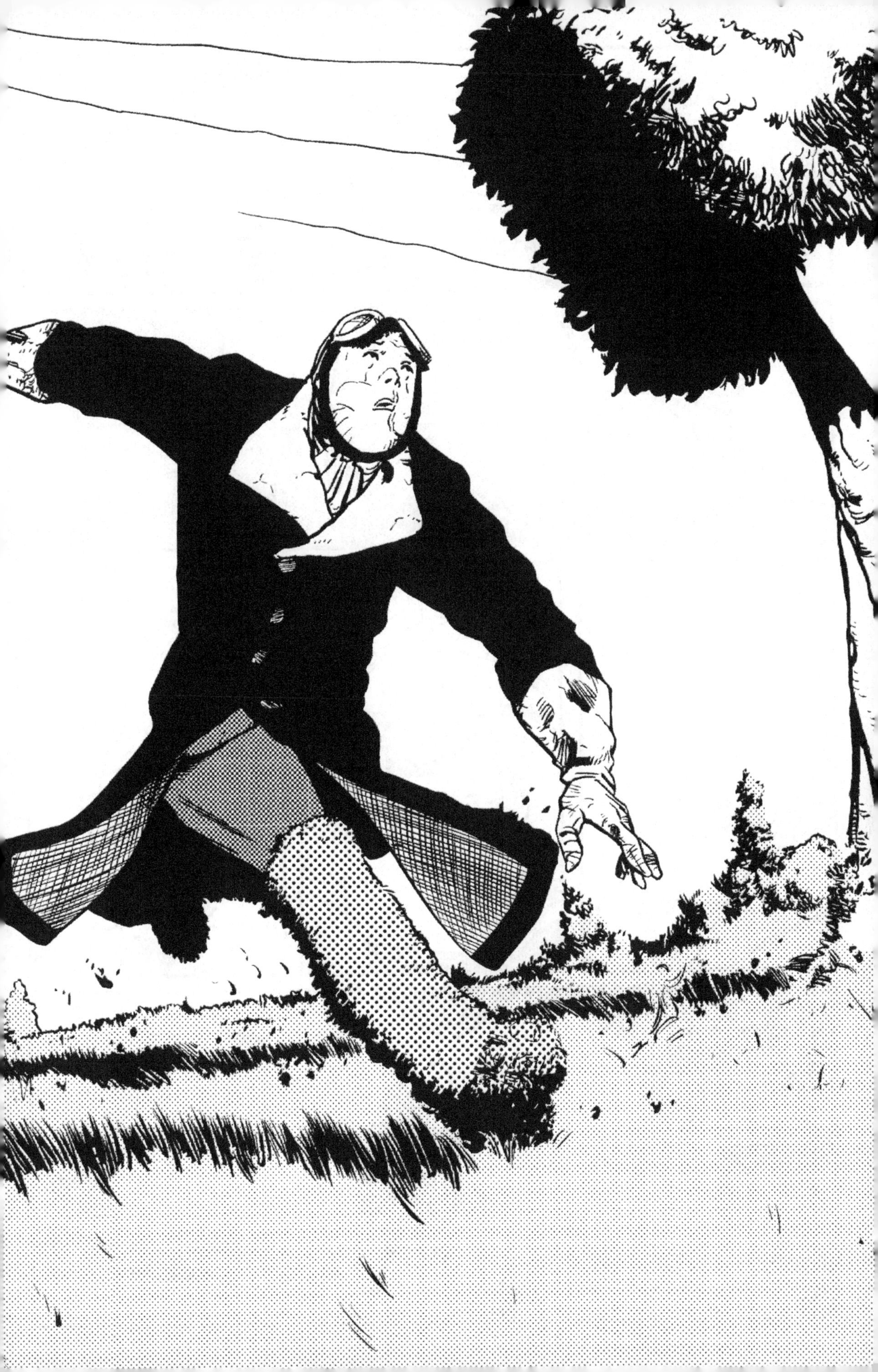

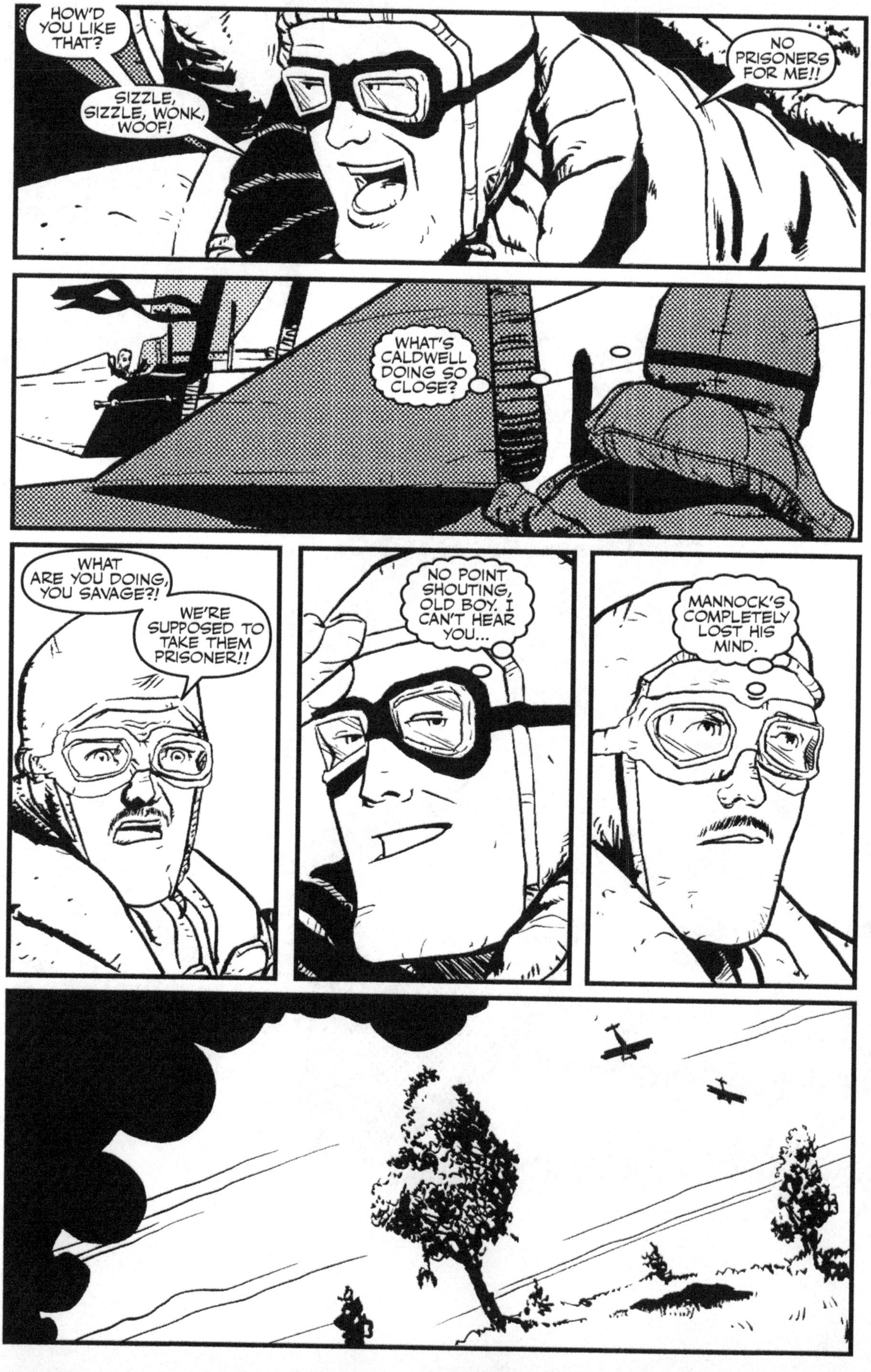
HOW'D YOU LIKE THAT?
SIZZLE, SIZZLE, WONK, WOOF!
NO PRISONERS FOR ME!!
WHAT'S CALDWELL DOING SO CLOSE?
WHAT ARE YOU DOING, YOU SAVAGE?!
WE'RE SUPPOSED TO TAKE THEM PRISONER!!
NO POINT SHOUTING, OLD BOY. I CAN'T HEAR YOU...
MANNOCK'S COMPLETELY LOST HIS MIND.

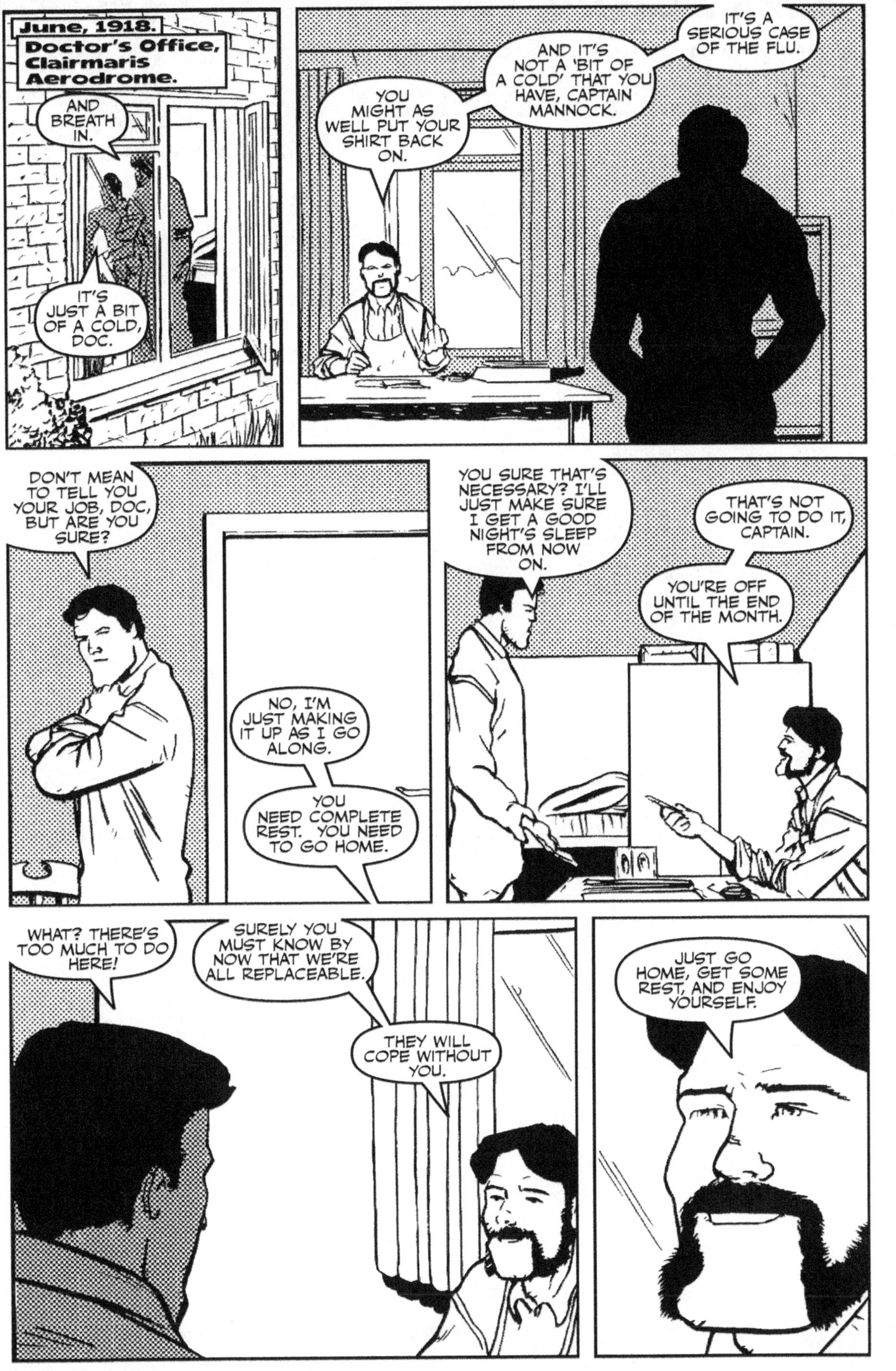
June, 1918.
Doctor's Office, Clairmaris Aerodrome.
AND BREATH IN.
IT'S JUST A BIT OF A COLD, DOC.
YOU MIGHT AS WELL PUT YOUR SHIRT BACK ON.
AND IT'S NOT A 'BIT OF A COLD' THAT YOU HAVE, CAPTAIN MANNOCK.
IT'S A SERIOUS CASE OF THE FLU.
DON'T MEAN TO TELL YOU YOUR JOB, DOC, BUT ARE YOU SURE?
NO, I'M JUST MAKING IT UP AS I GO ALONG.
YOU NEED COMPLETE REST. YOU NEED TO GO HOME.
YOU SURE THAT'S NECESSARY? I'LL JUST MAKE SURE I GET A GOOD NIGHT'S SLEEP FROM NOW ON.
THAT'S NOT GOING TO DO IT, CAPTAIN.
YOU'RE OFF UNTIL THE END OF THE MONTH.
WHAT? THERE'S TOO MUCH TO DO HERE!
SURELY YOU MUST KNOW BY NOW THAT WE'RE ALL REPLACEABLE.
THEY WILL COPE WITHOUT YOU.
JUST GO HOME, GET SOME REST, AND ENJOY YOURSELF.

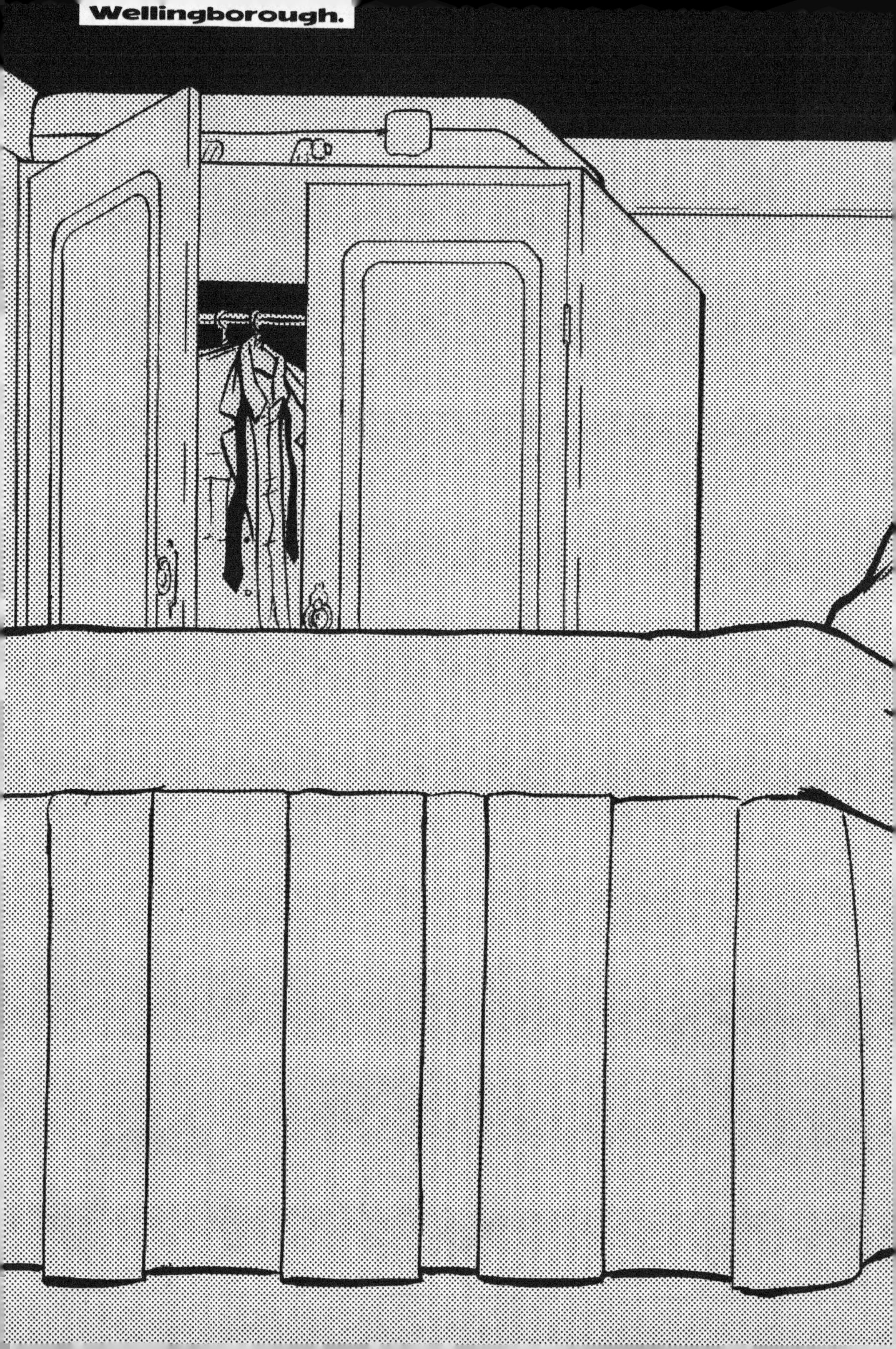
Wellingborough.

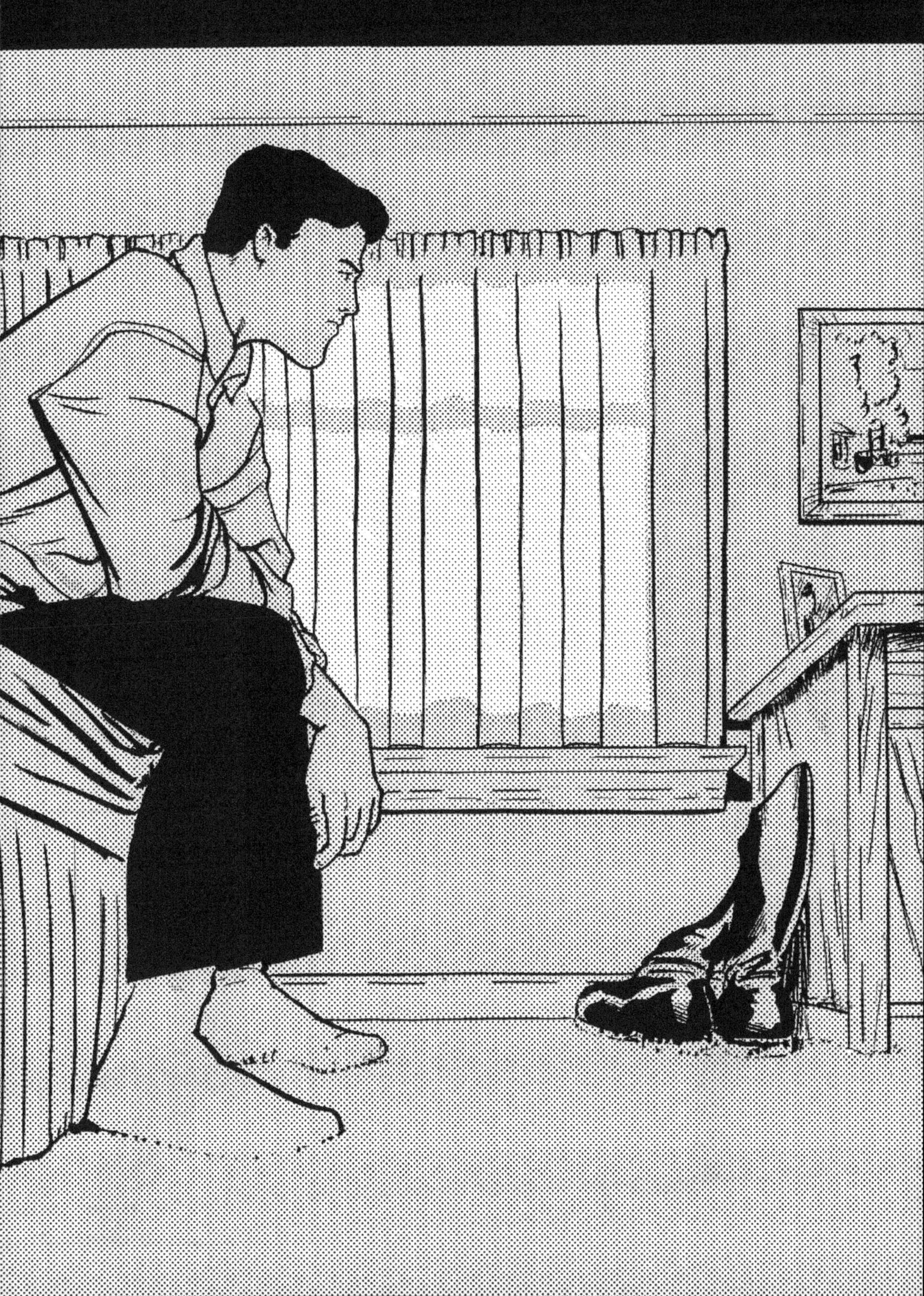

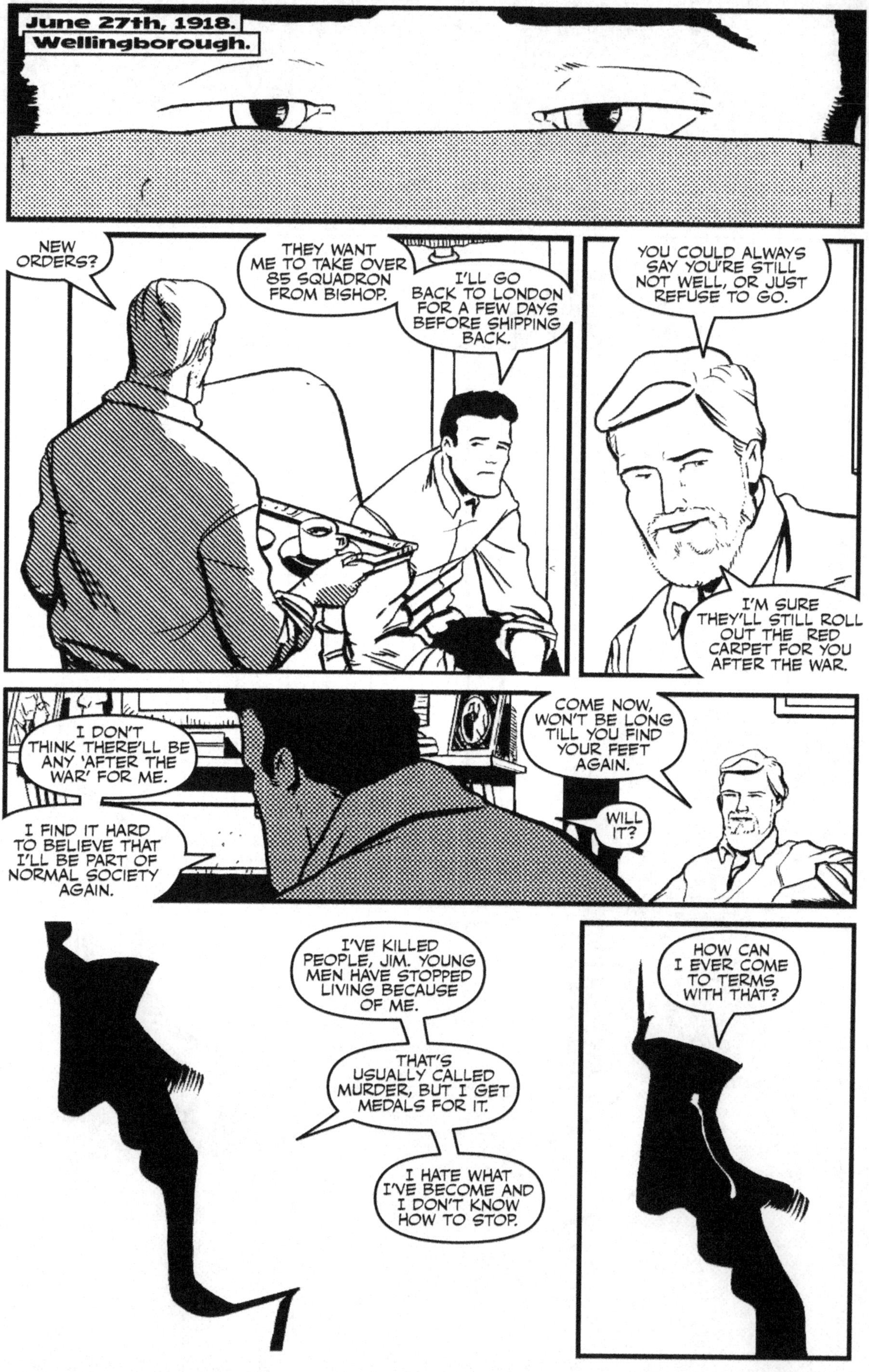
June 27th, 1918.
Wellingborough.
NEW ORDERS?
THEY WANT ME TO TAKE OVER 85 SQUADRON FROM BISHOP.
I'LL GO BACK TO LONDON FOR A FEW DAYS BEFORE SHIPPING BACK.
YOU COULD ALWAYS SAY YOU'RE STILL NOT WELL, OR JUST REFUSE TO GO.
I'M SURE THEY'LL STILL ROLL OUT THE RED CARPET FOR YOU AFTER THE WAR.
I DON'T THINK THERE'LL BE ANY 'AFTER THE WAR' FOR ME.
I FIND IT HARD TO BELIEVE THAT I'LL BE PART OF NORMAL SOCIETY AGAIN.
COME NOW, WON'T BE LONG TILL YOU FIND YOUR FEET AGAIN.
WILL IT?
I'VE KILLED PEOPLE, JIM. YOUNG MEN HAVE STOPPED LIVING BECAUSE OF ME.
THAT'S USUALLY CALLED MURDER, BUT I GET MEDALS FOR IT.
I HATE WHAT I'VE BECOME AND I DON'T KNOW HOW TO STOP.
HOW CAN I EVER COME TO TERMS WITH THAT?

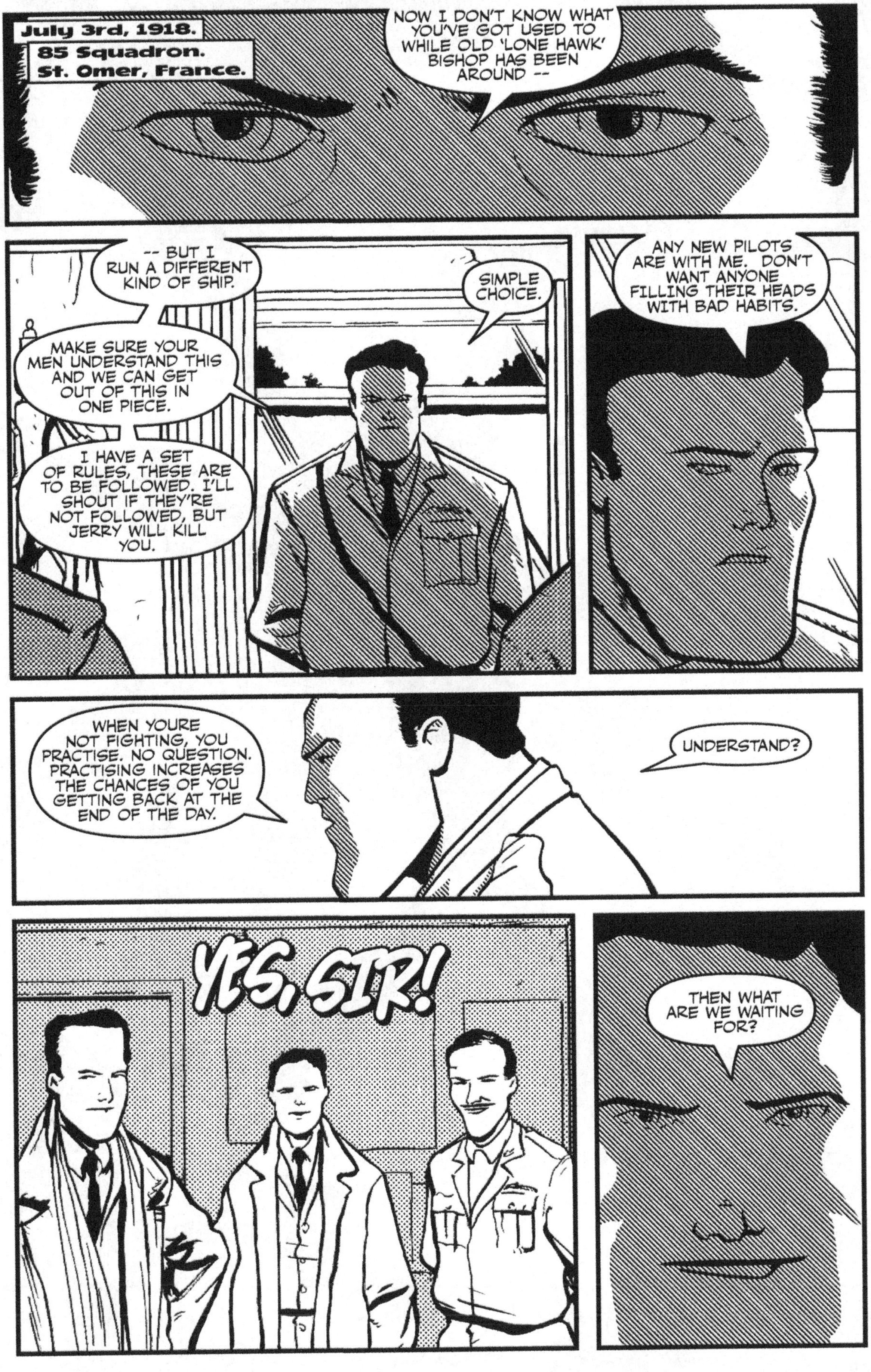
July 3rd, 1918.
85 Squadron.
St. Omer, France.
NOW I DON'T KNOW WHAT YOU'VE GOT USED TO WHILE OLD 'LONE HAWK' BISHOP HAS BEEN AROUND --
-- BUT I RUN A DIFFERENT KIND OF SHIP.
MAKE SURE YOUR MEN UNDERSTAND THIS AND WE CAN GET OUT OF THIS IN ONE PIECE.
I HAVE A SET OF RULES, THESE ARE TO BE FOLLOWED. I'LL SHOUT IF THEY'RE NOT FOLLOWED, BUT JERRY WILL KILL YOU.
SIMPLE CHOICE.
ANY NEW PILOTS ARE WITH ME. DON'T WANT ANYONE FILLING THEIR HEADS WITH BAD HABITS.
WHEN YOURE NOT FIGHTING, YOU PRACTISE. NO QUESTION. PRACTISING INCREASES THE CHANCES OF YOU GETTING BACK AT THE END OF THE DAY.
UNDERSTAND?
YES, SIR!
THEN WHAT ARE WE WAITING FOR?

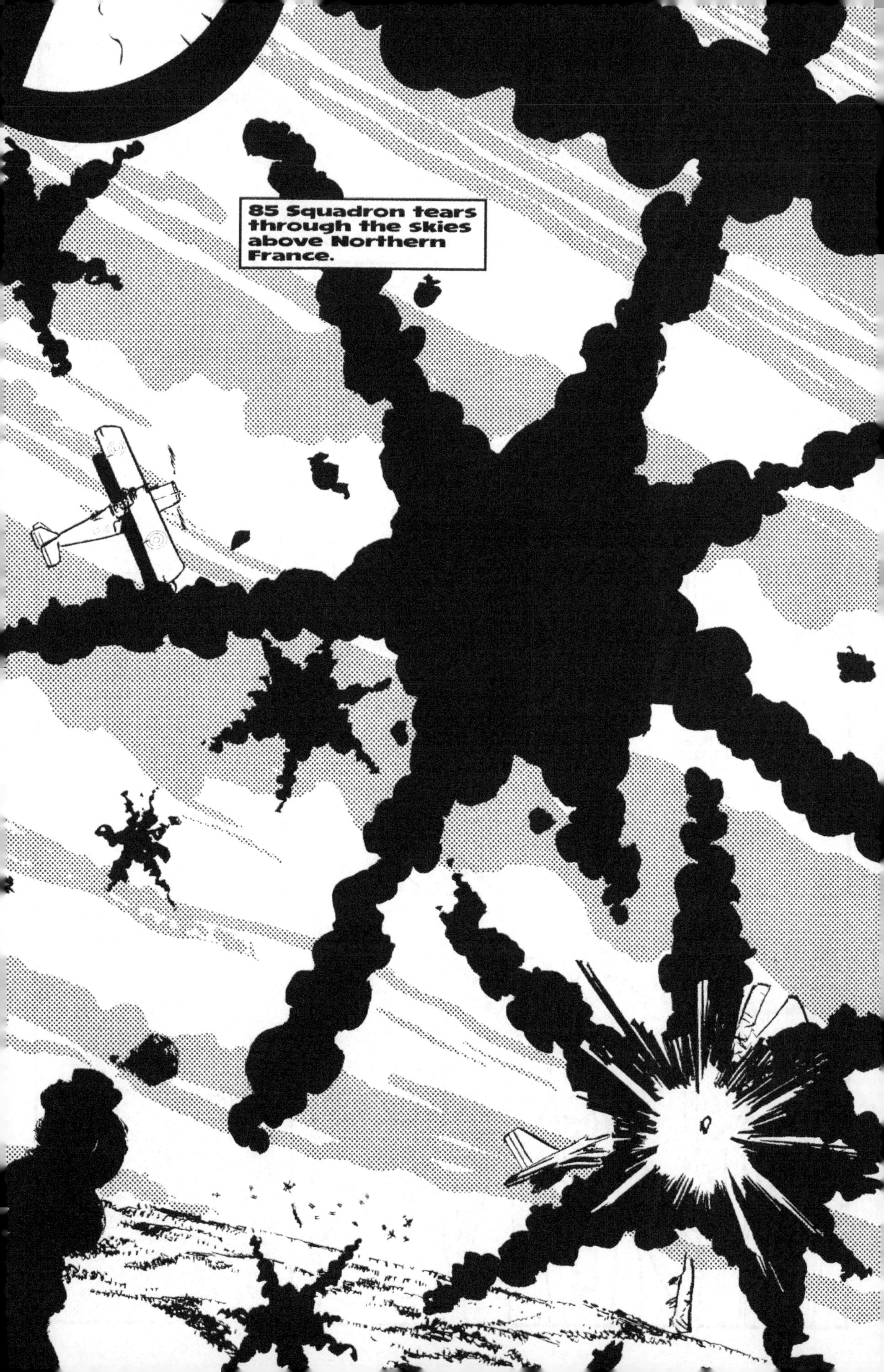
85 Squadron tears through the skies above Northern France.

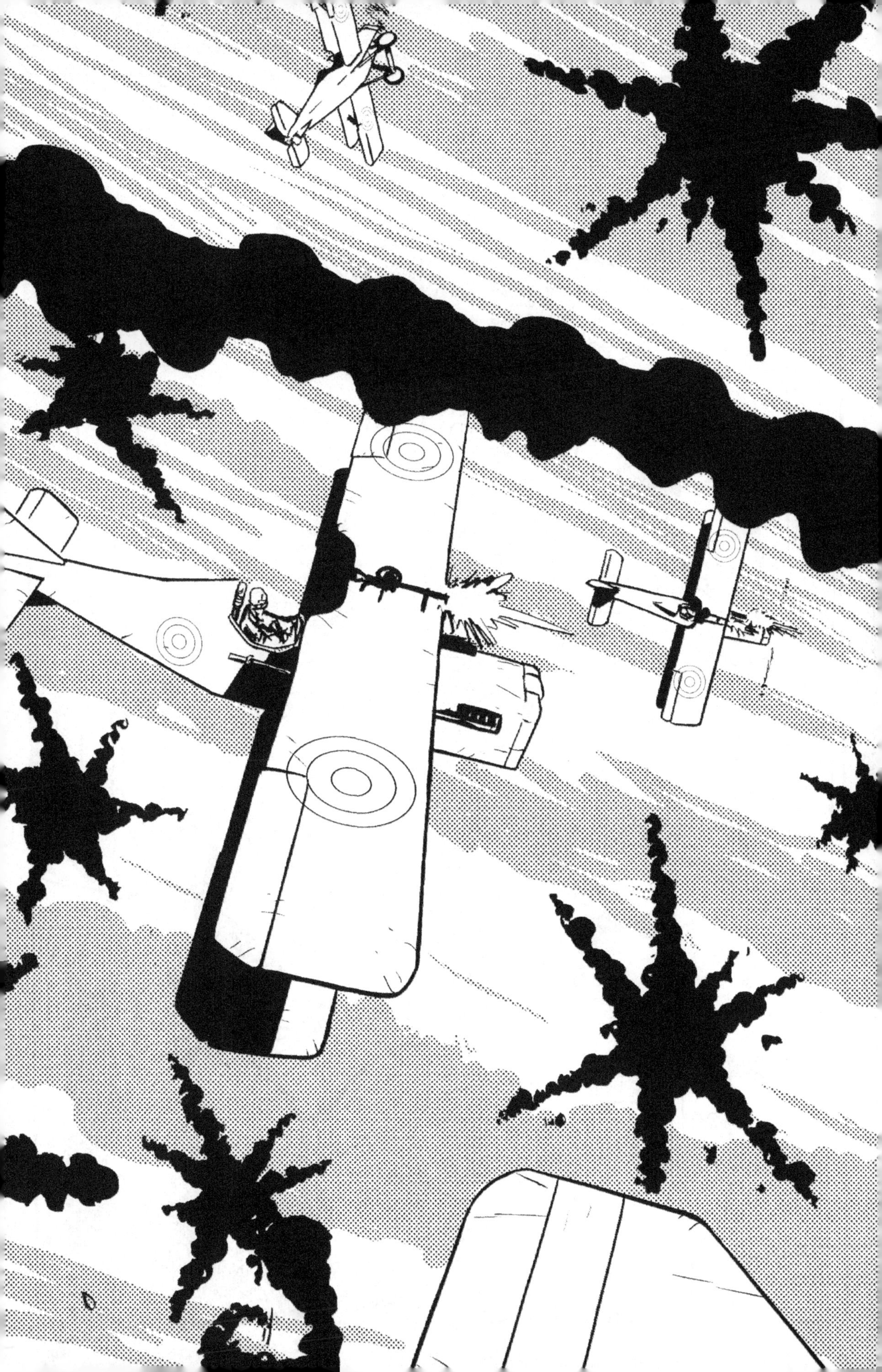

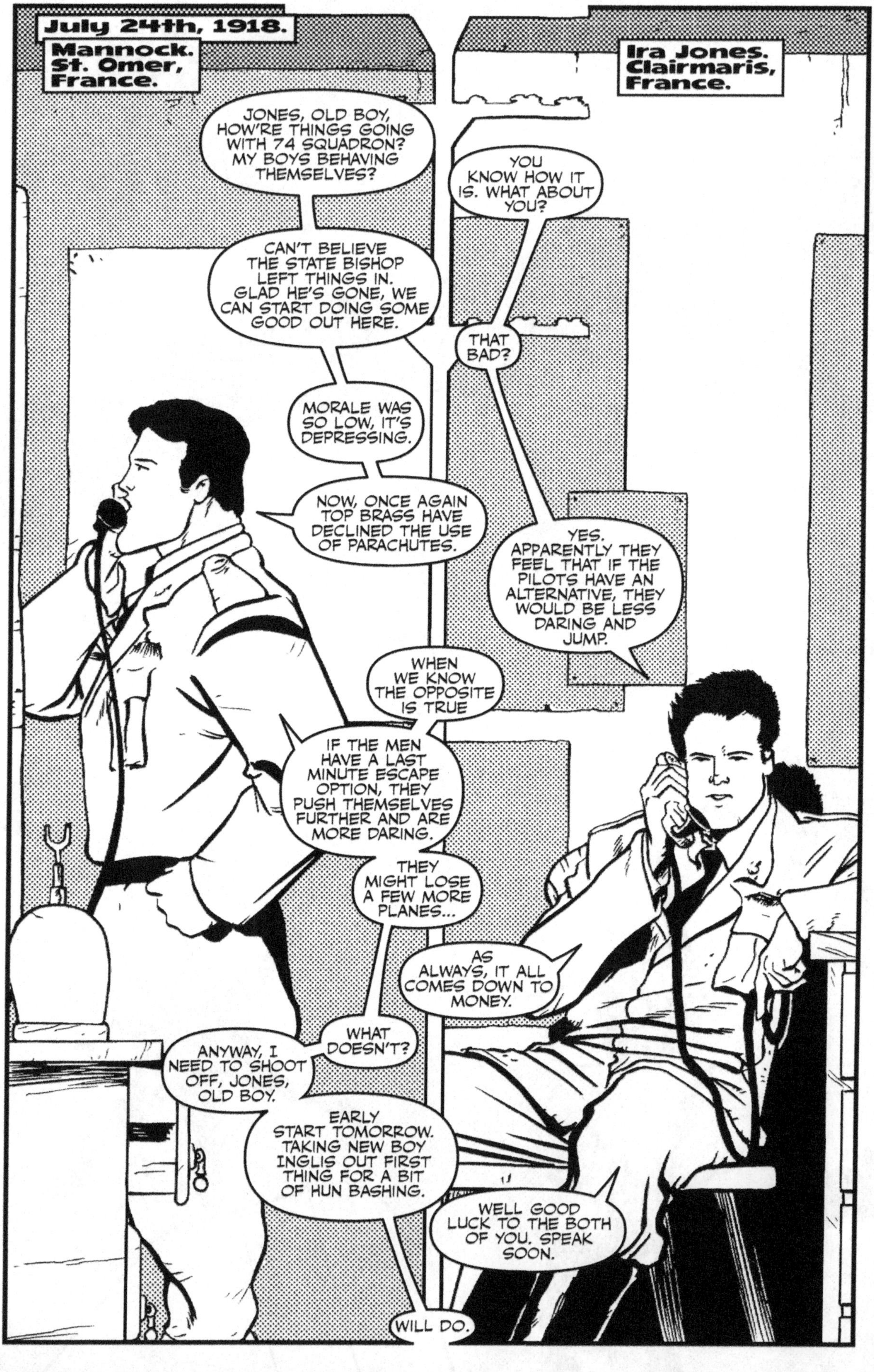

July 24th, 1918.
Mannock. St. Omer, France.
Ira Jones. Clairmaris, France.
JONES, OLD BOY, HOW'RE THINGS GOING WITH 74 SQUADRON? MY BOYS BEHAVING THEMSELVES?
YOU KNOW HOW IT IS. WHAT ABOUT YOU?
CAN'T BELIEVE THE STATE BISHOP LEFT THINGS IN. GLAD HE'S GONE, WE CAN START DOING SOME GOOD OUT HERE.
THAT BAD?
MORALE WAS SO LOW, IT'S DEPRESSING.
NOW, ONCE AGAIN TOP BRASS HAVE DECLINED THE USE OF PARACHUTES.
YES. APPARENTLY THEY FEEL THAT IF THE PILOTS HAVE AN ALTERNATIVE, THEY WOULD BE LESS DARING AND JUMP.
WHEN WE KNOW THE OPPOSITE IS TRUE
IF THE MEN HAVE A LAST MINUTE ESCAPE OPTION, THEY PUSH THEMSELVES FURTHER AND ARE MORE DARING.
THEY MIGHT LOSE A FEW MORE PLANES...
AS ALWAYS, IT ALL COMES DOWN TO MONEY.
WHAT DOESN'T?
ANYWAY, I NEED TO SHOOT OFF, JONES, OLD BOY.
EARLY START TOMORROW. TAKING NEW BOY INGLIS OUT FIRST THING FOR A BIT OF HUN BASHING.
WELL GOOD LUCK TO THE BOTH OF YOU. SPEAK SOON.
WILL DO.

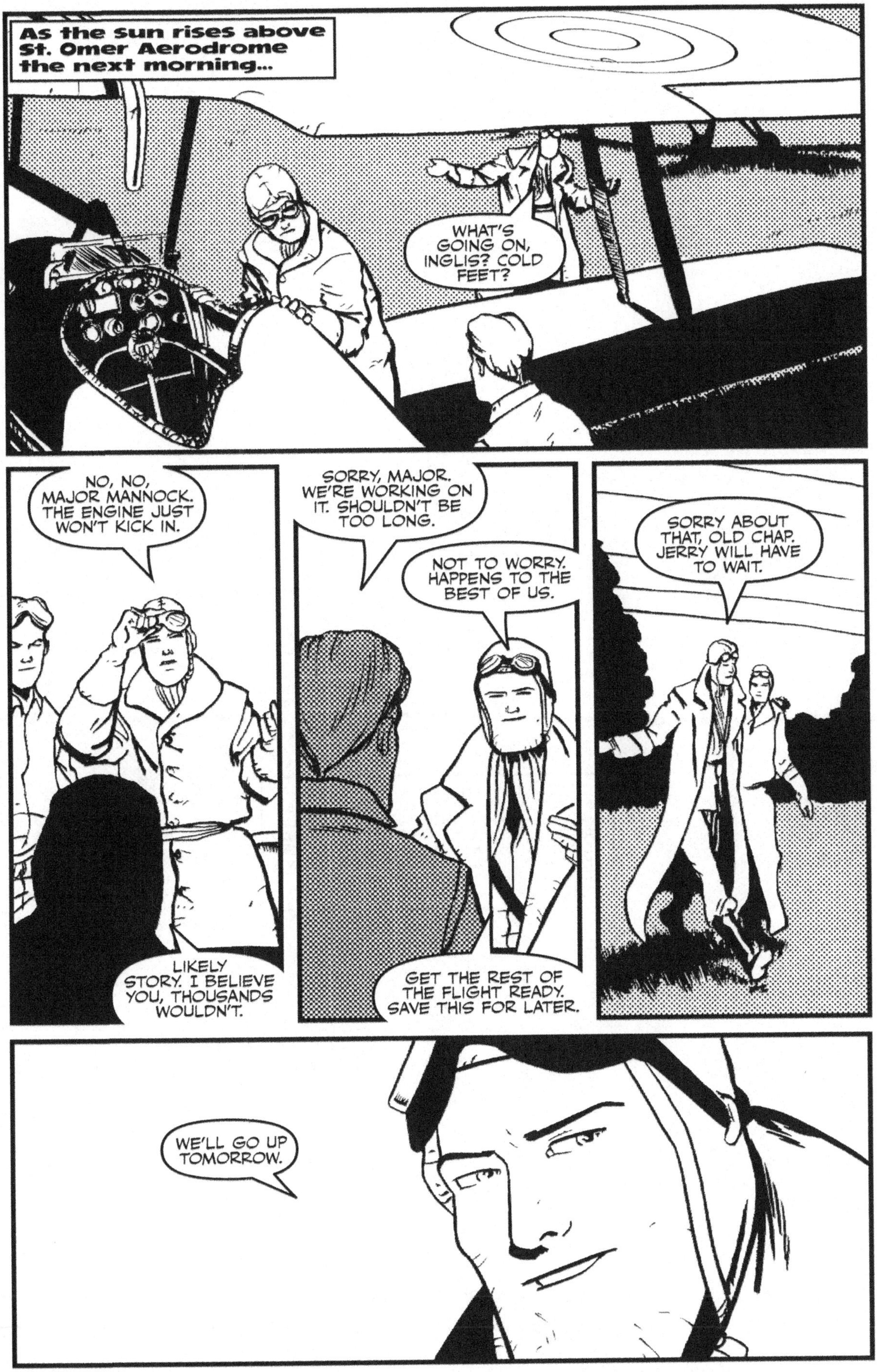
As the sun rises above St. Omer Aerodrome the next morning...
WHAT'S GOING ON, INGLIS? COLD FEET?
NO, NO, MAJOR MANNOCK. THE ENGINE JUST WON'T KICK IN.
LIKELY STORY. I BELIEVE YOU, THOUSANDS WOULDN'T.
SORRY, MAJOR. WE'RE WORKING ON IT. SHOULDN'T BE TOO LONG.
NOT TO WORRY. HAPPENS TO THE BEST OF US.
GET THE REST OF THE FLIGHT READY. SAVE THIS FOR LATER.
SORRY ABOUT THAT, OLD CHAP. JERRY WILL HAVE TO WAIT.
WE'LL GO UP TOMORROW.

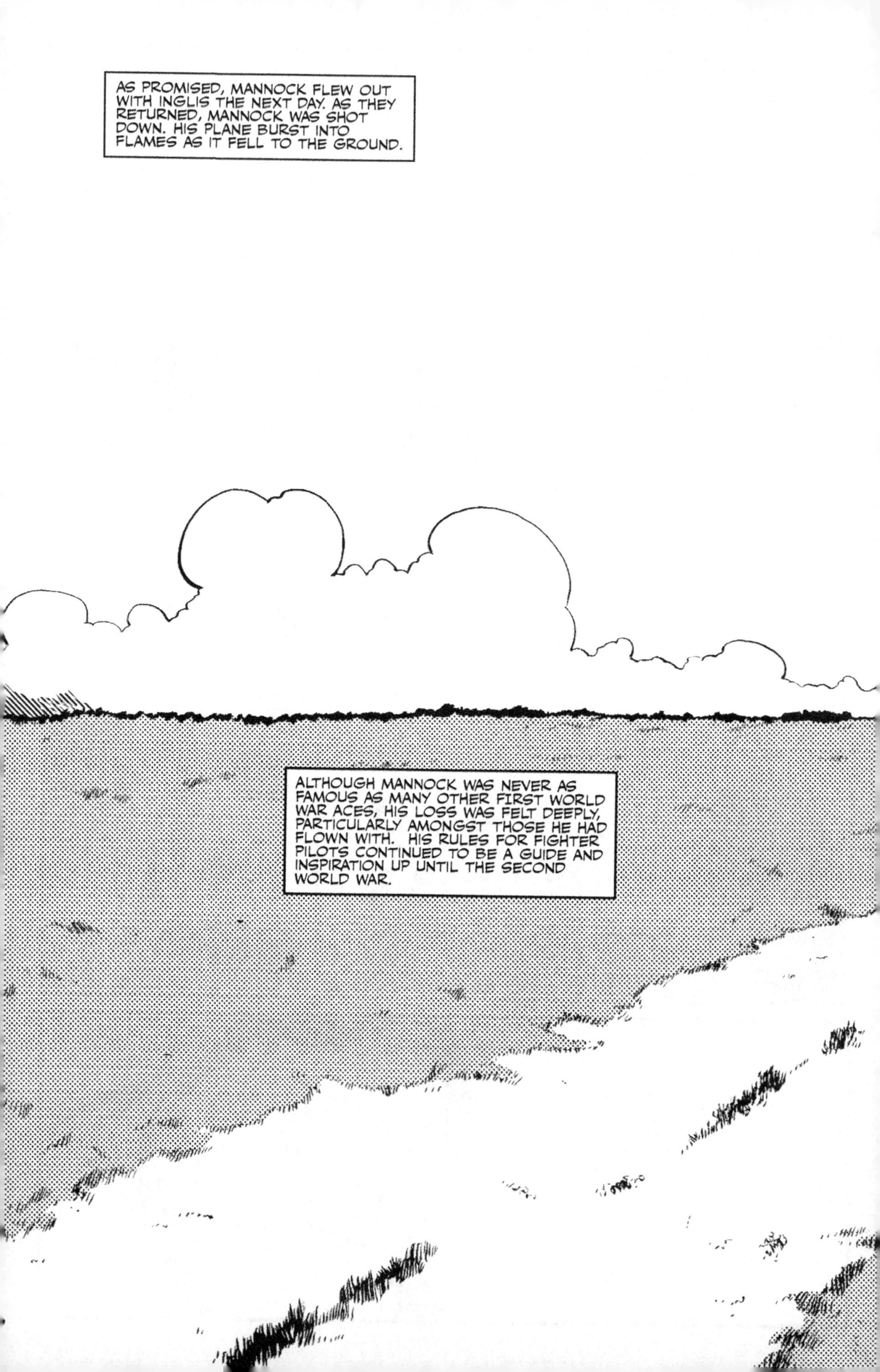
AS PROMISED, MANNOCK FLEW OUT WITH INGLIS THE NEXT DAY. AS THEY RETURNED, MANNOCK WAS SHOT DOWN. HIS PLANE BURST INTO FLAMES AS IT FELL TO THE GROUND.
ALTHOUGH MANNOCK WAS NEVER AS FAMOUS AS MANY OTHER FIRST WORLD WAR ACES, HIS LOSS WAS FELT DEEPLY, PARTICULARLY AMONGST THOSE HE HAD FLOWN WITH. HIS RULES FOR FIGHTER PILOTS CONTINUED TO BE A GUIDE AND INSPIRATION UP UNTIL THE SECOND WORLD WAR.

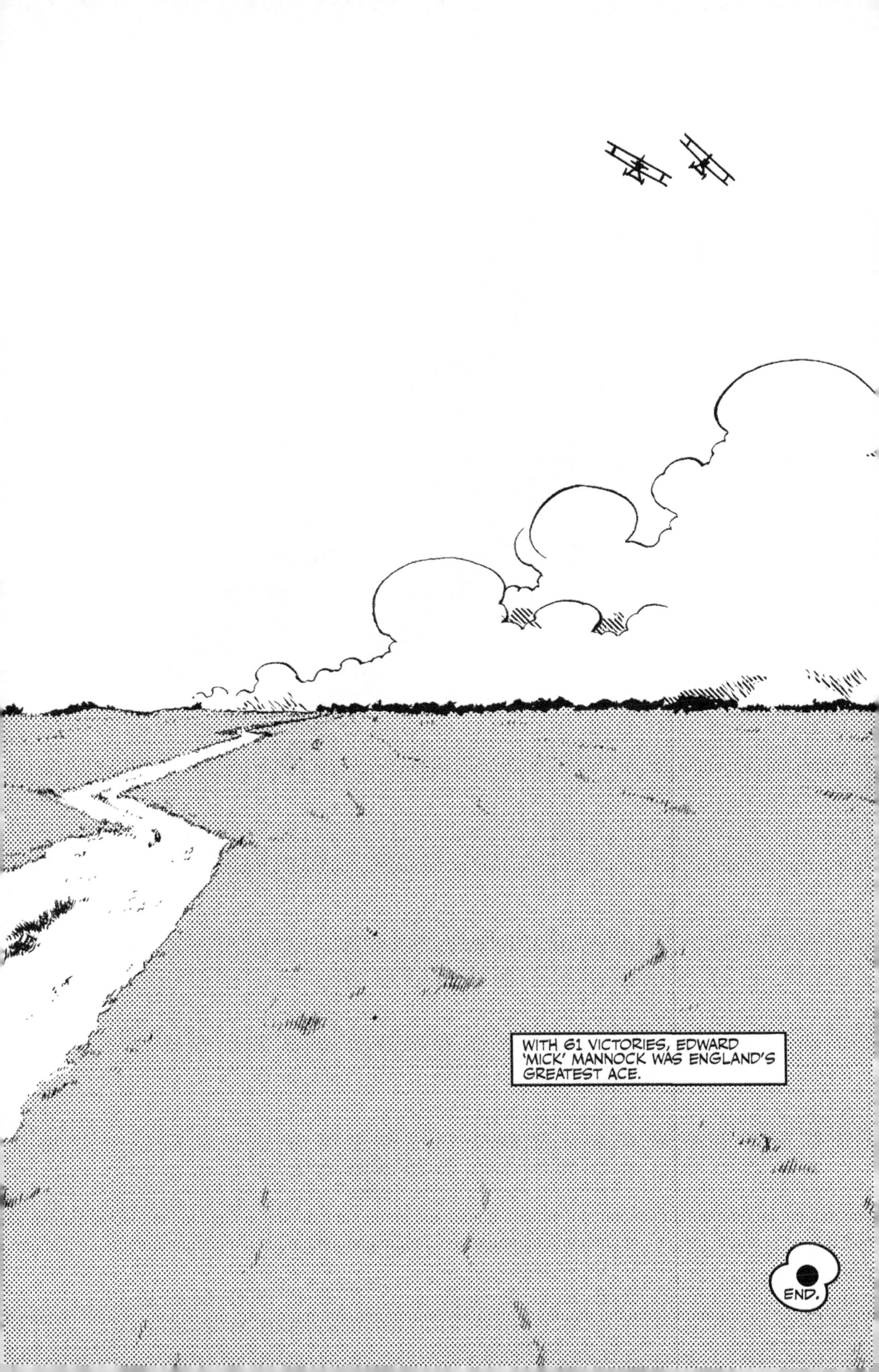
WITH 61 VICTORIES, EDWARD 'MICK' MANNOCK WAS ENGLAND'S GREATEST ACE.
END.

S.E.5a

At 11am
on 11th November 1918, the
First World War was
over.

Each year, at the
11th Hour, of the 11th Day, of the 11th
Month
we pay tribute to those
who fought during this, and
more recent, wars.

We will always remember them.

CALIBER COMICS GOES TO WAR!
HISTORICAL AND MILITARY THEMED GRAPHIC NOVELS

**WORLD WAR ONE:
MO MAN'S LAND**

ISBN: 9781635298123

*A look at World War 1 from
the French trenches as they
faced the Imperial German
Army.*

**CORTEZ AND THE FALL
OF THE AZTECS**

ISBN: 9781635299779

*Cortez battles the Aztecs
while in search of Inca
gold.*

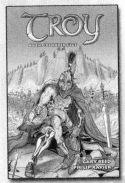

**TROY:
AN EMPIRE UNDER SIEGE**

ISBN: 9781635298635

*Homer's famous The Iliad and
the Trojan War is given a
unique human perspective
rather than from the God's.*

WITNESS TO WAR

ISBN: 9781635299700

*WW2's Battle of the Bulge
is seen up close by an
embedded female war
reporter.*

THE LINCOLN BRIGADE

ISBN: 9781635298222

*American volunteers head
to Spain in the 1930s to
fight in their civil war
against the fascist regime.*

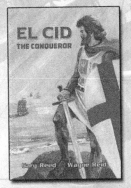

**EL CID:
THE CONQUEROR**

ISBN: 9780982654996

*Europe's greatest warrior
attempts to unify Spain
against invading foreign
and domestic armies.*

WINTER WAR

ISBN: 9780985749392

*At the outbreak of WW2
Finland fights against an
invading Soviet army.*

**ZULUNATION:
END OF EMPIRE**

ISBN: 9780941613415

*The global British Empire
and far-reaching influence
is threatened by a Zulu
uprising in southern Africa.*

AIR WARRIORS: WORLD WAR ONE #V1 - V4   *Take to the skies of WW1 as various fighter aces tell their harrowing stories.*
ISBN: 9781635297973 (V1), 9781635297980 (V2), 9781635297997 (V3), 9781635298000 (V4)

CALIBER COMICS PRESENTS

The Complete

VIETNAM JOURNAL

VIETNAM JOURNAL
BOOK ONE - INDIAN COUNTRY
DON LOMAX

VIETNAM JOURNAL
BOOK TWO - THE IRON TRIANGLE
DON LOMAX

VIETNAM JOURNAL
BOOK THREE - FROM THE DELTA TO DAK TO
DON LOMAX

VIETNAM JOURNAL
BOOK FOUR - M. I. A.
DON LOMAX

VIETNAM JOURNAL
BOOK FIVE - TET '68
DON LOMAX

VIETNAM JOURNAL
BOOK SIX - BLOODBATH AT KHE SAHN
DON LOMAX

VIETNAM JOURNAL
BOOK SEVEN - VALLEY OF DEATH
DON LOMAX

VIETNAM JOURNAL
BOOK EIGHT - BRAIN DEAD HORROR
DON LOMAX

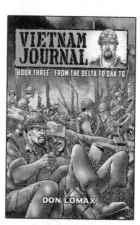

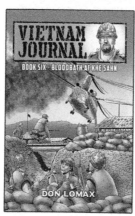

8 Volumes Covering the Entire Initial Run of the Critically Acclaimed Don Lomax Series

And Now Available

VIETNAM JOURNAL SERIES TWO

"INCURSION", "JOURNEY INTO HELL", "RIPCORD"

All new stories from Scott 'Journal' Neithammer as he reports durings the later stages of the Vietnam War.

VIETNAM JOURNAL
SERIES 2
INCURSION
DON LOMAX
VOLUME 1

VIETNAM JOURNAL
SERIES 2
JOURNEY INTO HELL
DON LOMAX
VOLUME 2

VIETNAM JOURNAL
SERIES 2
RIPCORD
DON LOMAX
VOLUME 3

FROM CALIBER COMICS
www.calibercomics.com

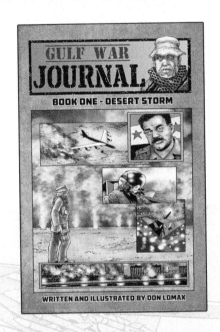

ALSO AVAILABLE FROM DON LOMAX

HIGH SHINING BRASS

High Shining Brass is based on the true story of an American spy during the Vietnam War as told to Don Lomax by agent Robert Durand who chronicles the tale. Durand was a member of a black-ops team, code- named "Shining Brass." The series depicts the horrific atrocities witnessed and performed by the once naïve special forces member as he attempts to perform his duties and understand the true meaning behind the madness. Durand's group was under the command of a combined force, comprised of every branch of the services, and headed up by the ever-popular Central Intelligence Committee. It's a journey into a shadow world of treachery and deceit—and reveals the way lives of Americans were traded about carelessly during the war in Vietnam.

ISBN: 978-1544962191 $14.99US

ABOVE AND BEYOND

Beginning in May of 2007, noted comic writer and illustrator Don Lomax teamed up with Police and Security News magazine to produce the series "Above and Beyond" - real life depictions of heroic acts by law enforcement professionals. Just as our soldiers here and abroad deserve recognition for their unwavering service, so do the men and women who protect and serve the citizens of the United States. Contained within these pages are just a few stories of these individuals who have demonstrated selfless bravery and heroic action under the most difficult circumstances and gone above and beyond the call of duty.

ISBN: 978-1635299601 $ 9.99 US

FROM AWARD-WINNING COMIC WRITER AND ARTIST
WAYNE VANSANT
COMES TALES FROM WORLD WAR II

An action/adventure tale of the French Legionnaire soldier, Battron, who is involved with the liberation of a freebooting French ship, the Martel, from a heavily guarded Vichy French port during WWII. The Allies want the ship destroyed; the Germans have sent serious resources and firepower to save it. But a critical security leak in British intelligence could jeopardize not only the mission but Battron's life. The key is the beautiful former mistress of the Martel's captain, enlisted in the hope she can convince him to join the Free French movement with his ship. But has she told the Allies all she knows? And can Battron and his skillful commandos complete their dangerous mission in time under the luming shadow of the pending Allied invasion of North Africa?

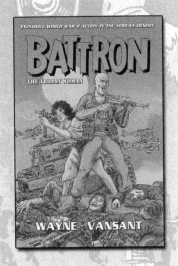

Collection of tales involving the German Waffen SS from acclaimed creator and comic artist Wayne Vansant. These stories deal with the German Panzer troops during World War II and collects the highly acclaimed Battle Group Peiper story, Witches' Cauldon saga, along with three short tales. Knights of the Skull covers the war experiences of young German troops on the Eastern Front to the massacre of American troops near Malmedy Belgium to the harsh conditions of a crushing winter and engagements against an unrelenting Soviet troop onslaught.

The epic and incredible telling of the early days of the United States during the Second World War. Days of Darkness covers the darkest days of WWII for the US, when the country went from the tragedy of Pearl Harbor to the triumph at Midway. Covering in detail is the attack of the US Naval base and the devastation of the fleet in Hawaii, then the action moves to the evacuation and fall of the Philippines to the horror of the Death March of Bataan, and finally to the dramatic Battle of Midway which stopped the Japanese juggernaut in the Pacific.

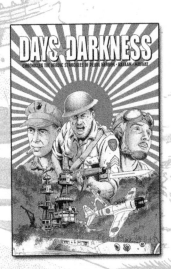

"Heavy on authenticity, compellingly written and beautifully drawn." - Comics Buyers Guide.

WWW.CALIBERCOMICS.COM

ALSO AVAILABLE FROM CALIBER COMICS

QUALITY GRAPHIC NOVELS TO ENTERTAIN

THE SEARCHERS: VOLUME 1
The Shape of Things to Come

Before *League of Extraordinary Gentlemen* there was *The Searchers*. At the dawn of the 20th Century the greatest literary adventurers from the minds of Wells, Doyle, Burroughs, and Haggard were created. All thought to be the work of pure fiction. However, a century later, the real-life descendents of those famous characters are recruited by the legendary Professor Challenger in order to save mankind's future. Series collected for the first time.

"Searchers is the comic book I have on the wall with a sign reading - 'Love books? Never read a comic? Try this one! ....money back guarantee..." - Dark Star Books.

WAR OF THE WORLDS: INFESTATION

Based on the H.G. Wells classic! The "Martian Invasion" has begun again and now mankind must fight for its very humanity. It happened slowly at first but by the third year, it seemed that the war was almost over... the war was almost lost.

"Writer Randy Zimmerman has a fine grasp of drama, and spins the various strands of the story into a coherent whole... imaginative and very gritty."
- war-of-the-worlds.co.uk

HELSING: LEGACY BORN

From writer Gary Reed (Deadworld) and artists John Lowe (Captain America), Bruce McCorkindale (Godzilla). She was born into a legacy she wanted no part of and pushed into a battle recessed deep in the shadows of the night. Samantha Helsing is torn between two worlds...two allegiances...two families. The legacy of the Van Helsing family and their crusade against the "night creatures" comes to modern day with the most unlikely of all warriors.

"Congratulations on this masterpiece..."
- Paul Dale Roberts, Compuserve Reviews

DEADWORLD

Before there was The Walking Dead there was Deadworld. Here is an introduction of the long running classic horror series, Deadworld, to a new audience! Considered by many to be the godfather of the original zombie comic with over 100 issues and graphic novels in print and over 1,000,000 copies sold, Deadworld ripped into the undead with intelligent zombies on a mission and a group of poor teens riding in a school bus desperately try to stay one step ahead of the sadistic, Harley-riding King Zombie. Death, mayhem, and a touch of supernatural evil made Deadworld a classic and now here's your chance to get into the story!

DAYS OF WRATH

Award winning comic writer & artist Wayne Vansant brings his gripping World War II saga of war in the Pacific to Guadalcanal and the Battle of Bloody Ridge. This is the powerful story of the long, vicious battle for Guadalcanal that occurred in 1942-43. When the U.S. Navy orders its outnumbered and out-gunned ships to run from the Japanese fleet, they abandon American troops on a bloody, battered island in the South Pacific.

"Heavy on authenticity, compellingly written and beautifully drawn."
- Comics Buyers Guide

THE BOBCAT

Described as the Native American *Black Panther*. 1898. Indian Territory. Will Firemaker is a Cherokee Blacksmith who is finding out that the world of ancient lore and myth of his Tribe, that Will had always thought of as tribal fairytales, are actually true, and they're telling him he must replace his best friend from the animal kingdom, The Great Cat, as the guardian of his people. This sends him down a path of shock and disbelief as beings from the ancient past begin to manifest themselves in the world of reality. And as malevolent forces rise up in the wake of the fledgling Industrial Age, the future rushes head on into the Old West. Tahlequah will never be the same...

CALIBER PRESENTS

The original Caliber Presents anthology title was one of Caliber's inaugural releases and featured predominantly new creators, many of which went onto successful careers in the comics' industry. In this new version, Caliber Presents has expanded to graphic novel size and while still featuring new creators it also includes many established professional creators with new visions. Creators featured in this first issue include nominees and winners of some of the industry's major awards including the Eisner, Harvey, Xeric, Ghastly, Shel Dorf, Comic Monsters, and more.

LEGENDLORE

From Caliber Comics now comes the entire Realm and Legendlore saga as a set of volumes that collects the long running critically acclaimed series. In the vein of The Lord of The Rings and The Hobbit with elements of Game of Thrones and Dungeon and Dragons.

Four normal modern day teenagers are plunged into a world they thought only existed in novels and film. They are whisked away to a magical land where dragons roam the skies, orcs and hobgoblins terrorize travelers, unicorns prance through the forest, and kingdoms wage war for dominance. It is a world where man is just one race, joining other races such as elves, trolls, dwarves, changelings, and the dreaded night creatures who steal the night.

TIME GRUNTS

What if Hitler's last great Super Weapon was – Time itself! A WWII/time travel adventure that can best be described as *Band of Brothers* meets *Time Bandits*.

October, 1944. Nazi fortunes appear bleaker by the day. But in the bowels of the Wenceslas Mines, a terrible threat has emerged . . . The Nazis have discovered the ability to conquer time itself with the help of a new ominous device!

Now a rag tag group of American GIs must stop this threat to the past, present, and future . . . While dealing with their own past, prejudices, and fears in the process.

CALIBER
COMICS

www.calibercomics.com

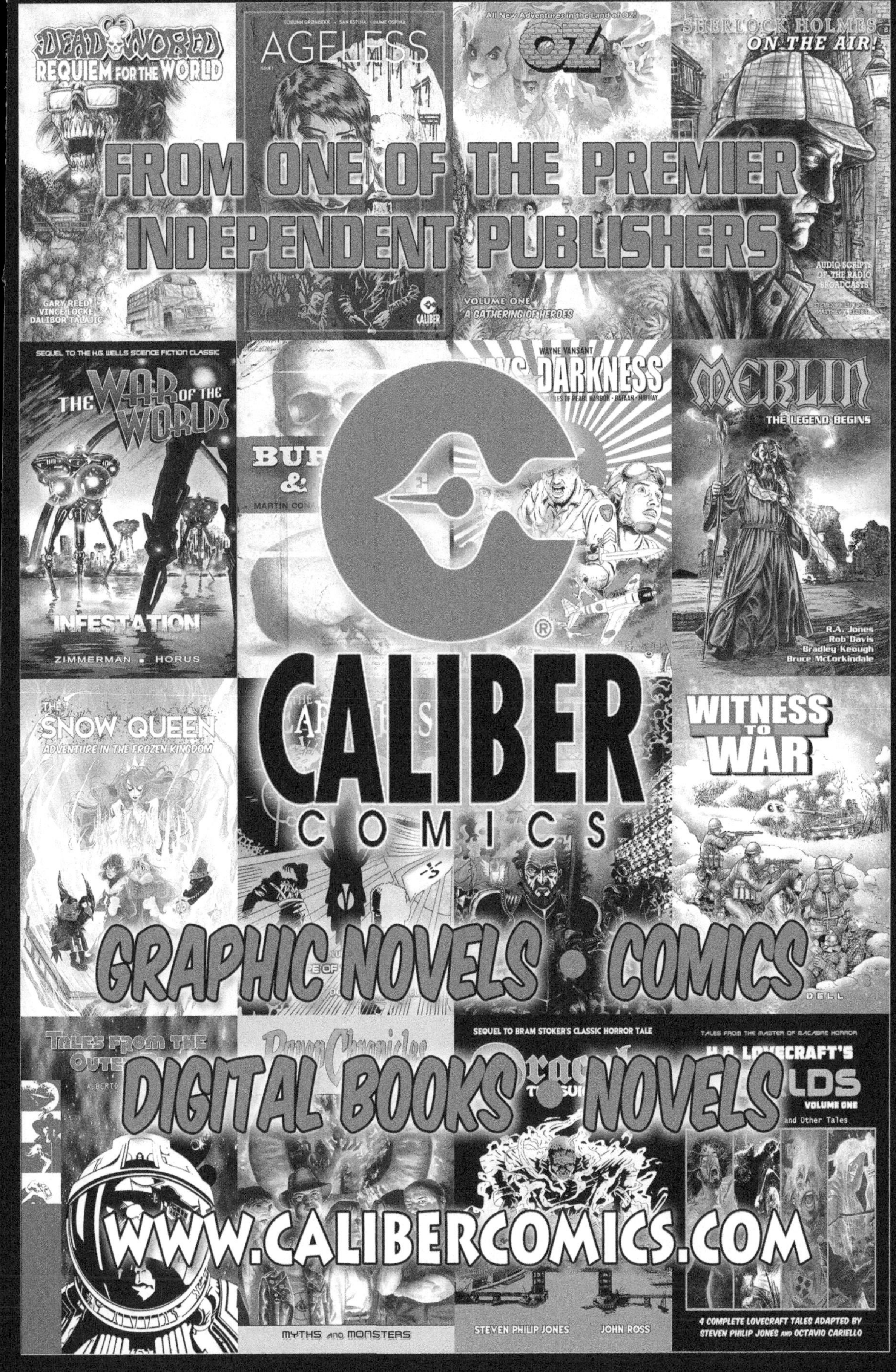
FROM ONE OF THE PREMIER INDEPENDENT PUBLISHERS
DEADWORLD
REQUIEM FOR THE WORLD
GARY REED
VINCE LOCKE
DALIBOR TALAJIC
AGELESS
CALIBER
All New Adventures in the Land of OZ!
OZ
VOLUME ONE
A GATHERING OF HEROES
SHERLOCK HOLMES
ON THE AIR!
AUDIO SCRIPTS OF THE RADIO BROADCASTS
SEQUEL TO THE H.G. WELLS SCIENCE FICTION CLASSIC
THE WAR OF THE WORLDS
INFESTATION
ZIMMERMAN ▪ HORUS
WAYNE VANSANT
DARKNESS
MERLIN
THE LEGEND BEGINS
R.A. Jones
Rob Davis
Bradley Keough
Bruce McCorkindale
CALIBER
COMICS
THE SNOW QUEEN
ADVENTURE IN THE FROZEN KINGDOM
WITNESS TO WAR
GRAPHIC NOVELS • COMICS
DIGITAL BOOKS • NOVELS
SEQUEL TO BRAM STOKER'S CLASSIC HORROR TALE
TALES FROM THE MASTER OF MACABRE HORROR
H.P. LOVECRAFT'S
VOLUME ONE
and Other Tales
MYTHS AND MONSTERS
STEVEN PHILIP JONES
JOHN ROSS
4 COMPLETE LOVECRAFT TALES ADAPTED BY STEVEN PHILIP JONES AND OCTAVIO CARIELLO
WWW.CALIBERCOMICS.COM

Made in the USA
Middletown, DE
05 April 2022

63608402R00066